—20TH— CENTURY DECORATING ARCHITECTURE & GARDENS

BOOK EDITED BY MARY JANE POOL

TEXT EDITED & CHAPTER INTRODUCTIONS
BY CAROLINE SEEBOHM

DESIGNED BY MIKI DENHOF

20TH CENTURY DECORATING ARCHITECTURE & GARDENS

80 YEARS OF IDEAS & PLEASURE FROM HOUSE & GARDEN

HOLT, RINEHART AND WINSTON
NEW YORK

Published by Holt, Rinehart and Winston,
383 Madison Avenue, New York, New York 10017.

Published simultaneously in Canada by Holt, Rinehart and
Winston of Canada, Limited.

Library of Congress Cataloging in Publication Data
Main entry under title:
20th century decorating, architecture, gardens.
Includes index.
1.   Interior decoration—United States—History—
20th century.   2.   Architecture, Domestic—United
States.   3.   Architecture, Modern—20th century—United
States.   4.   Landscape architecture—United States.
I.   Pool, Mary Jane.   II.   Seebohm, Caroline.
III.   House & garden.
NK2004.T83   747.213   80-12593

ISBN 0-03-047581-3

First Edition

Production by Karen Gillis

Printed in the United States of America
10 9 8 7 6 5 4 3 2 1

From Edwardian elegance to a stripped-down, plugged-in electronic world; from a house of many rooms to open-space living in a city loft; from the utter luxury of servants to the simple joy of do-it-yourself—from 1901 to 1980 the many changes in the way we live have been extraordinary. This book is about these changes. There are eight chapters on the eight decades of the century. Each decade has its own message about living at the time. For instance, in the Seventies and heading into the Eighties, the word is *nature*—to enjoy, to learn from, to conserve. Luxurious nature to live with as an integral part of the house. Now nature is more than scenic, it is a completely surrounding, sensuous part of life. As we live in sunroom-living rooms, garden bedrooms, solarium baths, and greenhouse kitchens, we plant gardens of growing things that move with the wind and flower with the sun, for color, for food, for shade. Plants, trees, and flowers are being collected like pieces of good furniture, and as something soft and appealing against wood and wicker, steel, and glass, and hard-edge art.

This return to nature is happening, despite, or perhaps because of, environmental and economic pressures, and drastic changes in family and household structures. Things are different now. There is a great urge to preserve and restore and at the same time, there is a flood of inventions, discoveries, breakthroughs to make everyday living a great adventure.

The newest houses don't look like houses you have ever seen before. Unlike the horizontal boxes of the Forties and Fifties and the slightly vertical shapes of the Sixties, houses now cling to the earth in undulating organic curves, or shoot up and out in every direction to make the most of nature's own heating and cooling systems. Technology and industrial materials have come home to make houses work like well oiled machines for the new, and very diverse, family groups. There are fewer rooms in these houses but a feeling of more space as activities flow into one another.

How do we live in these spaces? There seem to be two ways. One, is to feed the hungry eye and psyche with color, pattern, and craftsmanship, in rooms full of one's own treasures. The other way, is to create a serene feeling with just a few choice things. These rooms often belong to the young who still have a fresh, uncluttered eye, or to the old whose taste has been honed to a fine point, and who want to clear away the barnacles of a lifetime of collecting because they wouldn't want to take it with them if they could. To aspire, to collect, to refine—it is all part of growth that nothing can stop. This book documents these and other positive, creative forces thriving on encouragement and appreciation.

As you go through these pages you will see the flowering of decorating in this century, the impact of new architecture, our growing respect for nature. And, very important, you will be reminded of the beauty around us at home and its great gift to our civilization.

As an introduction, we asked three distinguished men who have worked in their fields for most of the century, to tell us what they have seen and to advise us. Billy Baldwin writes on decorating, Pietro Belluschi on architecture, and Russell Page on gardens. Their thoughts add immensely to the book's content. The photographs and text come from a magazine that is an exciting reflection of its time. Since the turn of the century, through an explosion of technology, catastrophic wars, and tremendous social change *House & Garden* has been reporting on how people live, guiding and giving pleasure to millions.

In 1924, Richardson Wright, Editor of *House & Garden* for 36 years, wrote this chatty account of the magazine's beginning. "One day, in April 1901, three architects sat around a drafting table in a Philadelphia office. Two of them were men in their prime. Their professional reputations were already established. Their work was known by those who took cognizance of such things as among the best being done in the country. Most of it was the designing of homes and gardens surrounding those homes.

"They talked, as architects eventually will when two or three of them are gathered together, about things concerning their profession—about the scheme Philadelphia had for cutting a wide boulevard from the City Hall

FOREWORD

(one of the world's ugliest buildings) up to Fairmont Park (one of the world's loveliest parks), about the perilous number of jerry-built houses contractors were running up in the suburbs to foist off on an unsuspecting public, and from the suburbs, their conversation passed on into the country.

"The three men were Wilson Eyre, Frank Miles Day and Herbert C. Wise.

"It had been suggested by a business man of Philadelphia that these architects start a magazine devoted to the development of the country home. They fancied the idea. It offered a pleasant diversion. The title "House & Garden" was suggested and accepted. Mr. Eyre offered to draw a cover for it. Mr. Wise was made editor. These three men undertook the creation of *House & Garden* as an *architectural lark,* it wasn't their intention to appeal to anyone save their architectural friends and their architectural following. They edited to suit their own high and unyielding standards of good taste. The making of money was farthest from their thoughts. "It remained an architectural magazine until 1903, when the pages began to appeal to a wide range of readers, showing practical articles about decoration and furniture and gardening, as well as architecture and building. Miss Margaret Greenleaf became editor. Then through the hands of several owners the property passed and through the guidance of several editors—Henry H. Saylor, 1909-1913; William A. Vollmer, 1913-1914; and on June 1, 1914, Mr. Richardson Wright, sat down at the editor's desk."

Mr. Wright and publisher Condé Nast who acquired *House & Garden* in 1915 firmly established the magazine's editorial excellence. Newspaper publisher Samuel I. Newhouse purchased the company in 1957 and brought the magazine to its present success. Other strong points-of-view carried *House & Garden* further into the century—Alexander Liberman, Editorial Director; editors Albert Kornfeld 1950-1955, William H. Lowe, Jr., 1955-1958, Harriet Burket 1958-1969. Now more than at any time in history, we want to create a world of our own at home. A love of home is basic and so is *House & Garden's* intent—to help people solve their living problems, reporting on ideas and things to make life easier, more comfortable, attractive. Eighty years has brought us from a magazine about architecture to a magazine about living. This book is based on these eighty years of terrific energy and insight. It is a history of ideas. It entertains. It reassures. It points straight ahead. To know where we are going, turn the page to see where we have been.

Mary Jane Pool
Editor-In-Chief
February 14, 1980

BILLY BALDWIN: "THE IMPORTANCE OF ROOMS PEOPLE LIVE IN"

Billy Baldwin, often referred to as the dean of decorators, has been creating attractive rooms for interesting people on two continents for over forty years. He is the author of two best-selling books—Billy Baldwin Decorates and Billy Baldwin Remembers—and here he writes about the flowering of decorating over the last eighty years and the basics of good decorating, which seem to remain the same no matter how taste may change.

When Mary Jane Pool showed me the *House & Garden* clippings she had gathered as material for this book—clippings from issues going all the way back to the magazine's debut in 1901—I smiled when I realized I'd seen most of the rooms before. Not only in the pages of *House & Garden* and *Vogue,* which arrived in a flurry of excitement each month at my boyhood home in Baltimore, but in real life as I was growing up. Indeed, I reflected, I am only two years younger than *House & Garden,* and nearly as old as American decorating itself, which only began in earnest at the turn of this century. This makes me one of the few decorators alive who has seen the germination, cultivation, weeding, and flowering of decorating in this country.

I suppose it was a book published in 1897 that started Americans thinking about decorating at all. It was an extraordinary and unpresumptuous little volume called *The Decoration of Houses,* by Edith Wharton (before she began publishing novels) and Ogden Codman, Jr., who became a leading architect in his time. Reprinted by W.W. Norton & Co. in 1978, the book contains principles applicable to good decorating today. Still, while the advance guard was realizing the importance of the rooms people lived in, the vast majority, including (and in some cases especially) the very rich, persisted in living in dark, stuffy, Victorian rooms full of antimacassars, horsehair, dismal pictures hung high and framed as hideously as possible, and cluttered with bad reproduction furniture and knicknacks. There was never a thought of an antique; the idea of collecting fine old furniture hadn't occurred even to the millionaires up and down Fifth Avenue. If someone wanted to reproduce a French room, he did just that—reproduced it down to the last spit-polished reproduction table. To early 20th-century Americans, antiques were *used furniture,* highly undesirable, and too chancy to sit on for fear of collapsing to the floor. Viewed retrospectively, it seems a

nostalgic but rather preposterous Life-with-Father setting, ripe for the appearance of a decorating revolutionary.

Elsie de Wolfe appeared on cue. She was born in Brooklyn, lived abroad a good deal, wore simple black dresses with pearls and white gloves, and was the first person ever to have her hair dyed blue. Elsie had a vision: The house one lived in, she said, should be attractive; there should be wonderful food; the people should be beautifully dressed; and it shall all be very, very comfortable. It was a colossal vision, one she tried to make real by selling good taste (which she defined unequivocably, in her crackling, crow-like voice, as "Suitability! Suitability! Suitability!"), which turned the decoration of houses into a profession. Her great contribution was not that she turned it into a creative art, for quite frankly she did not. But what she did became the foundation for all that was to follow: She purged those Victorian houses of their stuffiness and clutter, got rid of the bad pictures and the bad furniture, began painting walls white, and introduced the cult of the antique and the idea of comfort. Many of her ideas were imported straight from France and England. She had a house outside Versailles and another on Sutton Place, a gem of a street on the East River in New York City, a brief row of almost exact copies of houses in Chelsea, England, designed and brought to their charming perfection by architect Mott Schmidt and two of Elsie's dearest friends, Anne Morgan and Elizabeth Marbury. At the time, the great rooms in England and France were filled with antiques—real family heirlooms people had had forever. And the English had established the use of upholstered furniture with chintz slipcovers—a phenomenon scarcely thought of anywhere else. In England, you might find a couple of little French chairs, but never would a French room be contaminated by anything English. And so, Elsie de Wolfe did a revolutionary thing. In her house on Sutton Place, she used English flowered chintz upholstered furniture in a very formal French drawing room. Shocking! Unheard of! Instantly she was asked to do two million-dollar jobs: the original Colony Club, and the second-floor living quarters of what is now the Frick Museum, which was being built at the time. Suddenly having an Elsie de Wolfe room became the status symbol.

If Elsie de Wolfe revolutionized decorating, Ruby Ross Wood made it available. She entered the decorating profession by ghost-writing Elsie's book, *The House in Good Taste,* and then went on, with others, to build upon the foundations Elsie had laid. (Not only esthetic foundation, but professional ones as well: "You're a fool, Billy Baldwin," an elderly Elsie once told me as she stood barefoot on a sofa hanging a picture, "if you ever do anything for anyone without taking a commission.") Just after the war—in fact, Armistice Day, 1918—Ruby Wood and Nancy McClellan, a decorator who wrote what is still the definitive book on wallpaper, established on the fourth floor of Wanamaker's department store in New York the first decorating department in the world. It was called Au Quatrième, and in it could be found 18th and 19th century antiques from England, Italy and France, (Mrs. Wood loved the Directoire style), chintz, rugs, absolutely everything you could possibly need to decorate a house. And between her many articles for *House & Garden* and *Vogue* and her work at this department store, which made all the best things available, attractive houses were suddenly in great demand. Those two women were given millions of dollars by Wanamaker's to spend every summer in England, France, and Italy on the very best furniture and objects they could find. At one point they actually bought a whole Tudor house in England and had it shipped to Cleveland, where it was rebuilt for one of their clients.

Au Quatrième was also, it turned out, a kind of training ground for some of the people who would become decorators in their own right later: Rose Cumming, that marvelous woman with exciting color sense and rather bizarre taste, who sold fabrics in the thirties at prices you'd find exorbitant today, was there for about two weeks. "It didn't work out," Ruby told me later. "She wasn't very practical." (Actually, their tastes were not exactly compatible either. One couldn't possibly have had a good time in a room by Rose Cumming—unless one would have been miserable in one by Mrs. Wood.)

A saleswoman at Au Quatrième, Margaret Owen, became important to all the decorators a decade and a half later, when she was made the American agent for the remarkable fabrics and matching wallpapers of Paule Marrot, the Paris designer. They were cottons in flowers and prints in the colors of Matisse, the one great painter who had inspired me as a child. (I can remember seeing his pictures, feeling riveted by them, and then being led to them and told the aritst's name. Years later, when I became a decorator, I knew I was Matisse's disciple.)

A brilliant decorator working at the time was Mrs. Archibald Brown, head of McMillen, Inc., which, still under her direction after more than 50 years, has done some of the best decorating in America. Eleanor Brown was then a trustee of the Parsons School in Paris, whose president, William Odom, sent all the best furniture in Paris to Mrs. Brown for her decorating jobs in New York—an arrangement viewed with less than equanimity by Ruby Ross Wood. The two women admired each other greatly, but their decorating styles were completely dissimilar. Where Mrs. Wood's was casual, comfortable, and very English, Mrs. Brown's has always been luxurious and formal, and she loves Italian and

French furniture. She is decidedly contemporary about her use of pictures, and she pioneered in modern fabrics.

By the time I got to New York in the mid thirties, decorating was already in full flower. There was innovation, there were marvelous shows and openings of decorating exhibitions, people were turning out new fabrics and papers that in turn allowed the decorators to be more creative, and there was plenty of money from clients who had not yet felt the sting of a sobering income-tax law. New York was a wonderland for me. I was in revolt against Baltimore, a town in which there could not have been more than three or four French chairs. I didn't want to be stuck doing Chippendale all my life—I wanted to do high style.

I came to work for Ruby Wood, of course, who by then had her own shop on 57th Street. McMillen, Inc., was firmly established. Diane Tate and Marion Hall were doing absolutely marvelous work. Dorothy Draper came later, but she also had a very important influence, especially in freeing hotels and offices of stuffiness and bad taste, and introducing bright colors and big chintz roses. She did Hampshire House, one of the most exciting jobs ever done in New York. She was a very big and handsome woman who wore huge black hats—a clue to her one unforgiveable crime: She insisted upon enormous lamps and lampshades in even the smallest rooms. Elsie Cobb Wilson was decorating then, and a very talented woman called Mrs. Cosden. And Frances Elkins, who was, I think, almost the most exciting decorator we had ever had. She did a great deal of work in Chicago with her brother, the great architect David Adler (whose greatness was in that he created conventional houses in extraordinary materials: For instance, a wonderful 18th-century staircase would have spindles not of wood, but of crystal). Frances worked in California, where she knew instinctively how to use heavy handwoven rugs, leather, pottery instead of porcelain, in rugged, wooded, wonderful places like Santa Barbara and Monterrey. She herself lived in a perfectly beautiful old adobe house, which is now a club you can visit. Frances Elkins was one of the American discoverers and importers of the designs of a gifted Frenchman called Jean-Michel Frank who also decorated houses in France, using parchment walls and expanses of white needlepoint, but who was best known as the last genius of French furniture.

In Palm Beach, the strict formality of Mizener's famous Spanish architecture, with its velvets and tapestries, was beginning to give way to a more casual, suitable style. Mrs. Wood herself did the first great 18th-century British Colonial-type house in Florida, using the cottons and chintzes Floridians take for granted today, plus Chinese wallpaper in the drawing room.

You notice that during this period not many men are mentioned. For the good reason that not many men were decorators. In fact as Mrs. Wood hired me I distinctly heard here a remark that the last thing she'd have imagined was having a man on her staff. Nevertheless she had two or three outstanding male contemporaries: Freddie Jones, a brilliant decorator who died prematurely; his partner, Hobe Erwin, who was respected enormously by the ladies; and Robert Lochere, who began adding a real architectural element to decorating, and who used mirrors in a very modern way. Men in fact were pursuing brilliant architectural careers at the time. William Delano of Delano and Aldrich designed Ruby Wood's own house as well as very fine country and townhouses; John Russell Pope did principally Georgian country houses, and he is best known for the Mellons' National Gallery in Washington.

While all this innovation was going on in America, in France, Monsieur Boudin (whose first name I never heard uttered) of the firm Jansen, was doing some extraordinary decorating: his supreme gift was for the arrangement of furniture. And in London there was stirring a small but strong influence on the whole decorating world. And that was Syrie Maugham, wife of author Somerset Maugham. She was famous for her all-white rooms, full of texture and white-painted furniture, and wonderful style. She brought it to the United States in her shops in New York and Chicago, and houses she did all over the country. Syrie's contemporary and tooth-and-nail competitor was Sybil Colefax, who was later joined in partnership by the most knowledgeable of all English decorators, John Fowler. He was known as the great restorer of the great houses in England. He was entirely 18th- and 19th-century minded. And he knew more about curtains than anybody who ever lived. His color sense was absolutely brilliant (never a thought of an all-white room), and in his own living quarters at his shop, he had the walls hung with sample lengths of fabrics in different, wonderful colors.

During World War II everything in decorating seemed to hold its breath—but when the smoke cleared there was a whole new group of decorators ready to topple the world. Albert Kornfeld, then editor of *House & Garden,* asked me to help with a project that involved a lot of designs and sketches. For this project I was given my first published credit—William Baldwin of Ruby Ross Wood. It was a time of recognition for many new talents. James Pendleton spent a lot of time abroad collecting ravishing objects; we all bought from him. Valerian Rybar used to walk into a client's apartment and immediately tear down all the walls and redo them the way he wanted. William Pahlmann mounted design shows at Lord & Taylor none of us ever missed. George Stacey had at one time about the smartest clientele of anyone; he worked for all three Cushing sisters—Mrs. Vincent Astor, Mrs. John Hay Whitney, and Mrs. William Paley—all at the same time. And of course there was Mrs. Henry Parish III, whom everyone still knows as Sister Parish. We were the upstarts, and between our younger ideas and the fabulous growing array of fabrics, papers, and colors everywhere, decorating in America was just about as emotional an art as it has ever been. And we were all very different. Sister's decorating, for instance, has always been very human, inviting, easy to relate to. She uses a great many crafts, which not only raises the standard of the craft and the status of the craftsman, but gives the room a very warm and personal appeal. And I still maintain that she can do a woman's bedroom more seductively than anybody alive. I, on the other hand, have always been devoted to fresh, clear colors: I was—and still am—on this cotton kick; and I have always been irreconcilably opposed to clutter.

Among us was another force for good design, and a voice we all respected; Van Day Truex, the president of the Parsons School in Paris and New York. His advanced students saw every palace in Europe and every important house in New York. And he regularly produced beautiful exhibitions of their own designs. When Van left Parsons, he became design consultant at Tiffany's, where he ran a series of Tiffany Table Settings by New York decorators—an idea revived in 1979.

As decorators became more and more creative, art—as itself, and not as an ornament in a beautiful room—and sculpture—almost universally rejected before—began to appear in contemporary rooms. And, in a grand departure from the European antiques and FFF (Fine French Furniture) now coveted and collected by everyone who could afford them, people began to notice that America had produced some quite wonderful furniture, too. A lot of this recognition was due to people like Henry du Pont and his remarkable museum, Winterthur. At the time, American furniture was to be found mostly in country houses, and townhouses in places like Philadelphia, Boston, and Annapolis, splendid Georgian houses filled with very grand American cabinetry (by Early American, we do not mean only pieces of maple). But du Pont was interested in every kind of American furniture, from the most modest Pennsylvania kitchen to the grandest townhouse dining room. The appreciation swept all across America in a great reclaiming of our own country. And while I think it was more an interest in history than in decorating, decorating certainly profited. People began taking note of craftsmanship. Of course the idea of having crude New England kitchen furniture in a New York penthouse will always be incomprehensible to me, but what I do see even in the most rustic designs, appropriately used, is an enormous honesty, and a dedication that cannot be dismissed.

It seemed that, once the United States began to recognize itself as a strong decorating force, other countries did, too. We began to see a decided hands-across-the-sea kind of cooperation, and the Atlantic Ocean was now a two-way street. The most publicized English decorator David Hicks, whom I have often said revolutionized the floors of the world with his small patterned strip carpeting, liked the freshness, the color, the youth and boldness he saw in the States, and determined to take it all back to England. Here, he discovered contemporary paintings, and began using contemporary English abstracts, unframed, in rooms filled with 18th-century furniture. He freed England from the beautiful, stiff taste of the past. The French, who always have thought they were the best at everything (and at some things they were, no doubt about it) and had no need to borrow from anywhere else, suddenly discovered Le Style Anglais, rooms in which were to be found only 19th-century English furniture, and even furniture arranged in a decidedly English way. Some of the best decorating in France was actually done not by French people at all. There was American Roderick Cameron's Fiorentina in the South of France; in Paris, the houses of the Mexican designer Carlos de Beistegui and the Argentinian Arturo Lopez. Linda Porter, Cole's wife, was a definite influence on French taste. And never to be forgotten are the lovely houses of the Baroness Philippe de Rothschild, an American named Pauline Potter. Her flair for mixing the previously unmixable seemed the personification of American spontaneity, freshness, and style.

But share, borrow, trade, or steal as we have always done with our European (and in California, our Japanese) counterparts, there was never a doubt as to a room's heritage if it had been done by an American. From the very beginning, when Elsie de Wolfe began mixing the best of England and France, and reproportioning things to fit American-size rooms, American decorating has been uniquely itself. We have tended to simplify, to give rooms a fresher, younger look. Perhaps because we are a younger country, founded and built by people with open minds and a willingness to take risks.

And the trend continues. In California, the legacy of Frances Elkins is honored in the work of Michael Taylor. He bought her plaster models for lamps and a great deal of her furniture when she died, and has added his own personality, modernity, and wit. The style has branched into tree trunk tables, wicker, western warmth—but its roots are European, as Mrs. Elkins had been strongly influenced by Syrie Maugham. In the east, I think Sister Parish's partner Albert Hadley has made Mrs. Vincent Astor's red lacquer library a timeless triumph. He is a decorator with inspired ideas and great knowledge of the past—a quality too often given less than its due among young decorators today. With the result that their work lacks authority. Even born talent, as any great singer, musician, or painter can attest, needs to be cultivated either alone in the presence of the work of great masters, or in schools and classes. The greatest decorating in America has never been frivolous—it has been built upon solid foundations. Authority is not just a good shot, it's

confidence. As Van used to say when he saw a good room: "Its a statement."

Still, decorating today is more exciting and inventive than ever. More ideas are tried, more are accepted. Rather than reach a conditioned hand for the French or Italian chair, young decorators are designing a great deal of their own furniture. I may have designed a few bookcases and I certainly made a lady out of wicker, but in my time there was none of the emphasis on furniture design you see today. Because it's more suitable today. Decorating has evolved, and it keeps evolving. Arthur Smith, who was my partner until I retired, is doing things today I could never have done in my time. It has to do with how life changes, how people dress, work, keep house. And there is individual evolution, too. I have friends who lament, "What are we to do with the furniture? The children don't want it. They're interested only in modern." "Put it in storage," I tell them. "The grandchildren will discover it."

As for me, the country boy from Baltimore who wanted to do high style, I find myself interested only in simplicity in every way. There's even a hand-hewn wooden chair from the Cotswolds in my living room—something I'd never have allowed to cross my path even 20 years ago. You expect your taste to change. Not that you necessarily think it ought to, but that you're not surprised when it does. But no matter how taste may change, the basics of good decorating remain the same: We're talking about someplace people live in, surrounded by things they like and that make them comfortable. It's as simple as that.

PIETRO BELLUSCHI: "THE CONCEPT OF SPACE AS SHELTER"

Pietro Belluschi, former Dean of the School of Architecture and Planning at the Massachusetts Institute of Technology, winner of the American Institute of Architects Gold Medal in 1972, architect of The Juillard School in New York, the Bank of America building and St. Mary's Cathedral in San Francisco, has practiced architecture in this country for more than fifty years. Here he expresses his views on the design of houses.

Designing a house is probably the most interesting of all architectural exercises, although it is often difficult and demanding. One begins with a concept of space as shelter, space as a segment of infinity which a man attempts to retrieve as his own. A good house is such a space, a microcosm where man's dreams and desires can be fulfilled.

ROBERT B. MILLER

Whether or not the design of the house is improving in our time is a controversial question. On the whole, I would say no. Due to costs, minimum housing is now the rule. But even a house of the lowest possible cost can relate to the land and its neighbors and be acceptable. When I was a young man in Italy there were few individual houses. You lived in an apartment above small shops and the street was the community. When I became an architectural apprentice in Oregon in 1925 individual houses were the rule. Indeed, they were the American dream. In the early days in America, houses were simple structures designed by journeymen.

Some of the houses I did in Oregon in the 1940s owe a debt to the indigenous structures of the area—the farm houses and barns which were unself-conscious. They were not designed by architects; they were simply obeying the laws of nature and structure. Using wood as a material most readily at hand, they appear suitable and convincing. In houses I design I try to understand the essential qualities of wood, its potential and its limitations in giving meaning to space. Wood ages so gracefully, eventually matching the color of the surrounding tree trunks. From the Japanese we learned how wood allows all kinds of subtleties in design.

The planning of the interior of the house has always been my main concern. How will people behave, how will they move about, what views do they want—an intimate view of the garden or a dramatic one of the mountains or the city? It all has to fit, house and land, because the landscape is part of the experience of living, part of the excitement and pride of having a house.

Today, man is often hampered and frustrated in this quest. First of all, the loss of his instinct for nature and how to deal with it. His instinct has been blunted by the pollution of land, air, and water, by noise, by population growth, by other assaults on his senses. All of this and the fast-changing social mores, including the disintegration of the family, is affecting the house and the way of living in it. My own experience is an example. I lived in Boston until seven years ago in an old house on the Back Bay. A five-story townhouse. The main floor with living, dining room, and stairhall was several steps up from the street. The kitchen was downstairs in the basement because in 1880 there were servants. Now we live in Portland, Oregon, in a house I designed thirty-two years ago. It is one of the early open plans where the kitchen is open to the dining and living rooms and with a view of the outdoors. There are a few dividing partitions where privacy is desired. It has a well-loved garden on one side, with a view of the high mountains on the other. Within a block there is a forest where one can walk for miles. These two houses are samples of past and present, of the differing ways of our times.

Looking back over the past half-century, some architects have excelled in their appreciation of the environment. Richard Neutra contributed a great deal, particularly in southern California houses. He was less of a regionalist than others there and brought in Bauhaus architecture, but he refined it and made it fit. His wood houses are still among the best. Frank Lloyd Wright was great, particularly when he did Taliesin in Wisconsin. He had a tremendous influence on all of us in those days. There was Walter Gropius at Harvard but he was really the philosopher of the new architecture of the 1930s. Marcel Breuer was the creative one and, in my opinion, one of the great architects. Philip Johnson is a wonderful person and a very witty guy. We worked together on Lincoln Center in New York. He loves controversy and being an iconoclast, but you have to give him his place in architecture because he is a tradition shatterer and trend changer. In the east, I also admired Paul Rudolph's work. He is gifted, probably one of the most talented. And Louis Kahn's buildings have made an impact on all of us; he was an artist, even more than an architect.

On the west coast of America, in the 1940s and 1950s, architects did excellent houses. In Seattle and on the islands of Puget Sound, you will find some of the best ones. Bill Wurster, Neutra, Gardner Dailey, Paul Kirk, and some younger California architects, were able to capture the essentials of the house. They established a principle that houses need not be conventional and stylistic but should address themselves to the well being and satisfaction of their owners. They were concerned with the essence and substance of what a house should be. Finally, to me, the greatest architect of this century was the Finnish architect Alvaar Aalto. He was the one who knew the elements that make true architecture and was able to extract the essence of beauty from these elements. He never failed to do so and was never satisfied with doing the obvious. I admired him more than anyone else because he was a free spirit and never repeated himself.

Now I see a tendency by some of the younger architects to confuse a house with a work of art. That is, one that is simply an optical exercise in line and form and certain color and to mistake that for all the intensely human experience one has in living in a house. The house should clearly indicate crucial factors. What kind of space is it? Where is the fireplace? How do you enter? How much garden do you see? On which side does the

sun shine? How does the light come in? Does the house welcome guests, children, and so on? All these are fundamental things that make a house good, bad, or indifferent. But the new trendists seem to be confusing these factors with an intellectual exercise, with the abstract drawings of a house. This has little to do with a homeowner's dream, the desire for a satisfying shelter and the happiness it can create. Today, with much housing design becoming minimal, architects should rediscover these principles. Man needs to retain his instinct for nature and his own dwelling place in it.

RUSSELL PAGE: "GARDENS THAT LOOK INEVITABLE"

Russell Page has been making gardens for over fifty years. At present he is working in Belgium, Chile, Bermuda, Nassau, Long Island, and Connecticut on hotels, aboretums, conservation projects, private gardens, and on a new and expanded edition of his book, The Education of a Gardener. *Here he talks about gardening in this century with hints for anybody setting out to design his own small garden.*

Gardens are to do with growth and change, and through the last 80 years many new factors have modified them—sometimes for better and sometimes for worse.

Through the 19th century, gardens, in Europe at least, grew larger and more elaborate. The industrial Revolution created a new "middle class" on both sides of the Atlantic, and gardens tended by armies of gardeners were luxuriant manifestations of new money in new hands.

These gardens were what we choose to call Victorian. They were planned as a curious mixture of derivative formal elements and a very stylized form of picturesque gardening. Both these conflicting styles were interpreted in new materials, cast iron and synthetic stone. Monkey puzzles, bananas, palm trees, cactus, dahlias, cannas, and other newly introduced exotica from all over the world gave a rather bizarre look to northern gardens.

By 1900 more modest themes became fashionable—English cottage gardens, the writings of Gertrude Jekyll, William Robinson and others, and the saccharine water colors of Beatrix Parsons and many more, made borders of herbaceous plants and elaborate rose gardens, water, bog and rock gardens high fashion in Europe, but it was the First World War that caused the first major change in a century-long tradition.

I was recently visiting one of England's great country houses, looking at what was left of a large and elaborate garden. Two men struggled to keep an air of tidiness at least round the house. On asking how many gardeners there had been before 1914—I was told 80—and they all slept in the house!

By the middle 1920s, when I first began gardening, circumstances had changed and gardens became smaller and simpler. The bedding-out of whole gardens with annuals disappeared except in public parks, to be replaced by perennial plants, and (a new element) flowering shrubs, which could be used for formal and informal schemes and be kept in order with an occasional pruning. In the British Isles rhododendron fever set in due to the introduction of hundreds of new species from high Asia. British gardeners went mad about these and the Asiatic primulas and blue poppies that came with them. Formal gardens were reduced to the minimum required to make a seemly setting for a house if you had not already been obliged to move into a cottage, and "wild" gardening became the rage.

This was about the time that I set out to earn my living by making gardens in a modest way. People who had had 50 gardeners had by now maybe 10, and people who had 10 made do with 2. If garden owners were not digging themselves, they gave much time to pruning and weeding and propagating plants. Gardening was a pleasure and an interest for the amateur, and the sheer quality of gardens and of horticulture improved in consequence. Young, enthusiastic and hardworking, I was soon up and down the country building modest alpine and rock gardens, learning about plants from everybody who could teach me, from clients and from their gardeners, while I slowly felt my way to designing in a stricter sense of the word. Handling plants taught me much about design, form, and texture, and I wanted to use this knowledge to unite shapes and colors and textures to make gardens that would mature, I hoped, into original and well-designed entities fit to stand comparison with the best work of earlier designers.

In England, design had always taken second place.

Spending time and working in France I taught myself the elements of classical design, and then with some years of practical gardening behind me I became a landscape architect, as such, and in the few remaining years before 1939, found myself designing quite large schemes in England and France. By then the idea of using the garden for living as well as for looking at had made its way from America to Europe—people of means wanted their gardens tranformed to include terraces and loggias for outdoor living and their own swimming pool—new concepts for European gardens. Country house gardens in England and France took on a gayer look. A new kind of outdoor life brought people, literally, out into the open and induced a new and slightly different stimulus to garden design. Then came the Second World War, and the whole process repeated itself—1945 saw even more changes than 1918.

Of course there were still people who could afford to make large gardens, and I continued to work for them in many different countries.

On the whole, the great gardens and great gardeners of the last 60 years have been amateurs, working in their own gardens and in those of their friends—semi-professional in some cases. Distinguished professionals in this period are few. The outstanding designer of the last 50 years is surely Burle Marx—Brazilian painter, sculptor, and botanist. His influence and impact has been enormous though unfortunately limited in its range since, as far as I know, most of his work has been in terms of tropical vegetation.

Thomas Church was another first-class designer, in California and in temperate North America. Judging only from photographs he seems to have been singularly sensitive to plant material, to modern painting and sculpture, to the reticence and discipline of the Japanese approach as well as to the traditional forms of the smaller European and American garden styles of the last 300 years. Lawrence Halprin, whose garden work, too, I have only seen in photographs, has brought a remarkable eye to garden design using abstract forms and disciplined planting in a way that to me indicate a deep understanding of the motivation of certain Asian gardens and, more important, of the relationship between sheer geometry and the organic forms of plant life that informs all Islamic garden design to be seen at its best in the Mogul gardens of Northern India.

The amateurs who have shaped 20th-century garden design are many. Lawrence Johnston's garden, at Hidcote, is still the finest example of a small garden, as well designed as it is well planted. Inspired by it is Victoria Sackville-West's well-known garden at Sissinghurst. Here in the Kent countryside a basic framework of hedges and walls repeats and extends the courtyards and walls of the red brick castle. The planting, in each enclosure, tends to be dominated by one kind of plant, old-fashioned roses, perhaps, or Ghent azaleas with colored primroses, or by one range of color like the white and silver garden or the tawny copper and orange plot next to one of the cottages.

These two gardens have acted as an inspiration for hundreds of medium-to-small-sized gardens in England, whence the fashion has spread to other European countries.

A hint on designing a small garden—what do you want from your plot?—to grow flowers and plants, to sit about in it, or perhaps to have something pictorial to look at? Whatever the requirements I would set about the problem by choosing one simple idea for its plan and composition—and only one—and my planting would be thought out in the same way with a limited choice of plants deployed to look well and make the garden look bigger. If I try to introduce too many details unrelated to my basic plan I am only likely to achieve a confused and confusing result, which would be the opposite of what I think gardens are about and how they should look.

Over the last 50 years I have made a good many gardens in a good many different countries, differing climates and different types of soil. Each of these gardens was, and in most cases still is, necessarily unlike any other. All the aspects that a site offers will at once indicate possibilities and limitations. You have to design within these limits and possibilities and come up with a scheme that takes full advantage of both. The transient nature of gardens, other than purely architectural compositions, is what most appeals to us whether we are consciously aware of it or not.

I have lived to see many of my gardens mature and some abandoned or destroyed. Each of the ones I have revisited and liked years later, I have liked because they have seemed to me so closely linked to their surroundings and the nature of the ground they are built on. I like to feel that they look inevitable. Of course there are many possible solutions to the problems set by any one site. I usually hope to get a flash of insight into what the garden will be like—note that I don't say could or should—so I just try to keep this in mind and do everything that will bring me nearer to my original impression. I try to keep clear of variations that will distract from the essential nature of the garden I am making.

Imagine a narrow sloping valley, hemmed in by wooded slope, almost too steep to climb. There is a rocky ditch in the bottom with running if dirty water. The whole site is a tangle of weeds and brambles and assorted rubbish brought down by occasional brief floods from the mountains above. Now the small stream is cleaned and controlled and fills a series of small ponds, 11 of them, each flowing over a little cascade to the next pond below. Wide stretches of grass make easy walking on both sides of the ponds whose edges are planted with drifts of Japanese iris, Japanese anemones, phlox, which like a moist position, astilbes, spireas and ferns—wild rhubarb and gunnera make accents of giant foliage, and many varieties of hostas and other foliage plants are used as foils for more highly colored flowers. Through these low plantings rise groups of flowering shrubs suitable for the site. These include rose-species, barberries, magnolias, lilac species (not garden varieties), and many others. Clusters of Japanese cherries, mountain ash, magnolias and koelreuterias add their height to the flowering material, and certain evergreens and conifers especially some of the better chamaecyparis like C. Pottenii and C. Wisselii give sharp vertical accents. Autumn color plays its part: there are Japanese and other maples, sweet gums, sumacs and katsura trees. All this planting is linked to the surrounding woods by groups of Scots pine and white birch, both natives of the area. There are no dramatic statements, all is easy and flowing, and the gentle tinkling sound of water tumbling over the little cascade is the key to the whole scheme.

From England I learned to know plants, to love them and make them grow. France taught me to use geometry to design related and logical garden plans and the possibilities of using sunlight and shade to further explore the third dimension.

Islamic art and Islamic gardens, in particular, taught me a more subtle geometry and how to use it to make very basic and apparently simple patterns and forms and then to add all the luxuriance of living plants to make a special kind of world whose visual impact is unique.

How would I advise anybody who was setting out to design a garden? If it were I, I would first think very carefully of what kinds of plants I wanted to grow—this gives me some idea as to what conditions these kinds of plants will best succeed in, what soil they like, how large or small they will be when full grown. It may be trees, shrubs, flowering plants, or vegetables or a combination.

I tend, at this stage, to think of these as layers, high, medium, and low. Your plan must be as simple as you can make it, and the first thing to do, whether on paper or the ground, is to fix your lines of communication, how you get from one place to another, and as a general rule the shortest way from one point to another is the best. The exception is when you deliberately want to slow the pace, to stroll around and amongst your plantings. This is functional planning and basic.

After this, I would next look at the external surroundings, trees, woods, a view, the neighbors and their buildings—which would you like to include in your garden picture and which block out?

So far this is foundation work, and getting that part right will leave you with more precise spaces to plan for than the block plan of the site. Next you consider what you want to keep of what is already there—trees, mounds, or hollows or any other existing features.

Only then can you begin to see how much space you have for all the elements you may want to include. I start usually with the permanent structures, sitting areas of paving, swimming pool, tennis courts, and any other structures needed, and how most conveniently to link or divide them.

As soon as you have taken stock of all existing features and have decided on everything you wish to get rid of, you can then see how best to adapt the type of garden you aim to have to your ground. It may be formal or informal, or a combination of the two. I always find myself seeking how to suggest whatever I want in the simplest possible way. At this stage it is better to forget all the tempting picturesque details you may eventually want to incorporate.

Next comes perhaps a more interesting stage when you can decide where you want your trees and where shrubs, where you want sun and where shade, where hedges or barriers and where low plantings.

Unless you are an obsessive botanical name-dropper, a collection of one each of different kinds of plants makes a fidgety and dull-looking garden. Plant enough of each plant to show it at its best—one tree, three large shrubs, five small shrubs, seven subshrubs, five large herbaceous plants and ten to fifteen smaller ones is a useful ratio. You can make exceptions by adding an odd single plant from time to time to sharpen a color combination or make a contrast in texture and form.

As to flower color—I use the largest available area for closely related colors. A stretch of cream and different yellows works all the better if you point it up with a shiny leaved variegated shrub or an odd plant with blue-gray foliage. Rhododendron and evergreen azaleas are notoriously difficult to group well. I try to put all the reds together, for instance, but I would avoid putting pink or purple next the reds. Separate pinks from reds and reds from purple, or for that matter purple from yellow by breaks or patches of white.

White flowers are always useful as a bridge between dissonant color groups, and large groupings of different white flowered plants shows how subtly varied in tone white flowers can be.

Red flowers are difficult in the garden, they seem to make a dark hole. Orange tones need pointing up with the odd scarlet plant, and all the bright reds will sing together in harmony if you add a single note of magenta.

Rightly used, reds come near while blues seem to recede. The cold clear blues of some delphiniums, for instance, make their mauve and purple cousins look gray and misty; white delphiniums or lilies will help solve this problem.

Gray foliaged plants set off all flower colors admirably—lavenders, artemisias, caryopteris, teucriums, and larger dwarf buddleias, Buddleia alternifolia and Pyrus salicifolia, the silver pear. Unfortunately most of those silvery plants dislike too much cold and snow; many of them come from the Mediterranean area.

As all gardeners know, you can share delight with others. I have noticed all my life the generous spirit of all the many gardeners I have met. They are always ready to share their knowledge and their appreciation of plants and gardens, to give you plants and cuttings and seeds and information. In this respect all we gardeners can be called civilized people.

When I was in Cairo, in the last war, sometimes I used to visit a dervish monastery on the hills above the citadel, because it was quiet, had a wonderful view westward over the city to the pyramids beyond and a garden. The Sheik, the Abbot of the monastery, was an impressive old Albanian gentleman with a long beard who loved his garden. With no common language I could watch him gardening, using all the same economical gestures and movements that I had learned as a child from an old Lincolnshire farm laborer. We became good friends in that garden with never a word spoken.

1900/s

LIVING WITH TRADITION

At the dawn of the new century, living still reflected the grace and dignity of the past. A mixture of Victorian taste, combined with Edwardian opulence and show, dominated the large and spacious houses in which people lived. Interest in gardens was a feature of the period; the elegant formal gardens of Italy and France were copied by Americans, and outdoor garden decoration such as wicker and trellis increased in popularity. This increasing consciousness and observation of nature paralleled the most important style in decoration of the decade—Art Nouveau, literally new art, which had first appeared in the 1890s as an expression of dissatisfaction with the continued eclecticism of the Beaux Arts influence in design. Art Nouveau, as interpreted in France, Italy, Germany, England, and America, supplanted the old forms with organic, swirling shapes and movements originating in the natural world. Its ultimate outcome and simplification in America was the Mission style of Gustave Stickley. The work of Tiffany, Gallé, and Mackintosh, supported by international dealers such as Samuel Bing, transformed the taste of a generation brought up to value the more formal traditions of past epochs in interior design. In dramatic contrast, the prophetic work of Frank Lloyd Wright, pioneer of the prairie-house school in Chicago, began in this decade to influence architects all over the world for generations to come.

The walk from the rose garden to the greenhouses at Twin Oaks, near Washington, D.C., the home of Mrs. Gardiner G. Hubbard. Under the direction of landscape gardener Mr. Peter Bisset, a charming feature of the estate is the rose arbor which affords a connecting avenue to the rose garden.

ROOMS OF MODERN HOMES

U.S.A. and England, 1901, 1902

An architect is influenced in his first conception of a modern home by several considerations, perhaps one of the principal ones being suggested by the character of the life of the town in which the house is to be built. If it is to be in a fine, old-fashioned, country town, his ideas from the start are necessarily bound by certain lines, and the characteristics to be accentuated ought to be of the informal, hospitable sort. If it is to be built in a location involving the formal life of the city, a natural impulse is perhaps for stateliness and elegant formality. . . . The materials used will also have a bearing upon the nature of the architectural style. Elaborately carved mahogany, dark grained pine, a subtle blending of colors, will be found most suited to the more formal design of

An archway, The Read House, New Castle, Delaware

rooms, whereas more simple treatments, such as brick, pine, and white oak, will be found more acceptable and pleasing in the less formal, more domestic type of living quarters. It is of course essential that the architect take into consideration the use to which each room in the house will be put, whether it be for entertaining or for quiet family occasions. In the selection of furniture, an attempt should be made to produce a harmonious result, taking into account the proportions and materials used in the house, so that the rooms may, both in conception and execution, reflect the sincere expression of the tastes and the mode of life of their occupants. In this way, posterity may learn from these examples of harmonious design how to assemble and place the objects in a room. . .

Music room, finished in quartered oak. Brookline, Massachusetts, designed by J.A. Schweinfurth, architect.

Upper hall, with antique bronze railing to form a balustrade overlooking the living room; open fireplace 10 feet wide, faced in Harvard brick. Many pieces of the furniture were designed by the architect and owner, Mr. John P. Benson, Flushing, Long Island.

Living room, finished in quartered oak, with leaded windows and boldly expressive stairway. The Residence of H.C. Bennett, Esq., Jersey City, New Jersey, designed by Wilson Eyre.

Another view of the living room in Jersey City, showing vigorous detail of the frame of a decorative panel over the mantel shelf and brick fireplace.

Parlor, showing pictured wallpaper, depicting a view of Constantinople with its domes and minarets against a blue sky. Brookline, Massachusetts, designed by J.A. Schweinfurth.

Another view of the parlor in the Brookline house, with its plain-colored curtains and upholstery making a contrast to the vivid walls.

Sitting room with matching wallpaper and curtains, fabric-covered table and lamp. "La Rochelle," the summer home built for George S. Bowdoin, Esq., in Bar Harbor, Maine. Andrews, Jaques & Rantoul, architects.

Parlor, with interior finish of highly glazed pine, richly upholstered furniture. "Hill Stead," residence of Mr. Alfred Atmore Pope, Farmington, Connecticut.

Billiard room, with enclosed viewers' gallery, a collection of paintings on the wall, and fringed lamps. "Shooter's Hill," England.

Hallway, freely provided with woodwork in the form of pilasters, arches, and doorways. The Read House, New Castle, Delaware.

The exterior view from the northwest.

Hall of Riverdale house, looking toward garden.

A NEW WAY TO BUY A HOUSE

BY J. M. HASKELL

Riverdale, New York, 1906

"Very well! Here is my check for five thousand dollars. I shall take my family to Europe on the first of the month and will not return until the 10th of next December. On the 20th of that month I shall expect you to deliver to me, complete in all particulars according to my written memorandum of instructions, the house called for by these plans and specifications—complete as to structure; as to grading, sodding, and planting of the grounds; complete, too, as to furniture, with carpets down, curtains hung, pantry, kitchen, and coal cellar stocked, the house warmed and lighted, and dinner for six ready to be served at eight o'clock of that day. The price is to be thirty-five thousand dollars and it is agreed, too, that there are to be no bills for extras or additions, and further, that if the house complete can be built and equipped according to these plans and instructions for less than thirty-five thousand dollars I am to be credited with my share of the difference. Meanwhile I want to hear nothing further of the matter until I return. My financial agent will pay you additional installments of the cost pro rata as the work proceeds in accordance with my contract with you until twenty-five thousand dollars have been paid. The balance due you will be paid within thirty days of the delivery and acceptance of the house by me, and it will be accepted and your bond satisfied when I am satisfied that everything has been done by you as agreed."

Such, in effect, is the way the house builder of the twentieth century will buy his house, if the new method of Messrs. Hoggson Brothers is carried into successful operation; and that it can be done they offer as evidence the accompanying photographs of a thoroughly modern residence at Riverdale, New York, recently completed under their system. Acting as the owner's representative they attended to the making of the plans for the house by a New York architect approved by the owner; to the designing and planting of the grounds by a landscape architect; the building of the house and the grading by local labor under a local contractor.

The site of the house is on a slope of the Palisades overlooking the Hudson and facing east. To take the fullest advantage of the easterly exposure, all the rooms of the house are practically on that side, in accordance with plans which carried out the owner's wishes in every respect.

The house is of frame throughout with foundations of local stone. All of the rooms are furnished in enameled cream white woodwork with Colonial detail. The halls are paneled, and the ceiling beams show in the dining room, around which there is a rail 6 feet above the floor. The fireplaces are finished in brick, and the bathrooms in cream tile, with vitreous tile floors.

The second floor contains the bedrooms, bathrooms, and linen closet only. On the third floor are a large guest room, servant's room, bathrooms and attic. The cellar contains the arrangements usual in a house of this character.

The advantages claimed for this method of contracting are:

1st. That the owner is guaranteed a certain maximum cost with a variable minimum cost dependent upon the saving effected over the first estimates.

2nd. That the owner is relieved of responsibility and worry during the progress of the work.

3rd. That the inclusion under one contract of all parties engaged in the production of the house ensures a uniformity and unity of product not otherwise possible. In the case illustrated, the entire estate was finished, stables, pergolas, etc., erected, vegetable and flower gardens planted, and the whole delivered actually ready for use.

This proposition seems a reasonable one, and will doubtless become a well-established custom once public confidence is fully gained.

Fountain in garden.
A suggestion for relieving a blank brick wall.

Front entrance to the house.

The living room, finished in mahogany.

Garden at the west side of the house.

Bedroom with blue cartridge paper walls and white woodwork.

The Flower Garden.

Wooden Ornament of a Walk.

The Garden from the Porch.

"MORETON"

Hampstead, London, 1905

The Residence of Mr. F.F. Sidney, F.S.A. In the comprehension of the average Londoner, Hampstead is usually connected with nothing more than steep hills and the breezy heath, where cockneys spend their holiday hours and holiday money. Of the few who still delight in the old-fashioned village and its 18th-century red-brick houses are those unaware that, hidden in one of the old byways, is to be found a house which, but for the quickly gathering city grime, might have been bodily transplanted from the great limestone belt, which runs across England from east to west, from Lincolnshire to the Cotswolds; for over this house and the garden in which it stands there seem to fall

View from the East Shrubbery.

something of the quiet and dignity that are the universal possession of the old stone-built manors with which the district referred to abounds.

Moreton is built with rough-cast walls and stone trimmings in that transitional style that marks the earliest influence of the Italian Renaissance in England—Gothic, almost, in its constructional scheme and modified only in its decorative parts by the new method. Mr. Sidney has furnished the interior in closest sympathy with the whole architectural treatment. The ceilings, for instance, are in their original condition, and have upon them the texture and mellow color that plaster will acquire when left to itself. Externally, attention is at once drawn to the

Living Room of the House.

small niche above the entrance, where stone figures of Mary and Jesus, with a tiny lamp burning at their feet, seem to lead up insensibly to the Madonnas and Saints to be seen within—over the door, too, and on a shield of arms is the inscription "God is al in al thinges," borrowed from the well-known Little Moreton Hall in Cheshire, the home of Mr. Sidney's ancestors. The terraces of the garden are each bounded by a stone balustrade. The balusters are widely spaced, an arrangement for which

A Shropshire four-poster.

there is ample authority in early garden work, and their light and delicate character is a studied and effective contrast to the obvious solidarity of the house. Under the upper terrace is a square compartment with sundial and Irish yews ranged around, and to the west a flower parterre with box-edged beds, and for central feature a charming figure of gilded lead. Below these a broad, grassed terrace sets astride the site and overlooks the tennis lawn some 8 feet below.

At the back of the

The Descent to the Tennis Lawn.

house a little garden, of simple materials and clever welding together of existing trees, has turned an unpromising piece of ground into a pretty scheme where paved and cobbled paths divide the box-bordered beds. Around the fine

Under the old Holly Tree.

old yew tree at a crossing of the walks is a seat, fashioned of simple staves against the bole, and a yew hedge encloses all. This will, when fully grown, shut in this tiny and attractive lay-out from the surrounding work.

The box and yew gardens.

AN OLD-WORLD GARDEN

Levens Hall, Kendal, England, 1907

The walk separating the orchard and the topiary garden.

Levens Hall—main walk from the barrister's wig.

The gardens at Levens Hall are beyond question the finest surviving example of the topiary work that became so fashionable in Europe in the 16th century. . . . The various trees are usually surrounded by flowers set out in neat beds with an edge of clipped box for the border. Opening vistas are forms interesting for their picturesque fantasy—to many visitors the "judge's wig" is most amusing. . . .

The bagot "B," a modern example.

HERE AND THERE
IN THE TURIN EXPOSITION

BY VIRGINIA BUTLER

Turin, Italy, 1903

Any visitor to the First International Exhibition of Decorative Art in Turin could not fail to be convinced that modern art has made a place for itself in the world. . . . The lamps in the Tiffany exhibit were worthy of special notice from the way in which use and beauty were combined. The Rookwood ware shows that there is growing in the United States an artistic taste that breathes a freshness of thought and fancy to be expected in a country where natural, social, and economic conditions are different from those that have given birth to European art projects. The American exhibit of plumbing, bathtubs, and all those things purely practical also attracted much attention. The Scottish section was under the direction of Mr. Charles R. Mackintosh and his wife, Margaret Macdonald Mackintosh.

Cushion by F.H. Newbery

The space given to Scotland was divided into three rooms, opening into each other. The first one was done in silver, white, and rose; the second in white and a shade of golden gray with a frieze of pink and green that gave just the needed touch of color to save it from dullness; the third was in a rich purple and white. The woodwork and ceilings in all were pure white, and the effect was most pleasing and restful. Mr. George Logan's three-paneled screen of gray wood, inlaid with silver and semi-precious stones, attracted attention chiefly because of the unusual materials used. The two designs for tapestry, by Mr. David Gow, as will be seen from the pictures, while not startlingly original, are yet wonderfully graceful in pattern. Among the other artistic objects in the Scottish department were three sofa

Cushion by F.H. Newbery

Wrought-iron electrolier by Alice Nordin

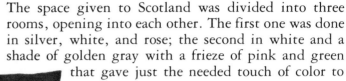

Favrile glass vases by Tiffany Studios

Tapestry Designs　　*by David Gow*

Faïence vases by the Rookwood Pottery Company

pillows, designed by Mr. F.H. Newbery of the Glasgow School of Art, which, as the illustrations show, have an originality of design not easy to duplicate, even in this age of sofa pillows. To the writer, the most interesting exhibit in the Holland room was the batik work on velvet, silk, and cotton stuffs. In looking at the finished work, one would never imagine that the material, especially the velvet, had been through such a process of waxing and boiling as is necessary to produce the impressive result. The idea comes from Java and is used for table covers, sofa covers, panels for screens, etc., and is extremely effective. Though the Turin Exhibition was not a financial success, it certainly was a success in every other way: and it is to be hoped that it will be followed by others, to further the progress of modern thought. . . .

Scottish interior by J. Herbert McNair

Bed by Bing's "L'Art Nouveau," Paris

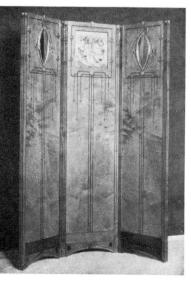

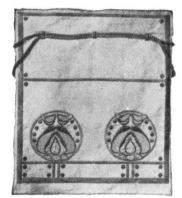

Cushion by F.H. Newbery

Inlaid screen by George Logan

AN ADIRONDACK LODGE

DAVIS, McGRATH & SHEPARD, ARCHITECTS

Lake Wilbert, New York, 1907

A comfortable night's travel on the Adirondack Montreal Express from New York and a 17-mile drive through the woods take one to the beautiful moutain lake in the heart of the Adirondacks on which this camp is situated . . .

The main lodge, about 30 feet above the lake, contains the living room and sleeping quarters, while the dining room, kitchen, and servants' quarters are placed about 200 feet from it on a rocky point projecting over the lake. The two buildings are connected by a rustic covered passage.

The buildings are constructed of spruce logs, 10 inches in diameter, from which the bark has been peeled, and stained with a rich brown wood preservative. The main lodge consists of a living room 25 by 40 feet, 8 bedrooms, 5 bathrooms and a gun room. Large closets and a native rough fireplace are provided in every room. The living room has a wide rustic staircase at one end and a stone open fireplace and raised alcove with cushioned seats at the other. The acetyline gas brackets are made to resemble kerosene lamps with glass chimneys and mica shades. The dining room is a large octagonal room 25 feet in width, open to the roof,

Rustic steps lead to boat landing.

which is supported by heavy hewn trusses. The upper part of the room is lighted by a row of small windows. Directly below are large panels filled with burlap. The walls and ceilings of the bedrooms are finished in a native spruce, paneled and stained in a variety of soft colors. The windows throughout consist of a single sash, hinged at the sides with the glasscut up in small panes, such as are always to be found in the old log cabins.

The long, wide veranda with its rustic seats and nooks runs almost around the entire building. The kitchen and servants' quarters are joined to the dining room by a butler's pantry and are almost entirely hidden from the lake by thick foliage. Adjacent to the kitchen is a commodious ice house consisting of a large ice chamber and two cold air rooms.

This camp was designed to give comfort to its owner in cold as well as hot weather. To this end, the walls were sheeted with ⅞-inch boards inside the logs, which were then covered with heavy building paper before the paneling was put in place, and double sash provided for all windows. Equal care was taken in protecting the plumbing pipes . . .

The living room with hewn beams and rustic staircase.

Opposite end of living room showing fireplace.

Rustic passage connecting lodge and dining room.

Octagonal dining room with open hearth.

Dining room veranda overlooking the lake.

A HOUSE FOR ONE THOUSAND DOLLARS

BY HELEN LUKENS GAUT

U.S.A., 1907

No style of architecture lends itself so amiably to all conditions of pocketbook as that known as the box-house. In moderate climates it adapts itself to every season, and makes an acceptable all-the-year-round home. These houses of one story, and occasionally one story and a half, may be fashioned according to the ideas of the builder, hence they are of almost innumerable and original designs.

The accompanying illustrations are of a house the cost of which was but $1000. The place was built by a woman who wanted a "rest home," a country place, yet because of many duties, realized it was out of the question to have it far from her city home, as too much time would be consumed in going and coming. She looked about, finding a cheap but sightly bit of land within 5 miles of the town, and easily reached by electric cars. It required but twenty minutes to make the trip from city home to country place, and at least once a week, on Saturday and Sunday, the family had an outing, enjoying entire change of air and scene in this cozy rest house in the lap of the Sierra Madre foothills.

This idea may be helpful to those who long for a country home yet think it should be located many miles from a city in order to be desirable. On the outskirts of every city are possible site opportunities, unpromising lots that can often be bought very cheaply, and, now that electric roads vein our country like arteries, can be reached in a few minutes. These sites are just as comforting and rest-giving as the more costly suburban lot or those located hundreds of miles away, in the latter case more so, in fact, because one avoids the fatigue of long dusty travel.

The foundation of this house is of posts, set on blocks of cement, and is enclosed by planed boards placed horizontally. The walls are made of boards a foot wide, which are planed on the inside and rough on the outside. These are nailed to the framework at top and bottom. Battens of unplaned wood 2 inches wide are used to cover the cracks between the boards on the outside.

The roof has 40-inch projecting eaves, and is shingled. Shakes are cheaper than shingles, and are frequently used for roofing, but such roofs often leak and prove unsatisfactory in other ways, thus shingles are advisable.

The house is unplastered. The inside finish is simple, consisting only of the planed side of the boards, which form the main walls. The cracks are covered with planed battens, 2 inches wide and ¾ of an inch thick. The effect is that of a wainscoting running from floor to ceiling. Handsomely grained wood adds greatly to the artistic effect, for the stains now so popular for finishing woodwork, and which often take the place of paint and varnish, bring out each detail of natural beauty in the wood. Ceilings are constructed in the same way as the walls, excepting that 2-by-4 beams are used. These are both artistic and substantial in effect. A brace, 1 by 3, circles each room about 4 feet from the floor. No other braces are necessary in these light-weight houses, for roof and floors strengthen and brace the structure sufficiently.

The best thing about this house is the veranda dining room, which in sunny California can be used almost every day of the year. The outer edge of the porch floor on the north is close to the ground. This porch is 10 by 26 feet. At one end is a low, wide railing for plants. Three-quarter inch gas pipe makes a framework for an adjustable awning, which, however, is seldom used, as the roof of blue sky is much pleasanter.

The house is complete and modern in every way, having the best of plumbing throughout, and is an excellent example of what can be done for $1000. Most of the furniture in the house is handmade from Arts and Crafts designs, and corresponds admirably with the rustic interior. Indian blankets, gay pillows, dainty curtains, and attractive pictures make the place an oasis of rest.

In cold climates such houses are especially adapted for summer homes for beach and mountains, but they are not really suitable for winter use.

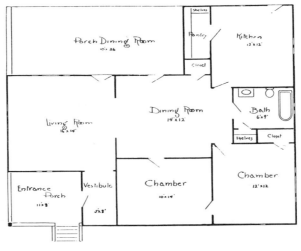

Floor plan.

Exterior of the house.

Veranda dining room.

Front view of Dr. E.B. Dane's garage, Chestnut Hill, Massachusetts.

THE PRIVATE GARAGE

ITS DESIGN, ARRANGEMENT, AND COST

BY I. HOWLAND JONES

Boston, Massachusetts, 1906

The most modern problem that the architect has to face is the private garage. Motoring enthusiasm has spread so widely that many country-house owners, even if horse lovers and possessors of a stable, have at least one machine. And the inaccessibility of public garages in this country being marked to a degree, as every motor tourist can testify feelingly, the need of one's own becomes imperative . . .

It is never wise to plan a building with only room enough to take one car, as the additional cost of making one large enough for two is so very little that the extra expense is always justified. Probably the one important thing to make the building a success is the ease with which the owner can enter and leave it. For this reason it should be arranged so that the cars can stand along the back wall with the door opposite. Another matter that should receive attention is that the house should be as fireproof as possible. A washing-stand should be planned for. It is well, too, to

finish a room in the second story for a chauffeur or perhaps two small rooms one of which could be used by a guest's chauffeur. The cost of a complete garage can range from $250 to $5,000 . . .

One of the most complete garages was built for Mr. E.B. Dane at Chestnut Hill, Boston, and was designed by Andrews, Jaques & Rantoul, architects. This plan is about as well arranged as possible. The carriage room is liberal in size, which allows the cars to be moved to and from the wash-stand and workshop with ease without taking them out of doors. The wash-stand is located opposite the center door and the car is run directly on to it on its return to the house. Then if a visit to the workshop happens to be necessary it is run straight into it, and can be taken back into the carriage room without the necessity of turning any corners, which are always difficult when a machine is not under power.

The second story has two rooms and a bathroom for

Car room of Mr. Dane's garage, showing granolithic floor.

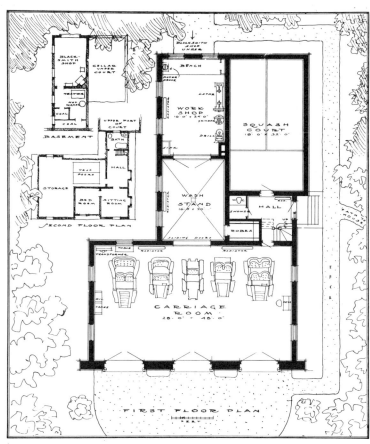

Basement floor plan of Mr. Dane's garage.

The garage seen from the house.

the chauffeur and also a large storage loft with a trap door from below. In connection with this building is a squash court, the floor of which is a little above the basement level. The workshop is a most interesting part of the building, and is fitted with most modern machinery. It is possible with this outfit, and the skill of the chauffeur, to make or repair any part of an automobile without ever having to send it away to have the work done. It contains a liberal-sized work bench, and the lathe, emery wheel, buffer, and drill, are all run by a little two horse-power electric motor, which stands on a shelf over one end of the bench.

The gasoline is stored in two 100-gallon tanks, which are placed underground at the side of the drive, about 50 feet from the garage, and the gasoline is pumped into a can with a small hand pump . . .

UP-TO-DATE BATHROOMS

BY CHARLES JAMES FOX, PH.D.

U.S.A., 1907

. . . For a first-class modern bathroom, several things are essential: spaciousness, light, ventilation, open plumbing, and last and most important, inorganic, non-absorbent, washable floors and walls . . . The small, musty bathroom of a few years ago with the unsanitary wooden floors and wainscoting is now a thing of the past. The ideal covering for the floors and walls is the baked clay tile. Tile is absolutely non-absorbent and germ proof. It is the most durable of all flooring materials, and it lends itself to the most artistic and decorative designs. Tiling of the entire wall is necessary. . . .

Colorful bathroom of Moorish design, with Roman or tiled pool-bath sunk in floor.

Bathroom with wall tile up to a height of 7½ feet, walls above and ceiling painted in a flat finish.

Cove base tiled bathroom (rounded tile for skirting or baseboard), with decorative tile panels on the walls and the ceiling.

Wall design for a green bathroom.

Decorative colored wall tile.

THE USE OF ELECTRICITY IN THE HOUSE

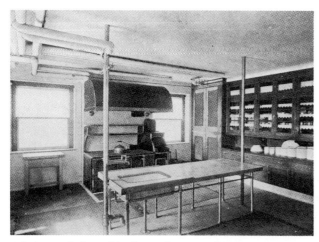

A light, simply designed kitchen, with range and hood. The central table has a sunken container.

Butler's pantry with wood paneled cabinets, glassed-in shelves, concealed serving equipment.

With electricity, housework no longer spells drudgery.

The electric range—driving all rivals from the field.

Water heater

Electric clothes dryer

Coffee percolator

Chafing dish

Cereal cooker and egg boiler

Curling iron

Flat-iron designs

Push-button breakfast

Ornamental flower garden with central circular grass plot and sundial. Residence of the Misses Mason, designed by Irving Gill, Newport, Rhode Island.

THE GROWTH OF THE ORNAMENTAL GARDEN

U.S.A. and Spain, 1902–1909

Much more goes into the making of a true garden than flowers, shrubs, and pathways. Such a garden, set down in the midst of the fields, would appear desolate and incomplete, lacking boundary walls and trellises, fountains and shelters, seats for rest and contemplation, and even tables for our attendant creature comforts. Especially is this true of the domestic garden, the garden that lies next to the house and forms a part of it, an outdoor living room for fair weather and reflective moods. . . . Garden development in our country is in so early a state, as yet, especially as regards the smaller private garden, that we seldom make use of our opportunities, even if we pay attention to them at all. The value of outdoor life is being insistently preached today by the medical profession and the garden is one of the means ready to hand for its accomplishment. Half the time spent indoors during six or seven months of the year might be more profitably spent in the garden—which should be regarded primarily as an outdoor family living room. Gardening, then, is an opportunity to add to the charm of home life and one's own health, by inexpensive means.

A floating summerhouse on a lily pond designed by Charles Frederick Eaton, Santa Barbara, California.

This is the trellised colonnade of a group of greenhouses at Villanova, Pennsylvania, designed by Messrs. Frank Miles Day & Brother for the estate of Samuel T. Bodine, Esq. They are built of coarse brickwork, ornamented by suitably simple and bold details in stone and wood.

*Summerhouses on the river, with a brick river wall, stone pavilions, and rose bushes.
Garden of the Prince, Aranjuez, Spain.*

A modern German treatment of a room furnished with wickerwork

THE GARDEN AND ITS FURNITURE

U.S.A. and Europe, 1906

As well a room without its furniture as a garden without its seats, tables, chairs, benches, tearooms, pergoglas, arbors, terraces. Accessories give vitality and accent to the scene. In the examples of minor garden furniture shown here, a simplicity of outline and careful adaptation of the material to its uses, having due regard also to exposure to the weather, results in that air of appropriateness. . .

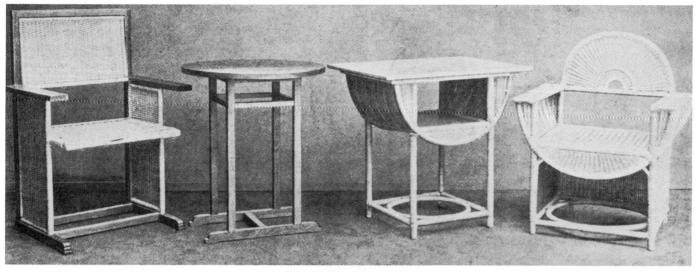

Examples of new outdoor furniture

 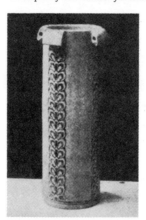 

Wickerwork garden furniture

Some novel pieces shown at a recent German exhibition

LIVING
WITH
PERSONALITY

As the great industrialists of America consolidated their fortunes, the notion of collecting works of art became a highly attractive pastime. It was in this decade that the dazzling collections of Andrew Mellon, Henry Clay Frick, and John D. Rockefeller, and of Europeans such as Samuel Courtauld, Ralph Giles and D. Davil-Weil were established, and that Edward C. Moore donated a generous fund to purchase decorative arts for the Metropolitan Museum in New York. The international dealer, Joseph Duveen, with a virtual monopoly on the sale of old master paintings, was personally responsible for introducing many of them into American homes. Interest in personal decoration increased as the art of the interior decorator began to be accepted. Edith Wharton and Ogden Codman wrote a book about it; Elsie de Wolfe and Ruby Ross Goodnow encouraged people to find new forms of self-expression in their houses. The tours of Diaghilev's Ballets Russes inspired a new infusion of exotic colors, fabrics, and harem styles into interior design. Artists such as Matisse, Bonnard, Picasso and Braque brought uninhibited color, patterns, and shapes into the world of decorating. New steel frameworks changed the shape of houses and buildings; the increasing popularity of the automobile made new demands on space. Finally, it was a decade that, because of the World War, waved goodbye to the old order and ushered in a new, more individualistic world.

1910/s

This is the trophy room of Theodore
Roosevelt's house in Oyster Bay, New York,
which shows the personality of the owner
to a marked degree. Game heads on
the walls, bear and zebra skins underfoot,
these are characteristic of the
virility of the whole house.

IN THE RESIDENCE OF ADOLPH LEWISOHN

New York City, 1917

The breakfast room bears the trace of English influence. Walls are paneled and painted ivory color. The mantel is ivory marble with colored marble inserts. A Chinese rug of old blue and old ivory tones with the walls. Fixtures are antiqued silver and the hangings old blue and silver. Hoffstatter was the decorator, C.P.H. Gilbert the architect.

Despite its rich dignity, the library is a comfortable room. Wall coverings and hangings are fawn, brown and gold. Some of the furniture is upholstered in fawn velvet and some in tapestry. The rug is two-toned fawn. Lighting fixtures are hand-carved walnut picked out with dull gold. Hoffstatter decorated the room.

The hallway has a magnificence eminently befitting its location. Against the Caen stone walls silhouette bronze railings. Antique tapestries are hung here. The carpet is plain red and the ceiling ivory. Italian walnut furniture with red upholstery finds a fitting place in such a hall. Baumgarten was the decorator.

To be understood, the color of the room must be seen. The walls are covered with plain gold paper. Woodwork and doors are painted dark green with the panels a light green. The floor is red tile. A mixture of Italian and Gothic furniture has been used. Multi-colored cushions and old brocade add interest.

ROOMS IN THE APARTMENT OF MR. JOHN BARRYMORE

New York City, 1918

Among the unusual accessories are a star-shaped lantern suspended over the couch and a brilliant carmine glass bowl that rests on the table in the bow window. The curtains at these windows are of two layers of chiffon, one mauve, the other green. In the little window is a rack of test tubes filled with colored water.

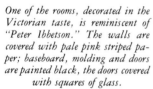
One of the rooms, decorated in the Victorian taste, is reminiscent of "Peter Ibbetson." The walls are covered with pale pink striped paper; baseboard, molding and doors are painted black, the doors covered with squares of glass.

Below: The big studio has several centers of interest, the main being the fireplace grouping of couch and prie-dieu with stools and chest drawn up on either side of the hearth. Over the skylight are curtains of saffron chiffon.

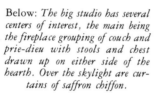
Below: The other center of interest is a music corner with piano over which is flung a cover of embroidered brocade. A bronze bird is perched on one edge. Light is given by a tall candle standard. An old mirror breaks the wall space.

Continuing the description of the Victorian room, we find curtains of pale mauve taffeta edged with a white bead fringe. Glass curtains are white gauze with crystal glass drops back of them. Crystal drops edge the molding.

The reception room has seen meetings between the leading figures of the world. One cannot but feel that here a man is surely a hero to this own chairs.

The personality of the owner is everywhere apparent. Love of books, of out of doors, of action—the record of a strenuous life—along this wall of the library.

INSIDE THE HOME OF THEODORE ROOSEVELT

Oyster Bay, New York, 1919

Left: Water buffalo, eland, a big fireplace flanked by elephant tusks, a service flag with three blue stars and one of gold—a man's hall in every detail.

Naturally one expects to find trophies of countless days afield. Game heads on the walls, bear and zebra skins underfoot, these are characteristic.

Africa and America meet around the trophy room hearth. The bison heads flanking the mantel and the lion skin on the floor suggest two of Colonel Roosevelt's best known books.

A more general view of the trophy room discloses in marked degree the virility of the whole house. Here is nothing fragile, nothing that does not stimulate by its very character.

CONCERNING COLLECTORS

U.S.A., 1918

Whenever I meet a collector of old, curious or rare objects, I hold him in especial regard. There is a man in whom Romance can never entirely die. He may be crusty, curt, uncivil and even miserly, but the very fact that he cares enough for ancient or unusual things to collect them proves that he has a door on some side of his heart. Sooner or later, if I find that door and knock, it is opened to me. Sooner or later if I show him I am interested in the same things, his tongue loosens, his eyes light up,' he bids me enter and pours for me the wine of friendship.

Age, wealth and position—the three things that build walls around men and make them unapproachable, have little to do with collectors. Such distinctions dissolve before the glow of common interest that the mere habit of collecting engenders.

Of course, like fishermen, collectors are clannish. If you come to scoff or out of vain curiosity the door will never open. The instinct of collecting is such an intimate side that no man would dare expose it ruthlessly to the world lest it lose its charm for him.

Ask a collector how he first got interested in collecting and, nine times out of ten, he'll say he "just happend to." There is more truth than fiction in that. The beginning of most collecting is just a happenstance that can come about in as many different ways as there are types of minds. The one universal element in all collectors would seem to be a form of whimsicality, of unaccountable affections and attractions. Some men have a postage-stamp mind; they are also often interested in geography. Others, like Horace Walpole, go in for china. The varieties are legion and as inexplicable as the choice of wives and husbands. No man has ever been able to give a satisfactory reason for marrying the woman he did (even Solomon was stumped by that!), nor have I met the man who could tell me exactly what it was that made him pick out and cling faithfully to his collecting specialty. The parallel can be carried even farther. For as a man gets accustomed to having a wife around and finds his curiosity growing into interest, so he gets accustomed to his hobby and becomes more and more absorbed in it. He begins to look up the history of his objects and gets chummy with the men who collect the same sort of things. From that point on it is a grand progress. He learns values, makes comparisons, studies his subjects, acquires discrimination; and eventually the day arrives when he has to choose between a box of cigars and an addition to the collection. He passes up the cigars. And thereby he becomes a confirmed collector, member of the clan; romance flames high in him and reverence is an added virture.

Romance and reverence, as a collector feels them, are mostly in the past tense. To him an old chair is more than something to sit on—it was a chair that belonged to So-and-So, who lived at such-and-such a time. It is a chair that shows fine or curious taste and the infinite pains of patient craftsmanship. Its wood has a patina that only time can give. So he annexes it to his collection and shows it proudly. Then, too, he had the romance of acquiring it. His is the last item in pedigree that includes the maker, the men and women who have owned it from time to time, the houses it has graced, the worthy folks who have admired it, the twists and turns of fortune that make it pass from hand to hand, and finally the good luck that made it his.

It is the weighing of this past romance against the possession of a modern luxury that determines the inveterate collector. He acquires a standard of values that is purely personal and not to be measured by dollars and cents. Apart from the intrinsic value of the object he seeks is the valuation his enthusiasm places upon it. Anything is at a premium so long as he wants it.

Naturally, not all collectors go in for antiques; the curiosity and the novelty are quite as collectable, and the man who seeks them is as much a collector as the millionaire whose hobby costs him fortunes. As there are grades of men, so there are grades of collectors. One may go in for Chinese porcelains and Rembrandts, the other for valentines and painted tin trays. Yet in both burns the same ardor of Romance and Reverence. They are brothers under their hides!

The only sins the collector recognizes are fraud and destruction. In both of these our Teutonic enemies have proven themselves peculiarly adept. It would seem that Germany was applying her policy of frightfulness to the art and beauty of the past, for she has deliberately caused the destruction of innumerable collections, destruction that men who love beautiful things can never forget. Her passion for substitutes and cheap wares is the result of a machine-made industrialism which holds no regard for the patient work of men's hands. Yet it is to this regard that all collectors are devoted and on which all collecting is based.

During the last four years the turn of fortune has forced many a fine collection into the auctioneer's hands. Happily for America, many of these collections have found a market here. This will surely have its effect. As time goes on Americans will be more a race of collectors than they have been.

Collecting is not a hobby of pioneer people. We are inclined to think of the English as the ideal collectors. They are a people of permanent homes—homes of long standing. Something of this principle is being worked out gradually here in the States—we are getting into the habit of settling down in one place, rearing a new generation in an atmosphere of permanency. The home is the basis of our national life; we have even crossed the seas to defent that home. Surely such a development, coupled with our recent opportunities, will stimulate the collecting habit. As we age and grow in national experience our material heritage will take on value and romance. It will give to collecting in America an increased impetus.

For collecting is nothing more than this—preserving the good of the past for the inspiration of the present. Collectors are men who cherish the legends of noble crafts, who keep the dust brushed from history, who perpetuate the appreciation of beauty.

A living room of distinction in the home of Frederic C. Bartlett, Esq., the well-known artist, in New York City, is spacious and contains an interesting arrangement of old Chinese banners and Gothic tapestries hung together on buff-tinted plaster walls. Two tall Chinese black lacquer screens cover one side of the room. Black, brilliantly flowered chintz slipcovers are used in combination with plain blue velour at the windows, a black and blue fabric on two chairs and a faded red on the davenport.

The daybed has become an almost indispensable adjunct to the boudoir. It is a comfortable piece of furniture and very pleasing to look upon, especially when upholstered in a gay, colorful fabric and piled high with an interesting assortment of pillows. This view is from the residence of William H. Earhardt, Esq., New York City. The architect was Addison Mizner.

White walls and white woodwork, silver fixtures and mahogany furniture make a dining-room combination hard to excel. It gives a cheerful, clean atmosphere, and is especially adapted to Colonial interiors. Less silver on the sideboard in this instance would have been preferable. Nelson & Van Wagenen, architects.

It is very much the sort of room we have all dreamed of having, with plenty of space for our cherished books and a background worthy of them. The furniture is covered in old chinz. A star-shaped lantern from Italy is the ceiling light.

This is the residence of Francis V. Lloyd, at Edgemont, Pennsylvania. Originally an old farmhouse, it was restored by Mellor & Meigs, architects. Note how the atmosphere of the original house has been preserved in the rough cast walls, beamed ceilings and original hardware. This view shows the living end of the combined living and dining room, with a comfortable seating arrangement.

A LITTLE PORTFOLIO OF GOOD INTERIORS

U.S.A., 1916

The woodwork is old white, with embellishments of blue and crimson on pilasters and capitals. Arched top shelves have been built in on every available wall space. An old sailing ship on the south end of the room is a quaint and artistic touch. Midway down one wall a niche holds a bust of Voltaire.

The door leading into the living room is made of a Chinese screen in blue and yellow. The 16th-century Italian table is filled with an interesting mélange of books, flowers and photographs, which give the room an air of livableness and personality. A quaint chintz-covered fireside seat is a final touch of comfort.

ESSENTIALS FOR MAKING A LIVING ROOM LIVABLE

U.S.A., 1915

The living room should be a formal, dignified room, well carried out in period style if possible, especially when there is a library or morning room for general day use; but it need not lack either in comfort or charm because of its formality. In fact, great emphasis should be laid on the choice of comfortable furniture and a real fire on its dignified hearth. Also, most important, the sun should be allowed to enter through its not too much curtained windows, while a great stimulus to livableness are plants and fresh flowers . . .

Above: An excellent arrangement creating a proper center of interest is to place a very long and somewhat massive davenport before the fire, and directly behind a table, equally long, about seven feet, and ample enough to hold a lamp on either end and plenty of books and magazines.

Right: There are few things that can lend such an air of charm, and can make instead of mar a room, as the lighting arrangements. Devices used here are admirable—good reading lights and wall brackets shaded. Nothing perhaps is more inartistic than electric bulbs in the ceiling.

Roominess in a small place may mean elimination of furniture; in general, however, proper arrangement solves the problem as here where the davenport is drawn away from the fireplace.

The living room should never be a passage, nor, if possible, should stairs or front doors be in the living room, for then it is open to strangers and servants, and there is often a time when that is not desirable . . . Two, or even three, different centers in the living room are advisable; the fireplace, primarily, with its long davenport and easy chairs; and also the window with seats and desk, bookcases close by, and a pleasant view of the outside world. It is stimulating to think that at this time, in spite of conditions abroad, there is a wonderful variety of beautiful things to furnish living rooms with right here in America. The opportunity to create delightful and artistic rooms was never greater than at the present moment . . .

The drawing room must be formal and yet not so stiff and unnatural as to make the guest uneasy. Here again the lights should be well shaded and an air of general repose created. The walls ordinarily should be plain and low in tone, with very few pictures, for seldom are there pictures that are good enough to lend beauty and distinction to a room.

Right: *Roominess can be created by setting the davenport beside the fireplace. By placing a low lamp at the end, comfort to a reader is insured and not too much light for the guest opposite. With any of these rooms, where economy is necessary, willow chairs can be introduced instead of the upholstery ones and made delightfully comfortable.*

THE TRADITION AND PURPOSE OF PAINTED FURNITURE

BY ELSIE DE WOLFE

U.S.A., 1915

Of the many mediums of modern decoration few are so sane, so easily used and so easily lived with when properly used as painted furniture. Its popularity is more than a fad, for, while its ultra expressions may pass, I venture to say that when many things considered less ephemeral shall have slid into the limbo of the forgotten, painted furniture will still be with us . . . There are reasons for the present vogue: painted furniture furnishes a splendid opportunity to introduce a vigorous color note into an interior for the sake of adding interest and enlivening contrast; and it is comparatively inexpensive. We need this vigor in our decorations. We need the wholesomeness, above all, the livableness . . .

Besides these reasons, such furniture has a tradition that comes through two channels: the finer work executed for wealthy patrons, and the rougher, cruder, but solidly substantial work fashioned and decorated by peasant owners' own hands. A revival of two types—the American farmhouse and the peasant—constitutes the bulk of the modern movement of painted furniture, and it is generally reproduced after their models. The trouble with much modern peasant furniture is that it tries to improve on its models. Beware of this when you are selecting painted furniture for your house. Look first to the lines of the pieces, then to the decoration, and then to the finish . . .

In the finer sorts of furniture, the painting was applied both inside and out. The designs were more decorative than naturalistic.

An original in fine condition. Its lacquer finish bears evidence that it was the work of Continental cabinetmakers.

Above: *An example of the sort of painted furniture of which the structural lines were those of a leading vogue in its day. Obviously a piece that requires an elegant setting.*

Right: *Paint was used, as on this console cabinet, to enrich the beauty of carved work and curved line.*

A revival of two types—the American farmhouse and the peasant—constitutes the bulk of the modern movement of painted furniture. Another type is represented here by furniture painted without decorations. Their lines are a revival of an old style.

An American bedroom done in the newer style of painted furniture by a student of the Viennese artist, Hoffmann. The walls are gray, rugs black and white and bed white with black decorations. Similar work is also coming out of the Paris studio of Iribe.

Left: The decorations on this console cabinet include, besides carving and painted decorations, heavy ormolu work. To be properly placed it would require a richly decorated room.

Above: The medallion on the back slat of these chairs is characteristic of the French and Italian masters who first painted furniture.

Many reproductions of the old models lack only age to make them perfect. This reproduction in satinwood with painted panels and floral decorations is a typical product of the present vogue for painted furniture.

DOES NATURE ABHOR THE STRAIGHT AND NARROW PATH?

U.S.A. and England, 1916 and 1917

Never before have we had such need of gardens. In this hour when the mind is torn with rumors of shell-shattered trenches and numbed with the statistics of suffering incomprehensible, it is well to seek in the garden the peace of green growing things. Does nature abhor the straight and narrow path, or is the straight path the longest in a garden? That is the question these examples illustrate. A path must have a definite *raison d'être:* it must lead somewhere and it must be part of the garden scheme. If concrete is used, there should be found some way to mitigate the mechanical nakedness—a grass or a flower border will help. There should be a definite reason for the path curving. Sometimes it avoids a large tree or skirts an embankment. On a level stretch, nothing is so loved as a grass path. It is a veritable part of the garden and lends itself to the most charming treatments with border beds. It requires, however, a maximum of care. The gravel path is easy to the foot, and after rain gives that rich earthy perfume so beloved of gardeners. The path with grass steps is a device long used in English gardens and is now being gradually tried out by landscape architects in America. Also of late, gardeners have seen the beauty and wisdom of the Japanese stepping-stone path. When properly laid, it is easy to walk on, and gives the garden an unusual interest.

There is balm in the kindly shade of trees, rest in the silent mirroring of a lake, and ennoblement in the faint high crest of iris—the flower of France. Such a glimpse can be caught in this garden of Mortan Nicholls, Esq., at Greenwich, Connecticut.

For the damp garden corner the old-fashioned board walk is still the best type of path; instead of the boards, use cedar branches, like miniature logs.

Apart from their picturesque charm stone steps are an indispensable feature in the rocky garden. They may be covered with rock plants or banked ferns.

This path leads definitely to the gate and shares characteristics of the wall.

Rose arches always enhance the inviting effect of any vista along the path.

This view of the grass step is in the garden of St. Catherine's Court, Bath, England, the estate of the Hon. Mrs. Paley.

Left: *Properly bordered, as in this case, with iris or phlox arranged in a definite color scheme, the old-fashioned gravel path has few rivals.*

A concrete path, with a naturalistic pebble finish.

The Japanese stepping-stone path is naturalistic.

Nothing is so satisfactory as a simple grass path.

Here the outdoor note is found in the lattice, the wicker furniture and the plants; the indoor note in the fireplace. It is a small room, showing many desirable points. For the tile floor might be used the alternative of wood painted to simulate tile. Fibre mats could be laid over it. Ivy can be trained up the trellis. The radiators are well concealed, and there is the added cheer of the fireplace. Barber & McMurray, architects.

THE PORCH ENCLOSED FOR WINTER LIVING

U.S.A., 1917-18

Because it stands for the transition between the house and the garden, between outdoor living and indoor comfort, the porch enclosed for winter has become a necessary adjunct to the house . . . One particularly good use for the enclosed porch is for a breakfast room. What an antidote to the morning grouch it is to breakfast in a sunny, gay porch with bright chintz shades and soft painted furniture! If a summer porch is to be converted into and used primarily as a winter living room, summery furniture should not predominate. There are now on the market some wonderful pieces of furniture that seem admirably suited to winter use—comfortable chairs, semi-formal tables, natural wood finishes. Wrought iron, which is coming again into vogue, finds its place in this room. It has a dozen uses—for radiator grilles, lamp standards, plant stands. Furnished well, glassed-in porches can be indispensable extra rooms . . .

The old-fashioned settle is always a useful adjunct to porch or terrace.

City dwellers will find the roof capable of many porch treatments if ingenuity is used and a little paint.

Lattice will prove a pleasing background for some porches. Here wicker is used with gay-toned cushions.

This porch has been converted into a conservatory, with winter rugs. James Greenleaf Sykes, decorator.

The upholstery and rug are in tones of dull gold, old rose and blue. The wicker willow is stained mahogany. Casement cloth at windows. Courtesy Joseph P. McHugh & Son.

Casement cloth is used here to subdue the strong light from the windows. The plant stand against the wall gives the relief of growing green things. W. Adams, architect.

The modern porch is a thing of many colors. This outdoor living room is filled with Canton furniture, with Tango and Prussian blue color accents. The floor has Tango-colored tile with a border of blue. The curtains are copper-colored, made of dyed theatrical gauze.

One often gets in the way of thinking of porches as places where we sit only to hide from the blistering sun. If the truth be told, we use the porch as much for entertaining. A new use for the popular refectory table is on the dining-porch where it will accommodate a large family.

Each porch tries to outdo in brilliancy of color and novelty of furniture and arrangement the porch of the preceding season and the porches of emulative neighbors. The all-year porch above is the ideal arrangement. It can readily be changed from summer to winter garb.

If a porch is any sort of a porch it should boast a chaise longue, *that delight of the summer novel fiend*. As in the porch above, flowers are indispensable. They give relief to wicker and painted furniture, and make the spot more livable with their color and scent.

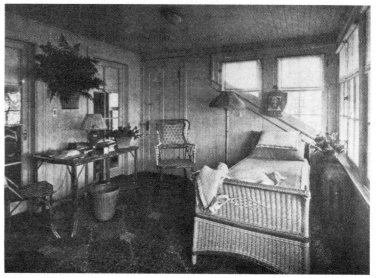

Wicker, reed, willow, painted furniture and wrought iron are the best choices for the winter porch living room. Here reed has been used. Casement-cloth curtains filter the strong sunlight. From the home of Gardner Steel, Esq., Pittsburgh, Pennsylvania. Louis Stevens, architect.

In this sleeping porch the rug is orange fiber squares, and the wicker furniture painted delft blue. White Holland shades at the window have blue painted designs. On the bed is a spread of yellow linen trimmed with blue. The walls are white enamel. Agnes Foster Wright, decorator.

THE ACCOMMODATING DAYBED

Which Can Be Used In The Bedroom, Living Room Or Studio

USA, 1919

A couch has always been indispensable in a comfortable bedroom, but as it has always been a problem to make it attractive, we welcome the return of the daybed. Its use, however, is not confined to the bedroom, for in the living room it can serve as a couch or window seat, and is a much better solution to the extra needed bed than the dangerous folding bed or unsightly rug-covered cot. Its graceful design looks appealing anywhere . . .

Lacquer and cane, to match the bedroom suite, are a pleasing combination. Chamberlain Dodds, decorator.

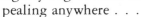

Vari-colored pillows give the daybed the necessary finish and add notes of interest to the room.

A soft rajah silk in yellow and blue is used on this daybed.

In the Royal House at Bedford, Massachusetts, built about 1641, there is still a rare daybed after the Queen Anne style, the cane bottom being covered with rich upholstery, as was the fashion of that day.

For studio use, or in a small apartment, the daybed supplies room for an extra guest. Here the covering is soft blue silk and the hanging a foreign peasant fabric in bright colors to add interest.

CONCEALING THE RADIATOR

Successful Methods By Which It Can Be Boxed or
Incorporated into Built-in Furniture

USA, 1919

To have a radiator standing forth in full view in any room is a piece of inexcusable barbarity . . Any self-respecting architect will see to it that radiators are placed in the least obtrusive position feasible, and with a little additional expense will conceal them with more or less ingenuity. When radiator concealment can be planned for at the time the house is built, it is much easier to manage successfully than when added later. The most logical position for radiators is either under or near windows. If this is not feasible, another good installation is in the lower part of built-in bookcases. The examples on this page show various good methods of concealment . . .

Above: *In an old house where the radiator is set in a window it can be concealed by a cupboard, which makes a plant table.*

Left: *This radiator grille is made of plaited iron, behind which the radiator is set, thus concealing it successfully.*

When shielded by an asbestos base, the radiator may even be concealed in a bookcase without injuring the books.

Beneath a long window or a row of windows, the radiators can be concealed by a built-in seat with the grilles set low in front, that do not obstruct the passage of warm air. Cupboards on either side give a balanced grouping for the design.

For sun-room radiators one may have built decorative covers such as these, which are also useful as shelves or tables.

NIPPON IN NEW JERSEY

*The Japanese Garden
on the Estate of P.D. Saklatvala, Esq.*

Plainfield, New Jersey, 1918

*Shobu-no-to, The Iris Teahouse, is at
one end of a little pond where goldfish
drift indolently about under the watch-
ful eye of a bronze crane. Through the
wistaria-covered pergola the path from
the teahouse crosses a stone bridge to
Matsu Yuma, the Pine Tree Hill.*

Above: *From the teahouse, one looks
out in one direction to the dense shade
of trees, and in the other to a sunny
opening where water, rock and stump
lend contrast to the iris and little
pine trees growing on the right bank.*

Left: *No less a personage than Mary
Pickford herself has posed in worship
before the statue of Buddha, a tribute
at once to the genuineness of the
220-year-old figure and to the perfect reproduction of the Japanese atmosphere.*

Above: *The effects obtained here would indicate a genuinely old garden, although as a matter of fact the whole development is relatively recent. A bit of the curved bridge may be seen in the left background.*

Right: *Two antique stone Fu dogs guard a shrine hidden among dwarf rhododendrons, mountain laurel and ferns. A stone lantern and moss monkeys in the trees help give a character typical of old Nippon.*

Here, instead of accepting the commonplace that "all small houses are alike, excepting that some are worse than others," the architect, Bloodgood Tuttle, has said that some small houses may be better than others. This is "The Hearth," a modern English cottage.

AN ARCHITECTURAL EPIGRAM

The Possibilities and Limitations of the Small House, as Shown in "The Hearth," an English Cottage. Designed by Bloodgood Tuttle, Architect.

BY C. MATLACK PRICE

Philadelphia, Pennsylvania, 1918

Until recent years the small house of real architectural merit has been lamantably rare. The vicinity of Philadelphia for some years has demonstrated that the small house may also be well designed, and it may be we are on the threshold of an era of more general public appreciation of the distinction between "architecture" and "building." In appraising the small house as architectural design, the most natural beginning is to place it beside the most generally familiar criterion—the modern English cottage. Spontaneous admiration of the English cottage, however, is very unsafe. We are likely to be so charmed by the exterior that we forget to consider the interior . . . Considering first the exterior, without question the English architect has made most of his problem, with expressive craftsmanship. In the cottage illustrated, for example, the stucco has been tinted cream color with a slight accent toward pink, while its texture has been made as rough and as expressive of troweling as possible. Most notable of all, the exposed timber-work has been carried out in the good old hand-wrought manner, with wooden dowel-pins instead of nails. The use of steel casement windows throughout, with leaded glass, is another detail strongly contributing to the picturesque total. The interior plan is as unusual as the exterior. Bedrooms have been compactly contrived in remarkably small compass, and the principal space has been given to the big living room, with its open timber trusses, and most interesting of all, its dining alcove. Here is a declaration of emancipation from an odd habit, a tangible expression of a belief that a dining room is not necessary in a cottage plan. Further incentive may be given to the "dining alcove" idea in small plans by the numerous choices in modern furniture outside the confines of distinctly "dining room" furniture—gate-leg tables, straightforward Windsor chairs, for instance . . .

The plan follows the good English idea of reversing the usual American disposition of service quarters and living quarters. By placing the kitchen and service entrance nearest the road, the rear of the house is left free for access to the garden.

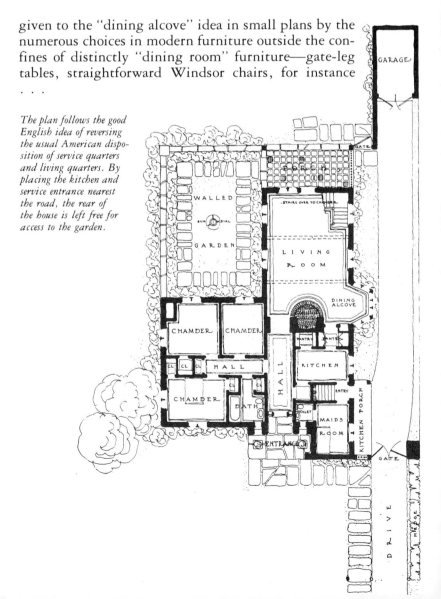

The driveway gate, leading into the garage, is so designed that it is not only a natural part of the house, but an interesting architectural story itself.

Right: Along the side of the house appear comfortable casement windows, the solid cluster in the bay lighting the dining alcove in the big living room.

Below: "Apart, yet a part," the cheerful, sunny dining alcove in the big living room does away with the necessity of the dining room as a separate room.

Left above: One is impressed, in this garden gate, not only by the fact that it is built of wood, but that wood is a very interesting and friendly material.

Right above: The entrance to "The Hearth" owes much of its charm to architectural restraint—the things he did not do to it.

Left: The interiors of "The Hearth" are conspicuously free from triviality, and show wherein a small house may also be large.

Right: Through the frank architectural expression of its construction this living room openly declares that a house, even though small, may proudly be a house instead of a plastered-and-papered packing box.

A SAMPLER OF REMARKABLE AMERICAN HOUSES

USA, 1917, 1918, 1919

The decorative and constructive possibilities of cobble are enormous. Laid almost dry with wide interstices between, the beauty of the individual stone is further enhanced. Above is an ingenious use of small cobbles in an interesting house. The mason must have been a patient man.

This residence in La Jolla, California, is constructed of unburnable materials—the walls, floors and roof are of reinforced concrete, the window and door casings of metal, and a pergola of concrete and stone. This unburnable house was designed by architect Irving J. Gill.

The seeming nudity of the exterior of this house, designed by Irving J. Gill, is simply an expression of the extreme simplicity of the interior, from which wood has been eliminated. Tile, marble, mosaic and concrete floors are again coming into use, easier to keep clean, simpler to manage, good-looking.

This home-like California residence, designed by Irving J. Gill, is of fireproof construction. People today are quite content with woodless wall surfaces, frameless doors and windows, and polished cement floors, showing sheer pleasure in emancipation from flimsy construction and tawdry decoration.

The Villa D'Amicenza, the residence of Harrisson Bennett, Esq., is like a bit of Italy transplanted to Weston, Massachusetts. In front lies an Italian garden, with a balustrade capping the rubble wall and accented by heavy cement flower jars. Steps lead down to the lawn from this garden.

Antique details have been introduced into the Italian villa's construction. Soft gray walls are accented by wrought iron and blue Venetian blinds. In contrast, right, an oriel chimney on a projecting corbel of stone models, with a sundial, creates historic old-world charm.

The residence of Lieut. Col. C.G. Edgar, in Grosse Pointe, Michigan, is Italian in feeling. A walled-in garden on one side and a terrace wall give formal approach to the house and enclose the turn of the drive. The material is stucco, the roof tiled. The architect was Albert Kahn.

The walls of this residence, in Mason City, Iowa, are made of native stone. The floors are concrete, covered with tile. The roof is reinforced concrete poured in forms. This is another example of the unburnable house. The architect was Walter Burley Griffin.

This careful study of the Long Island farmhouse is the residence of J.M. Townsend Jr., Esq., Mill Neck, Long Island. The shingles are whitewashed, shutters blue-green, chimneys white with black caps. Honeysuckle and box at the entrance add intimacy. W. Lawrence Bottomley, architect.

The way up to the residence of Frederick Dana Marsh, Esq., in New Rochelle, New York, is by a rocky, winding path. Exterior walls are hollow tile covered with gray stucco and broken vertically by timber work and rows of narrow casement windows. The architect was Henry G. Morse.

Brick, wood, stone, slate, stucco and leaded work have produced what the architect, John Russell Pope, wished for in the house of Allan Lehman, Esq., Tarrytown, New York—the old-world charm possessed by such historic Tudor houses as Compton Wynyates in Warwickshire and Ockwells Manor in Lancashire.

It's hard to improve on Colonial architecture, and the house of E.J. McCormick, Esq., in Brooklyn, New York, is an excellent example. Faced with brick veneer and limestone trimmings, it relies for decoration on the classic simplicity of recessed doors and windows. Slee & Bryson, architects.

Somehow, you don't expect a tropical patio garden in Boston. It comes as a pleasant surprise. The pink brick walls and red flooring, the cement stairs leading to the gallery, the little fountain set low in the floor, the great wrought-iron lantern swung from the ceiling, the trailing vines and young palm groves, the Far East rattan furniture—all combine to make a room of rare beauty and a warm oasis in what is generally thought a severe climate. Harry B. Russell, architect.

A TROPICAL PATIO GARDEN

Boston, Massachusetts, 1919

There is intriguing architectural detail on this side of the patio. The stairs climb up past great steps that spill their trailing vines. The little casement window and the angel suggest an Arabian Nights' romance. And the doorway and balcony are exquisite.

Along the opposite side runs a gallery with its vine-swept rim. Here too a little angel floats complacently against the white wall. From this view one can appreciate the unusual beauty of the wrought-iron lantern. The color of the cement is rose gray.

An iron grille gate closes the entrance to the upper floor, its silhouette standing out against the rose gray cement stairs and pink walls. High up in a cage hang a pair of love birds—a quaint little touch in a romantic garden.

LIVING
WITH
TECHNOLOGY

Freed from the constraints of war, buoyed by an economic boom, this decade saw an explosion of energy in interior design. In response to the elaborately decorated objects inspired by Art Nouveau, a new style of furniture and decoration emerged that became known as "moderne." Cubist and geometric lines, influenced by industrial developments in machinery and materials, replaced voluptuous curves and shapes. Art Deco (called Art Moderne in America), a largely French expression of skilled craftsmanship in metals, glass, and other unusual idioms, sometimes with Mayan and Aztec influence, was triumphantly displayed for all the world to see at the 1925 Paris Exposition. The cabinetmaker Jacques-Emile Ruhlmann, an acknowledged leader of

the style, and Jean Michel Frank from France, Josef Hoffmann, cofounder of the Wiener Werkstätte in Austria, and Eileen Gray, Irishborn experimenter in lacquer and industrial materials, were some of the talents who influenced designers everywhere and delighted a generation ready for anything as long as it was new and fun. Their luxurious ideology contrasted with the Bauhaus movement, with its philosophy of "less is more," which had begun in 1919 but expanded in Germany after the War to bring a new functionalism to design. New home technology accelerated the liberation of women from domesticity and turned living into a plug-in world of speed and efficiency.

This is a room furnished in the modernist taste by Lord & Taylor, showing an interesting fireplace group. The walls are peach color and the chair coverings are in beige and brown tones.

The modernist feature in this view of a New York studio is found in the wall painting of the "cynical eye" above a futurist book and plate rail.

THE MODERNIST TASTE

BY RICHARDSON WRIGHT

Paris, 1925

In Paris this summer was held the Exhibition des Arts Décoratifs et Industriels Modernes, an international showing of the modern tendency in the arts of architecture, decorating and landscaping and in the various allied crafts . . . From the architectural viewpoint it was a mad and colorful conglomeration by day and a not unlovely fantasmagoria by night. There were enough architectural vagaries to make this American delegate wonder if the show were the product of madmen or simply the tricks and pranks of highly sophisticated architects who wanted to create the most serious and sustained exhibition of bad taste the world has ever seen. Or were they really striving for a hitherto unpronounced interpretation of living Nature? The same doubt did not arise on seeing the gardens, the sculpture, the books, the glassware, silver, ceramics, or some of the other individual exhibits, except perhaps certain sections of furniture. And since furniture and decoration are interests closely allied to House & Garden, I will devote my remaining space to them.

The illustrations chosen for these pages are of modernist interiors, two from a New York apartment and the remainder French, some of which were shown at the exhibition. They are the least radical of many that were available. The first thing that strikes the observer are the lines of the furniture. The pieces look elephantine and out of proportion. So a great many of them are. They appear to have been made for people who are very much overweight. The modernist has a weakness for heavily overstuffed or tufted furniture of the

sort that made popular the red plush sofa in the regretable days of the General Grant era. On the other hand, much of the craftsmanship is superb, for good craftsmanship is a form of tradition that has not yet been abandoned on the Continent. Rare and unusual woods are used and used effectively. Macassar and Gabon ebony, rosewood with ivory inlay. The chairs are, in the main, comfortable; but the lines of the furniture, however stimulating as novelties, cannot be said to delight the eye for a long time. They are too heavy, too ponderous, too serious looking. One wonders if the average American would want to live with such furniture.

Contrasted with this is the brilliancy of the coloring and the manner in which colors are combined. Raw, primitive reds, blues, yellows

In the same New York studio, the walls are pale lemon yellow with design in yellow, orange and gold. The panel is tan and brown sateen. The lamps are futurist.

and greens are thrown together in fabrics and wall decorations that fairly shout. The designs are modernist in the extreme. And whereas the furniture designs are mainly rotund, the fabric designs are often angular. They are lively and amusing and full of laughter.

The combination of these two types, the heavy and the light, the ponderous and the lively, make the modernist interior strangely incongruous. They remind one of stout men sitting down to a vast meal and then getting up and trying to do some such lightsome step as the "Charleston" . . .

The modernist movement in the arts today is laboratory work; all kinds of experiments are being made. I wish, though, that more of the experiments were thrown away and fewer of them put on exhibition. To perfect the electric light, the talking machine and the telephone Edison and Bell probably tried and abandoned thousands of experiments before they announced discoveries practical for public service. The trouble with the modernist artist, architect, furniture and fabric designers is that they apparently put every experiment on the market as a full-fledged, complete and brand-new discovery. The Exhibition des Arts Décoratifs was simply a vast array of these experiments, fully fifty percent of which should have been discarded before they reached the region of L'Esplanade des Invalides. And yet out of this chaos some order may eventually come, some new feeling, some new styles, some new reevaluation of architecture and decoration that we can take seriously and adopt.

This is an example of the modernist type of built-in,
overstuffed sofa. The frame and cabinets are oak. By
Dim.

For the Exhibition Ruhlmann designed a round room
with futurist paper and a domed ceiling frescoed in the
modernist taste.

An office, designed by Ruhlmann for the Exhibition.
It was in sombre brown. Note the modernist shape of
the large chairs.

Above: Rosewood was used for this bed and ebony
inlaid with ivory in the bureau of this room by Dim.
The walls are fabric-hung.

Far left: Dining room in the modernist taste designed
by Ruhlmann for the Exhibition.

Left: A wall group by Dim—a console in gilded wood
with a black marble top, mirror squares.

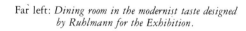

AMERICAN MODERNIST ROOMS

U.S.A., 1928-1929

Above top, left and right: *In this bachelor's apartment in the modern taste, bedroom and living room furniture of rubbed black lacquer, chromium-plated metal, serve both decorative and practical purposes. The living room chair is upholstered in green leather, frame edged with black bakelite. Entrance-hall pieces at the left are of black lacquer, polished copper hardware. The mirror is by B. Fischer, furniture and metalwork by G. Rohde. In the New York apartment of Norman Lee.*

Right: *This section of a modernist living room decorated by Abraham & Straus reveals fluted opaque glass columns holding the lights flanking the chimney breast. In the center is a narrow niche lined with silver leaf and filled with small objets d'art, instead of a mirror or painting.*

Left: This interior, furnished in the modernist taste, shows an interesting fireplace group. The walls are peach color and the chair coverings beige and brown. All the rooms shown except the bedroom, bottom left, have been decorated by Lord & Taylor, New York.

Below left: A novel color scheme of citron yellow, silver and black distinguishes this dining room decorated in the spirit of today. Furniture finished in silver leaf gleams against a background painted cool lemon yellow.

Below: This fireplace group in a modernist living room shows interesting uses for mirrored glass. Both the fireplace surround and the pyramid shaped lighting fixtures are made of mirrors. The walls are painted Nile green and the upholstery fabrics used to cover the very modern chairs are new handblocked materials in tan, green and seal brown.

Above: This bed of silvery gray wood inlaid with pewter has attached cabinets. The walls, slightly rough, are white, as are the satin hangings and voile glass curtains.

Left: In this bedroom the furniture is pale yellow maple. Peach brocade panels against cream walls; hangings beige satin over beige-shading-to-apricot chiffon. Room by Macy.

In the drawing room of the Vicomte de Noailles in Paris, the walls are covered with squares of vellum parchment; burnished bronze doors.

THE MODERNISM OF JEAN MICHEL FRANK

Some Notes Pertaining to New Wall Treatments as They Are Used by This Brilliant French Decorator

BY GEORGE CAYEAUX

Paris, 1929

The path the modernist decorator treads is a narrow one. It is so easy for him to slip off into the abyss of the bizarre; so easy, on the other hand, for him to tumble into the morass of mere ugliness that often results when he tries to straddle traditional and contemporary styles. Yet it is possible to be modernist without losing one's balance, without creating rooms that will be out of date in a twelvemonth or be so outrageously bizarre as to hold the owner to the titters and scorn of his friends. One of the very few Modernists that seem to be treading this narrow path successfully is Jean Michel Frank, the young Parisian decorator.

M. Frank's departure from the usual treatment of rooms begins with the walls, and yet, in one of these at least, he is merely reviving an ancient custom. In some rooms he covers the walls with large squares of vellum parchment, giving it a tone that is light and elusive and at the same time reminiscent of ancient times. In other rooms he uses split straw marquetry to cover the walls, sides of furniture and panels of doors. Here again he is harking back to an old usage, for the 18th-century maker of little boxes used

straw to advantage, and English collectors today are always on the watch for straw marquetry pieces made by French prisoners of war. In applying these two mediums to wall surfaces, M. Frank produces rooms of unusual

In this same room, decorated by M. Frank, the carpet is deep tête-de-nègre and the curtains of beige heavy silk. The furniture is upholstered in white leather—the last word in "modern."

interest, subtle color and unexpected pattern.

Since these mediums have been used in rooms, illustrated here, it would be interesting to see just what kinds of furniture and accessories are successfully combined with them.

In the drawing room of the Vicomte de Noailles in Paris the decoration is the last word in "modern." The walls are covered in squares of vellum parchment and the doors are of burnished bronze. The carpet is deep *tête-de-nègre* and the curtains are heavy beige silk. The upholstered furniture is in white leather and the small screens, at either end of the sofa, are veneered with natural-colored split straw. In the far corner of the room, on the piano, rests a lamp, with a parchment shade, which is made of thick strips of plate glass held together with bronze bands.

Between the windows is a very interesting example of a cabinet veneered with split-straw marquetry in natural color. The chair by the side of it is also veneered in split straw and covered in beige velvet. On top of the cabinet is a light shaded by sheaves of thick split ivory set into a bronze base.

A writing table, veneered with split straw, stands at one end of the drawing room. In form it resembles an old spinet and the writing surface is covered with pale beige leather. The small armchair of white galosha is covered in oyster white plush. To the left of the door is a huge fragment of pink rock crystal, which contains a light.

In one of the salons of the Noailles house, the tapestry panels have been set into a frame of split-straw marquetry tinted dark brown.

Split-straw marquetry has been used in libraries recently completed for the Count Pecci-Blunt and the Baron de Lellemand. The former is an oval room with high ceilings, since it serves both as a library and a music room. Its plaster walls are painted white. The niche at the end of the room where the piano stands, the back of the bookcases and the panels of cupboards below, as well as the inside window shutters, are in blond straw, giving the room a rich glow of sunlight. All the trim is in gilded bronze. There are lights concealed behind frosted glass over the bookshelves and windows. The bookshelves are of plate glass. The carpet is beige and the furniture, which is made of pearwood, has beige leather upholstery. A gold mirror hangs over the fireplace and gold mirror tops are used on the small occasional tables in the room.

The Baron de Lellemand's library is a more *intime* room. Here straw has been stained a dark brown toning in with dark walnut bookshelves. The furniture also is walnut upholstered in a patternless fabric, and the curtains are beige leather.

The library of the Count Pecci-Blunt in Paris has its plaster walls painted white with the woodwork covered in split straw, gilded bronze trim. The furniture is made of pearwood.

In the library of the Baron de Lellemand, dark brown straw marquetry covers the doors and door reveals. The curtains are very pale beige leather.

THE NEW MODERN DECORATION IN EUROPE

BY GILES EDGERTON

France and Vienna, 1922

To originate a work wholly without tradition as though no art had ever existed before in the world, seems to be the intention of the modern school of art in middle Europe. Whether the expression is architecture, sculpture, or the making of furniture, fabrics, silver or porcelain, the effect must be (in form, color and texture) new to the existing art world.

It is this absolute determined originality that sometimes produces a sense of shock in the minds of those more accustomed to being led into art adventures down gently sloping paths of traditon and memory. But the whole scheme of interior decoration in Europe today is to experiment, to test, to evolve from the unknown and mysterious new expressions of beauty in home-making, or what seems beauty to the "new art" movement in decoration . . .

In time, as the craze for the "new art" increased, the most adamant of the producers began to crave some sort of authority, some whisper of paternal wisdom, and the Secessionists as well as Lalique turned to Nature for help, feeling quite safe on her green threshhold. And for a number of years this phase of art was dominated by curving vines, rounded flower petals, strangely elaborated leaves, always curves, ovals, twined about other curves; an essentially graceful art, without fire or ecstasy except in color.

This epoch of art, for we would not be allowed to call it a "period," has continued its grip on Europe up to the present day, especially in architecture and interior decoration. Then there was a cessation of art expression during the War. And today a vigorous uprising, especially in Vienna, along the earlier, finer Secession lines, and in France still an appreciation of Art Nouveau but some new flexibility . . . A recent exhibition in New York reveals to us the old spirit of Viennese art in its purest forms and richest trappings. In these rooms, shown in our illustrations, the decorations and furniture are all designed and executed by Joseph Urban, that Viennese genius who has done so much for stage de-

coration in this country with his scientific knowledge of color and his fearlessness in creating new forms of decoration. In these schemes we see Urban's great cleverness in the use of simple materials for ornate effects,

An entrance hall in the Viennese style. In the center, a painting by Gustav Klimt; Hoffmann vases.

A New York room in Viennese style. Wallpaper by Pechi, silver tea sets by Hoffmann.

the original forms of his furniture and cabinets and the interesting manner in which he has incorporated all paintings into his scheme of wall decoration.

There is no trace here of that tortured spirit of a dozen years ago. It is sincerely and earnestly the presentation of the New Art as one skilled believer in it can set it forth.

Pechi's wallpapers and silks are used to decorate the wall. Black woodwork predominates, and all the little cabinets and alcoves, which show porcelains and silver are lined with a cool strong shade of green. Floating curtains are cool, apple green chiffon with an interlining of sky blue. If one could write as simply, freshly and surely as Urban uses color you would easily picture these rooms so startling, fresh, their beauty resting so completely on the new art of Vienna as Urban sees it and accepts it.

We were fortunate in securing pictures of modern French rooms decorated by Sue et Mare, which show Art Nouveau at its best, blended with the very latest development in interior decoration, involving somewhat a return to old period designs and to a degree the breaking of faith with the former cast-iron standards of new art. For instance, in one drawing room there is a combination of new art decoration and furniture of the 19th century which brings back much of the old elegance of France's traditional school. The wall lamps of metal and alabaster are unquestionably Art Nouveau, as is the mirror in its curved frame of gilded wood and the ebony fireplace with rounded corners.

The walls of this salon are quite in the newest mode covered entirely with tightly drawn satin in a delicate shade of mauve, which makes a charming background for the rich velvet furniture.

Altogether this acknowledgment by some of the best modern French decorators that there is beauty in the past, and value in tradition as a background for decoration is really working out for more harmonious and elegant interiors than we can remember to have seen in the purely Art Nouveau house.

In this French bedroom,
definite suggestion of Louis
Philippe in these chairs,
with Art Nouveau mirror,
and walls covered with tightly stretched mauve satin.

Left: A baroque note is given this detail of a French
bedroom in the shell pediment over the door. Plain silk
wall decoration. Right: Blue and green mosaic bathroom.
The bath has a marble surround; marble bracket.

The study in M. Bernheim's Paris home has walls hung
in fluted folds of green velvet. The gold furniture is
Louis-Philippe style.

In the Paris drawing room of Mr. Kapferer, the walls are
gray and yellow damask, with a typically Art Nouveau
fireplace of yellow marble.

M. Monteux's French salon with Art Nouveau side lamps
of metal and alabaster. The mantel also new art, chairs
Louis-Philippe in feeling.

Darting lights of the Far North inspired the design above. The border is engraved in swirling lines and handles on both tray and compote are carried out in the same spirit. International Silver Company.

MODERN DESIGNS IN SILVER

Europe and U.S.A., 1928

From the edge of the lip, around the curved ivory handle down to the narrow base, this silver water pitcher is one continuous flowing line. It comes from Denmark and is shown through the courtesy of Eugene Schoen.

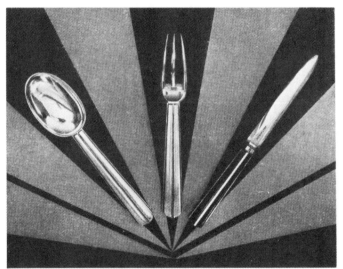

The grooved design of the handles on this fork and spoon is a new note in flat silver. The knife handle of ebony inlaid with ivory is also highly desirable. These are examples of French silver, imported by Wanamaker.

Infinitely pleasing in its suggestion of strength and orderliness is this square dish of straight lines and varied levels. By courtesy of Reed & Barton.

A charming feature of this tea caddy is the carved jade handles. Gorham.

The simplicity of this compote design accentuates the beauty of the silver. The bowl section is without ornament, the base gracefully fluted. Reed & Barton.

An absence of meaningless ornament and a simplicity
of form mark this tray, the motif of which is engag-
ingly named, "Ebb Tide." In common with the best in
contemporary silver design, this piece avoids all suggestion of the bizarre. International Silver Company.

This graceful cocktail shaker of Danish origin is
fluted from top to base. The tray on which it stands
has a pie-crust edge also fluted. The shaker is courtesy
of Eugene Schoen.

The convivial grape, exquisitely wrought in silver, sur-
mounts the top of this cocktail shaker. The silver glass is a
graceful variant of accustomed forms. Georg Jensen.

The border of this sandwich tray is engraved in a design of
half circles and inset at intervals with pieces of jade. Jade
tops the handle of the serving spoon. Gorham.

The ubiquitous skyscraper motif is again apparent in the
handles of a silver salad spoon and fork. Sections of these are
given an oxidized finish. From Gorham.

If we wander through the courts of Granada, we are reminded that once the tile was not despised. Later, find the shining blue of Delft in the interiors of Vermeer and Van Hooghe. Here, in a modern house, is the renaissance of the tile.

THE MODERNIST WORK OF DUNCAN GRANT AND VANESSA BELL

BY RALPH PATTISON

London, 1925

For some time past, "period" rooms have been the fashion in England. Elizabethan, Jacobean, then Queen Anne, right up to Victorian. But is there any reason why we should not consider our own day as a "period"—the only period for us that is not in some sense artificial—and set aside, at any rate, one room in our own house that shall be truly representative of the best in it? . . .

Many leading British artists in the modern movement (which is derived largely from Cézanne and the French Impressionists, though it must not for a moment be supposed, as some critics have suggested, that it despises the Old Masters) have turned their attention to decorative work.

Among these are Duncan Grant and Vanessa Bell, who even before the War were associated with a group of artists who produced work of this kind under the leadership of

Roger Fry. The War, unfortunately, put a stop to the enterprise, but not before they had produced many charming things in the way of furniture, stuffs, and pottery, practical as well as beautiful . . .

The illustrations to this article are

A carpet, designed in the English modernist taste by Vanessa Bell, is in several shades of reds and browns and beige pink.

taken from decorative work done by Duncan Grant and Vanessa Bell during the last few years. They turn their versatile hands to anything, from the complete scheme of decoration to the painting of a bowl or the designing of a carpet. Among the pictures is a view of a room in the Tavistock Square house of Virginia Woolf, the brilliant author. The narrow frieze round the top of the wall is an amusing wallpaper, made simply by an *écriture* of brush strokes in subdued violet on a white and lemon yellow ground.

The chimney piece in one of Duncan Grant's rooms is a good example of the transformation of a very ordinary feature into something dignified and beautiful. The ugly cast-iron Victorian grate was removed and an open fireplace made, edged with specially designed tiles. The original marble mantelpiece was allowed to remain, with a painted design above it . . .

An unusual alcove in a dining room painted on paper with deep blue and pale gray *ecriture* and a yellow ochre border, giving a Chinese effect.

A chair designed by Duncan Grant has a cross-stitched motif of gray and emerald.

A fireplace by Duncan Grant has a painted decoration of arum lilies and leaves in white, greens, yellows on crimson; pale bluish pink walls.

Panels by Duncan Grant and Vanessa Bell in Mrs. Woolf's London house. The walls are pale dove gray, the panels white with tomato red borders, and *fonds* in sienna pink and maple yellow.

In this room in a London house, in which hang pictures of Matisse and Derain, the doors and woodwork are decorated in the modernist taste.

MODERNIST ARCHITECTURE IN AN ENGLISH SUBURB

England, 1927

Above: Symmetrical placing of ranges of unmullioned windows and snowy expanses of cement wall in combination with the extreme rectangularity of the residence give to the rear the appearance of one of our own sunlit foodstuff factories.

Left: Another view of the rear seen at an angle to the house shows the stairway from the garden to the loggia. A pool underneath the loggia receives rainwater from the roof, which is conducted by way of earthenware drains in the outer walls.

Below: A style of building truly representative of the present age is the aim of modernist architects, such as Professor Behrens of Vienna who designed this English country house. Such designs as the facade below have an arresting quality, but whether or not this style will endure is questionable.

Above: *This English country house is an example of advanced modernistic design. Unusual indeed is the massive living-room fireplace. The odd-appearing windows flanking the fireplace are of metallic tinted glass illuminated by lights set between these and outer windows.*

Right: *Simplification of lines to make vertical or horizontal planes is a dominating feature of modernist architecture. Absence of all curves from the architecture of this hallway is obvious. Even the clock above the door bears evidence of simplification. A triangular window at the stair landing is an interesting touch.*

93

THE HOME OF J.H. CARSTAIRS,
JOHN RUSSELL POPE, ARCHITECT

Ardmore, Pennsylvania, 1925

The house, Georgian in feeling, has been executed in native stone so pointed up that it appears to be whitewashed. Canopied bay windows and entrance portico are features of an era later. The lattice-filled doorway proves another pleasing innovation.

Throughout the main rooms the backgrounds are dignified Georgian in style. On the other hand, the furniture is French, some of it Empire, thus giving the rooms a lighter touch. In the living room the walls are old blue with ivory moldings and trim.

The paneling in both the living room and dining room is made by the simple device of molding on a plaster wall. The dining room walls are an old yellow.

Above: *The entrance court is walled. On this side of the wall lie the terrace and rose garden. An iron gate leads to the terrace. From terrace, steps lead to the rose-paneled garden, whose central feature is a pool.*

Below: *In the courtyard before the entrance is the long pool, with the driveway passing each side of it to the gate. Box is massed at each end, and the pool is flanked by low-growing perennials.*

A PORTFOLIO OF GOOD INTERIORS

U.S.A., 1921-1929

Opposite page, top left: *As a contrast to the cream marble mantel and the numerous decorative accessories in light tones, the background of this engaging small dressing room is shining black wallpaper sprinkled with bright gold stars. It is in the New York residence of Miss Rose Cumming, who was also the decorator.*

Opposite page, top right: *In the New York home of Mrs. Clifford McCall the background is blue-green as a contrast to the copper moire curtains, the mauve toile chairs, copper velvet and flowered chintz, and eggplant colored rug. Diane Tate and Marian Hall, decorators.*

Opposite page, bottom left: *The background of this Directoire hall affords a fine study in contrasts. The wall above the sofa is paneled in small squares of mirror and flanked by plain panels outlined with old paper borders in green, black and white. On the opposite wall is a section of the Cupid and Psyche paper bordered in the same manner. The dado is light mottled green and the sofa covered in green silk. McMillen, Inc, decorators.*

Opposite page, bottom right: *The outstanding feature of this dining room in the residence of Alfred E. Hamill, Lake Forest, Illinois, is the architectural treatment of the background. Flanking the fireplace are gray marble pilasters with capitals in royal blue. The walls are eggshell white plaster and the doors blue with gray and white moldings. David Adler and Robert Work, architects.*

Above left: *The charm of this bay window in the home of Mrs. S.R. Hollander, Hartsdale, New York, depends upon the net glass curtains, which soften the light, and the glazed chintz of terra-cotta, black and green on buff, which gives color to the ensemble. The furniture is Sheraton, walls Italian yellow and woodwork Venetian red. John Wanamaker, decorator.*

Above right: *When there can be created something more graceful than winding stairs, architects will doubtless design them. Meanwhile, we can rejoice in this broad sweep of guarded rises and treads as they mount to the upper landing and beyond in John Sloane's house in Far Hills, New Jersey. John Russell Pope, architect.*

Left: *Although the entrance hall in the New York home of Cornelius N. Bliss is narrow, a sense of space is achieved by the careful grouping of furniture. On one side is an arrangement of two Directoire walnut tables and black and gold chairs. Long windows on the opposite wall are hung in tête de nègre satin, with a pair of black and gold Empire benches. The floor is black and white marble. Elsie Cobb Wilson, decorator.*

COLLECTING OLD WHITE FOR DECORATION

In China or Furniture, Paintings or Curtains, the Ivory of Age
Lends A Fascination to the Modern Room

BY RUBY ROSS GOODNOW

U.S.A., 1921

I can't remember how I began to collect old white things—I think by dreaming over unattainable white treasures of other people, for certainly my first loves were priceless things, like old Chinese porcelains, and ivories, and pearl-broidered satins, and Whistler paintings. And when once your eye is trained to the appreciation of a special quality, that quality becomes the outstanding thing in any composition. An old yellow silk-hung chamber where a great white lacquered bed held the place of honor, like a fine lady in a fine room, always seemed to me the room of the white bed, rather than the room of the yellow silk. My Aubusson carpet—a delicate pale colored thing, its mauve field irregularly spotted with white stars, its great circular white medallion holding a violet and pink vase—seems to me not the rug of the vase but the rug of the white stars. One sees what one likes to see in objects of art, and perhaps some of my choicest white loves might be to you anything but white.

Collecting a color is good fun, because collections of objects are usually hard to place. No matter how exquisite snuff boxes may be individually, they are difficult to display agreeably. Collecting a color may be the keynote, the secret basis, of all your decoration. Given a collection of old white things—fabrics, ivories, paintings and such—your soft white becomes a pervading glamor, which spreads itself over your rooms, coloring everything. The aging of white is exactly opposite to the aging of color. While colors constantly lose their intensity, white takes on a thousand lovely tones . . .

When I found an old pair of white kid gloves of the Directoire period, with naïve pictures and Spanish verses printed on them in black ink, with their edges minutely scalloped and yellowed white ribbons laced through the wrists, I had a much greater thrill than if I'd found a snuff box or a fan or a bandbox. My lovely

pair of old gloves now have a proper place in my bedroom beneath the glass that covers my dressing table. The cost, I think, was five shillings, but their charm is priceless.

Most of my white finds represent so much fun and so little money that I feel my passion must be an inspired one. And when I find irresistible white things I cannot possibly afford, I buy them for some more fortunate one who may have the right room and the adequate dollars and the proper appreciation. When I found a quilted petticoat of white satin, of the Louis Seize period, I could not possibly afford it myself, but I bought it and covered a small old sofa frame with it and used it in a drawing room, just beneath an old flower painting in which white flowers shone against a dark ground. When I found a fragile triangular white lace shawl for fifteen dollars I kept it for myself, and made a hanging for the head of my bed, a perfect

In using white, it should be disposed about a room sparingly lest its value be lost by too great repetition. In this living room corner the desired effect is obtained by the small white objects set at distances apart.

hanging and yet utterly undreamed of. This bed is a graceful white and gold one, Louis XVI in feeling. Its four very thin white columns terminate in gilt swans. The swans at the headboard hold this old lace shawl in their beaks . . .

The graduation of difference in white is limitless; for instance, there is the difference of degree, or digestion. A fresh white muslin curtain in a freshly whitewashed room has charm and simplicity, but it cannot be compared in degree with a yellowing satin curtain in an old room where white paint has taken on the polished quality of ivory. A glass—two glasses—three glasses of buttermilk are refreshing, but a glass of cream would be surfeiting. It is all a matter of quality. White must be used sparingly, preciously, to remain the motif of an arrangement, and not be lost in too great repetition. One recalls the amusing trial of Whistler, when the critic testified that a certain "Symphony in White" contained many other colors—green, and brown, an so forth. "And does a Symphony in F contain only F—F—F?", asked Whistler. "F—f—f—fool!"

A collection of white is best shown against some definite tone—canary, or pink, or gray, or blue—but some tone that itself, in combination with deeper color, suggests white. White not too insistent, each white object being a subtle support, should be used like a recurring motif, a delicate repetition, of another white object. The play of tones and colors in white is great, but one has learned that it is more successful to use a lighter white against a deeper white than vice versa. A white porcelain figure—of itself a shining clear white—is fine against a yellowish stuff, or against deep cream. My living room, for instance, is very faintly cream, its white marble mantel is bluish white, and the two large jardinieres are of pinkish white, and yet there is no suggestion of one white melting into another. The painting above the

This white bedroom has fascinating white touches—lyre fixtures, strung with pearls, white satin curtains hung over peach-pink taffeta.

An old white lace shawl hangs over the white and gold bed. The walls, ceiling and woodwork are pink, the draperies silver gauze.

mantel is from an old Italian screen, and shows a gorgeous blackamoor leading in a proud white horse. On the mantel shelf beneath are two little blackamoors

One of the white rooms I most enjoyed doing was a bedroom in a New York house built around a lovely old bed of white and gold. I have never seen such paint, as smooth and shining as a bowl of thick cream. This old bed is Italian, with four posts of equal height, and a great hanging head board with the monogram of the owner carved and gilded within an oval. The bedspread is made of an old brocade of a white ground patterned with little Watteau-like groups in yellow and pink and violet. A valance of pink silk hangs under the bedspread.

This room also has many notable touches of white against white, the most amusing being the lyre-shaped fixtures strung with pearls instead of crystals. To the appreciative eye these pearls make no more claim to preciousness than do crystal. They are no more affectation than are the white satin curtains at the windows. Imitation pearls are beautiful things: why not use them?

White satin is always beautiful, and age but mellows its beauty. I've had a dream of a room paneled in painted white satin.

This bathroom has a mixture of white satin and painted curtains. The chair is painted white, with white, dark and light blue upholstery.

Left: *The rug here has white stars that outshine the violet and pink rose in the central medallion. The mantel panel is white.*

ROOMS
BY
ELSIE
DE WOLFE

New York City, 1924, 1925, 1926

One of the features of the delightful living room that Elsie de Wolfe decorated for herself is the use of only small pieces of furniture that are all in scale with the room.

Pine paneling and old yellow flowered paper in Elsie de Wolfe's living room make a colorful background for the furniture covered in quilted blue silk and brown taffeta.

The fireplace end of Elsie de Wolfe's living room, showing a pleasing furniture arrangement, has an unusual mantel decoration consisting of a row of Chinese figures.

Below: In this living room of John McMullin's apartment in New York City, the sofa is beige damask. On the black and white table are white Bristol glass ornaments; the radiator box holds a collection of shells, figurines, cacti.

Right: Walls painted to resemble pine paneling make a restful and dignified background for the fine eighteenth-century furniture in a small guest room in Mrs. Ernest Iselin's residence in New York City.

The curtains in this bedroom are yellow glazed chintz bound in red, with a painted cornice board. Blue taffeta for the dressing table, red and gold chairs. It is in the home of MRs. Bernard Pollak, New York City. McMillen, Inc., decorator.

This entrance hall, with its distinguished background painted oyster white and ornamented with large landscape panels, is in a country house, the residence of Mrs. Charles Steele, Westbury, Long Island. The furniture is English, French, Italian; curtains, yellow damask. Elsie Cobb Wilson, decorator.

Eighteenth-century wallpaper with medallions of birds and flowers on a blue ground enhances the New York dining room of Mrs. Ernest Iselin. Nancy McClelland, decorator.

ROOMS BY AMERICAN DESIGNERS

U.S.A., 1925-1929

This sideboard in Mrs. Emily Vanderbilt's New York home is black enamel with gray insets and black glass shelves. The decorator was Margaret Owen.

Here the paneled background is yellow, the curtains of sapphire blue taffeta and the chair coverings blue and yellow striped silk. Diane Tate and Marian Hall, decorators.

PANELING WITH PAPER

BY NANCY MCCLELLAND

U.S.A., 1925

There seem to be a hundred new ways of using wallpaper today, apart from its utility for minor decorative objects like lamp shades, boxes, desk sets and screens.

Small wonder that it has been whimsically called the "tapestry of the poor," because of its extraordinary capability of giving the effect of a much richer and more costly decoration. At this particular moment, when architects, mural painters and interior decorators will all bear witness to the fact that the decorated wall is steadily growing in favor, wallpaper is a valuable asset, worthy of careful consideration.

As in the case of many other decorations, however, one must have real knowledge and appreciation of wallpaper in order to get the best results. Used without special thought, left to a paperhanger to install according to his own notions, wallpaper is simply wallpaper. Used by an artist of fine discrimination it may be made to take the place of tapestries, of printed fabrics, of woven stuffs, or even of paintings and statuary. To a certain extent wallpaper actually gives a room the effect afforded by these decorations, which it imitates.

It is only recently that we have learned the delight of partially papered walls, as compared with walls that are wholly covered with paper. We have just discovered that what is left out accentuates and enhances what is there. Yet, as a matter of fact, the use of wallpaper in panels is a well-known fashion of the eighteenth century. Not everyone, even in the luxurious days of the Louis, could command a wall decoration specially painted to order by Watteau or Boucher or one or another of the famous mural decorators of the century. Wallpaper done in delicate arabesques or studied designs offered an inexpensive substitute for the works of the great artists. So came the fashion of setting paper into wood-paneled walls.

In many ways this fashion seems to be peculiarly well suited to our requirements of today, for it is an admirable enlivenment of our flat backgrounds of paint and picture-moldings, and gives new interest to the composition and arrangement of rooms.

Not every wallpaper, however, adapts itself successfully to use in panels. There must be a design of more than ordinary interest and vigor to obtain the desired result. Perhaps that is why scenic papers, which are easily separated into groups of pictures by combining three or four strips, are used in panel fashion with the least difficulty. All-over designs like toile de Jouy papers may also be used in this manner with great effectiveness, and chintz and brocade patterns of wallpaper used in panel effect will give a room the quality of being hung with stuffs.

Whenever old paper panels are available, one has a decoration worthy of special attention. Wellplaced, so that they form part of the architectural plan of the room, well lighted, and well seconded in color, they will more than repay the

A Chinoiserie paper treated with a coat of orange shellac gives the effect of an old Chinese paper and makes a singularly effective overmantel decoration in this New York living room of Mrs. James Preston.

Old paper panels make a dignified wall decoration for a small dining room in the New York home of Leigh French. The background is marbleized to give the illusion of statues standing in the two niches.

In the New York home of Agnes Foster Wright a charming wallpaper panel of a cupid standing on a pedestal with a basket of flowers decorates a small hallway.

Old Chinese papers set in panels give color and add interest to a long side wall in a country house. All the papers shown in these photographs are from Nancy McLelland.

An old paper of Venetian scenes in tones of warm gray and sepia has been used in the home of Henry O. Rea, in Sewickley, Pennsylvania.

people into whose daily life they enter.

Leigh French, the New York architect, has chosen to put in his dining room two old paper panels, which are part of the set of "Apollo and the Muses," made to imitate bronze statues. A picture of this room is shown above.

What may be done by using an old scenic paper in panels is illustrated by the picture of the dining room in Sewickley, Pennsylvania above. Such a wall decoration is almost a complete furnishing in itself, before anything else is in place. Many of the modern papers in allover designs may be successfully used as panels, although they were not primarily designed for this purpose.

A PORTFOLIO OF INTERNATIONAL INTERIORS

England, France, Italy, 1927

Above: *The drawing room at Wormington Grange, Gloucestershire, reveals the comfort and livableness characteristic of the majority of English interiors. On the mantel is a collection of colorful china noted for its decorative value. Pictures and flowers add interest.*

Above right: *Easily the dominant note in the decorative scheme, the background in the drawing room of Hartlebury Castle, England, the Episcopal seat of the Bishops of Worcester, presents a striking example of stucco ornamentation. This treatment consists of plaster walls painted green and decorated with scrolls in ivory stucco relief.*

Right: *A beautiful wood mantel, a good example of the rococo taste that came into England in the 18th century, dominates the fireplace end of the drawing room at Warbrook, in Hampshire, residence of W.B.E. Ranken.*

Above top: *In this French dining room, the walls are robin's egg green, ornamented with cream moldings and panels of 18th-century wallpaper in grisaille. An Aubusson rug covers the marble floor. Above: The entrance hall of this charming French house is an inviting interior with marbleized walls, Directoire furniture, and an effective black and white marble floor. Its most unusual feature is the arched niche holding an interesting example of a Directoire stove, fitted with shiny brass ornaments.*

Above top: *This interior is in the Versailles home of Madame Juliette Massenet, daughter of the celebrated composer. The paneled drawing room shows an exquisite marble mantel cornered between two small windows, and an amusing sofa alcove fitted with a mirror. Above: In Madame Massenet's bedroom, the walls are hung in cream-colored rep as a background for a collection of remarkable color engravings, and as a contrast to the brilliant red and white toile de Jouy hangings used to ornament both bed and alcove.*

This library is in the apartment in Florence of Madame Ruby Melville Nadi. The bookcases are marbleized. The walls are the gold color of Sienna marble with the moldings and baseboard marbleized in a contrasting shade of reddish pink.

In Madame Nadi's loggia-like bedroom the architectural treatment of the background is painted in the Italian chiaroscuro manner, with the wall spaces between the cream-colored pilasters painted in cloud effects. The chandelier is green Venetian glass.

105

BOOK ROOMS OF BEAUTY AND CHARM

BY ALDOUS HUXLEY

U.S.A., 1921

In most houses books are apt to be too much scattered. Each sitting room will have its bookshelf, and the overflow will find its way into the bedrooms. There is too often an unnecessary and generally hideous multiplication of small and flimsy pieces of furniture for the reception of books. As more books come into the house—and books are things that tend, insensibly but steadily, to increase and multiply with the passing years—the owners find themselves forced to acquire new receptacles to accomodate them.

This is the wrong way of storing one's books. The method is doubly inconvenient. When volumes are scattered by twos and threes, by dozens and scores, here and there over the whole house, it is often impossible, without a great deal of unnecessary trouble, to lay one's hand on any specific work at a given moment. To find one book, one may have to look through ten or a dozen bookshelves placed in as many rooms. The other undesirable consequence of this method of storing books is that it leads, as we have already pointed out, to the multiplication of superfluous pieces of furniture. The presence of many little bookshelves dotted here and there all over the house gives a certain air of restlessness. The books themselves, seen in small quantities at a time, do not produce their full decorative effect; the little shelves are generally uninteresting, and often positively ugly. Every consideration, practical as well as esthetic, emphasizes the desirabilityf of forming a book room or, at least, of turning a part of one of the ordinary living rooms into a storehouse for the accomodation of our literary possessions.

The essence of a book room is that the shelves shall be a more or less constructional feature of the room. The presence of books in such a room is not fortuitous; they do notoccupy a casual piece of furniture which might be removed at pleasure. No; the books and the shelves that accommodate them are an integral part of the room, almost an architectural, furnishing feature, like a window or a fireplace.

Massed in a single room, one's books become orderly; it is possible to find the volume one requires with out a lengthy search. At the same time the books are seen to their best effect, and a room of remarkable beauty and charm will have been created.

We have spoken purposely of a book room, and not of a library, because the words "book room" are the more intimate, the less solemn term. The distinction between the library and the book room is largely a matter of size. The people who possess enough books—several thousand at the least—to create a library on the grand scale are comparatively few. But innumerable households treasure the several hundred volumes that might be stored in a small and intimate book room. A library is a place in which one stores a great many books one is never likely to want to read—books of reference, old folios, complete works of writers once famous, but now, it must be confessed, a trifle dull. In a book room one keeps the book one likes to have always at hand, the books that one really reads.

The book room in its most complete form is, of course, a miniature of the library, that is to say, a small instead of a large room, of which the walls are completely lined with shelves. In a great many rooms the projection of the chimney leaves two shallow recesses on either side of the fireplace, which may easily be fitted with shelves. This will generally be found a particularly happy arrangement. The bookshelves on either side of the hearth serve to bring out the architectural qualities of the chimney piece.

In houses where there are recessed cupboards in the walls, a very pleasing effect may be produced by fitting one of these cupboards with shelves, and turning it into a book cupboard. Niches may be treated similarly. Indeed, the problem of what to put in the niche is, perhaps, best solved in this way. One great advantage of the converted niche or cupboard is the fact that it can be provided with a glass door. Books, as any housewife can tell you, collect dust at a greater rate and in larger quantities than anything else in the world.

Glass-fronted bookshelves mean a great saving of labor to those whose business it is to keep the house and its contents clean. Unfortunately, it is not always at all easy to give one's bookshelves the protection of a glass door. The niche and the narrow cupboard can easily be fitted with doors. But when we come to glazing shelves of any size the doors become so large and often so ugly, they take away so much from the beauty of the books, that we generally prefer to give the dust free play. Dust is, happily, not among the worst enemies of literature. A book may have slept under the accumulated dust of two or three centuries and still be very little the worse. From the point of view of the books, therefore, glazing is not imperative. The problem must be left to each book lover to solve as he thinks fit. Some will prefer to sacrifice the full beauty of their books to the goddess of cleanliness. Others will swallow the dust for the sake of the decoration. It is all a matter of taste.

The form of the shelves is another point to be considered. Perfectly plain deal shelves are always adequate and inoffensive. Where greater elaboration is desired, the beauty or ugliness of the shelves will depend entirely on the quality of the moldings employed. When the room has a cornice, care must be taken to see that the cornice of the bookshelves shall be in harmony with it and that the two cornices coming together shall not produce too heavy an effect.

The most satisfactory treatment for the lower part of the shelves up to dado height is, generally speaking, to close them in with paneled doors so as to form cupboards. If the books are brought right down to the ground the volumes in the lower shelves should be the portentous folios of earlier days rising through quartos to the octavos of today.

Above: *Fortunate is the man who has a paneled book room, for the flatness of the panels affords a pleasing and dignified contrast with the irregularity in color and size of the books, as is demonstrated here.*

Below: *One of the decorative advantages of books is that they fit conveniently into narrow spaces. In this book room an effective use is made of pilasters to create narrow spaces. Cupboards are built in below.*

Above left: *Books ranging from floor to ceiling give a room a richness of color that is unique. The lower shelves should be for folios and the others for quartos and octavos.*

Left: *The book room in this New York residence is enclosed by built-in bookshelves surmounting cupboards. The doors are glassed to preserve the books from dust. Vernay, decorator.*

Right: *Books and the shelves that accommodate them are an integral part of this room, almost an architectural, furnishing feature, as in this Spokane room decorated by Mrs. John Adson.*

Delicate grilles frame vistas of a real city garden in the New York residence of Mrs. R.G. Reese. Painted metal flowers above the door and consoles holding gay pots of flowers further the garden idea.

OUTDOORS WITHIN WALLS

At least one room in a town house should be furnished to suggest a garden

BY RUBY ROSS WOOD

New York City, 1926

The usual problem in the city is to make a room that will take the place of a view. There are several small private parks in New York, like Sutton Place and Turtle Bay and Beekman Terrace, where one may have a real garden vista outside, and bring it indoors in some connecting room. Then there are hundreds of remodeled private houses that have the old ground-floor kitchens made into garden rooms that serve as sitting or dining rooms. One charming room of this kind is shown above, where a green formal garden opens directly from a room that seems its very reflection. A sensible city garden view is a green one, which one can enjoy most of the winter months, and a green painted window trellis keeps the illusion when the living greens are dead.

When there is no roof for a garden room, no faraway view of the park or the river, or of sktscrapers, and if there are other apartment house walls appallingly nearby, what is one to do? Can the garden illusion be obtained? Here is an answer, using a small room that was a left-over bedroom in an apartment, with an exposure completely obscured by a nearby building. The problem was to shut the outside out, not to bring it in. This little room is a veritable sermon in chintz, for it begins and ends in the pattern of the yellow chintz curtains, pale canary yellow with big bunches of white lilies and

The garden room in Mrs. John Vietor's New York apartment grew from a carved pine overmantel framing an English garden scene. The pale green of the walls is carried into the curtains of glazed chintz sprigged with flowers.

Over the desk is a group of watercolors of hyacinths, and old English porcelain jardinieres hold masses of fresh flowers. The seat of the Queen Anne desk chair is also flowered needlework. Ruby Ross Wood, decorator.

Suggestive of the cool, simple interiors of Japan is the garden room above, with its assortment of furniture on slightly exotic lines, its colorful Chinese rug, and its background of unusually fine Kakemono paintings.

Off the room left is a conservatory with walls of glass suggestive of the sliding windows in Japanese homes. These rooms, in the New York home of Mrs. Walter Douglas, are on the top of a tall house overlooking Central Park.

Over this daybed, covered in gray silk sprigged with bunches of flowers, hangs a painting of Mrs. Vietor's garden. Watercolors of hyacinths are on this wall, and a needlework chair is in the foreground.

A flower box surmountd by a trellis fills this city window, and brings a bit of real garden into the room. Paula Robertson was the decorator.

pink, wine and yellow primroses. The walls are paneled with moldings and painted in three very light, sharp yellows. The windows are hung with a pale yellow gauze curtain, very full, and then with long curtains of the chintz with double fluted ruffles of plain yellow and green chintz. The carpet is the color of the primrose leaves. The chairs are covered in old quilted petticoats of yellow sprigged in pink. The gloomiest, smokiest day of the winter has no effect on this little sunshiny room.

A suggestion of the outdoors may be given a city room by a double window in which are glass shelves holding decorative plants. A collection of flower prints accents the garden feeling. Designed by Harry C. Richardson.

If you really care about gardens and want to make a room part of your own, settle on some one thing and collect prints, objects and chintzes relating to that. Whether it be roses, fountains, lilies, birds or butterflies, you will make your room infinitely more interesting if you make it a hobby. There are so many gardenish things one can bring into brick-walled apartments, so many chintzes and wallpapers that are gardens in themselves, there is no excuse for being without a garden atmosphere in any sort of abode.

CONCEALING THE UNSIGHTLY TELEPHONE

U.S.A., 1923

It is a curious fact that the telephone, probably the most indispensable of all our modern luxuries, has been allowed to retain its original unprepossessing aspect. Even when painted to harmonize with the surroundings, it strikes a discordant note by the very ungainliness of its lines, which no amount of painting or decorating can transform.

There is only one thing to do with the telephone—conceal it . . . Hanging cabinets, chests, small commodes or built-in cupboards are ideal places in which to keep it. There is no lack of convenience, for when the bell rings, one merely has to open a door to take out the instrument. When not in use how much better to have it tucked away

in some charming piece of furniture than to be constantly confronted with its ugly lines.

Small chests of drawers in oak or walnut can have the three drawers in the midddle taken out and a door put on. Into this place the telephone fits nicely. The sketch below shows a chest that would be suitable for a living room, library or hall . . .

If there is a built-in cupboard in the living room the telephone might have a compartment of its own with a separate door. A chair or settee nearby adds to the convenience.

Only the ringing of the bell betrays the presence of a telephone on this desk. It is cleverly concealed in the four large books, which have been made into a cabinet for the purpose.

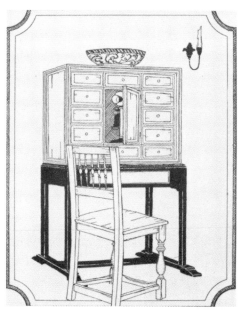

A happy solution for the telephone in an Italian hall is this small, sturdy chest of drawers on a table. The three center drawers have been taken out to provide space for the telephone.

Left: *The bookfront commode provides a place for the telephone behind the sliding front.*

This wall cabinet is both decorative and practical. It conceals the hall telephone. Within reach are a pad and pencil, in the drawer.

THE RADIO BECOMES A DECORATION

U.S.A.,1925

After having coped with such decorative problems as unsightly radiators, telephones and phonographs, the matter of adapting the radio to a certain scheme of decoration presents few difficulties to anyone possessed of a little ingenuity. In the first place the horn has been dispensed with, the majority of sets being equipped with a loud speaker—that unfortunate term—a small box-like arrangement at the top. In addition to these compact sets are the countless pieces of furniture, distinguished in line and workmanship, designed especially to hold a receiving set. These cabinets, for they are mostly cabinets although occasionally we find a radio set in a desk or commode, are made in various period styles, in staple woods or painted to conform with the decorative scheme.

An excellent example of a cabinet designed especially for a radio is the Chippendale model shown below. It is effectively placed between bookshelves, its dark wood a nice contrast to the paneled walls painted a light coffee color, with red moldings . . .

When a radio is used in a library it may be enclosed in a cabinet such as this Chippendale one, designed to harmonize with the room. This cabinet is courtesy of the Aeolian Company.

In a sunroom a small receiving set may be placed in a niche in the wall, as shown above. From the Radio Corporation of America.

This handsome cabinet comes in walnut or mahogany, containing both a radio and phonograph. From the Brunswick-Balke-Collender Company.

In this attractive small sitting room, a radio receiving set is placed in a small hanging cabinet. It is not apparent when the doors are closed, as these are fitted with pieces of mirror and decorated with painted flower designs. This cabinet is courtesy the Freed-Eisemann Company.

The all-electric kitchen offers the most convincing solution for the problems of domestic management that thousands of housewives now face. It requires intelligent handling, but less actual labor. Its cost of maintenance and its general convenience more than compensate for the initial cost of installation. In this all-electric kitchen the equipment includes a range, fireless cooker, percolator, grill, ovenette, vacuum cleaner and ironing machine. Edison Company.

THE EIGHT-HOUR KITCHEN AND SAVING TIME ON TUESDAYS

U.S.A., 1920, 1921

Whether we like it or not, this is the era of the short working day, in the home as well as in the factory. The only constructive course for the house-manager is to reorganize the mechanics of her shop, as it were, so that the time-element can receive due attention . . .

Kitchen equipment divides itself into devices for the preparation of meals; apparatus for cooking and serving; and appliances for cleaning up. It is of interest to see how largely electrical devices have come to be used in all of these departments . . .

Ironing done by machinery is simple and pleasant; the new inventions save time and wash-day nerves. As for electric vacuum cleaners, they cost not even as much as an electric iron and far less than the cost of extra cleaning folk at the wages prevalent today . . .

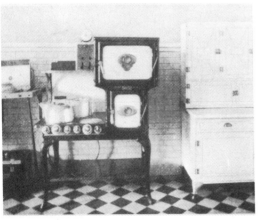

Left to right: This style of electric range is equipped with a fireless cooking oven. The clock can be set to cut off the current at the desired time. Westinghouse Electric Co. In some home refrigeration systems, the machinery is placed in a compartment at the bottom of the refrigerator with the coil box and ice-making trays in a section above. Courtesy of the Frigidaire Corporation. A dishwasher of this type should be priced at about $145.

The cost of this electric kitchen motor aid should be about $130—plus attachments, up to $160.

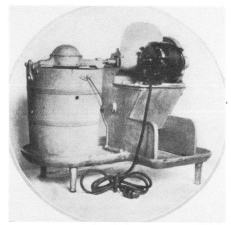

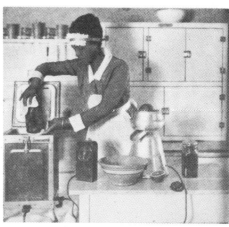

Left: This arrangement for freezing the American dish, ice cream, shows an ordinary motor attached to an ice crusher and freezer. The electric machine is courtesy of the Edison Company. Right: This type of motor unit can be used for dozens of kitchen purposes in addition to turning the ice cream freezer, such as polishing silver, sharpening knives. Edison Company.

When it comes to canning and preserving in an electric-equipped kitchen, effective sterilizing can be done in an electric fireless cooker, a few jars at a time, of course.

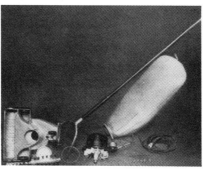

The sewing machine is an absolute necessity. This is a rotary model, hook-type, with additional devices of hinged pressure foot and speed adjustment. Cost: $72.

The vacuum cleaner is not a highly complicated piece of machinery, but it requires care. It should be oiled once a month, and dust removed after each operation. Courtesy the Hoover Co.

A vacuum cleaner of the tank type, with attachments. Courtesy the Duntley Pneumatic Cleaner Co.

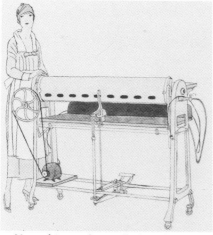

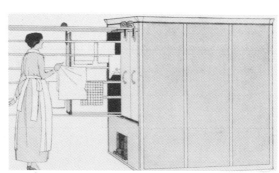

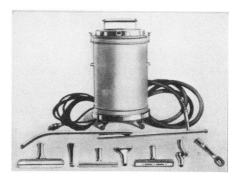

Motor-driven, electrically-heated ironing machine, foot-operated. Courtesy Wallace B. Hart.

In this heated air dryer, electricity, gas or kerosene supplies the heat and fresh air circulates. This type has an overhead sliding rack.

This ironing board, which folds up against the wall, has an attachable sleeve board. It is very practical for the small laundry or kitchen.

Left to right: Do not detach an electric iron, or any electrical appliance, by yanking the cord. The right way is to free the cord by pulling on the socket. When through with an electrical iron, not only detach the plug but also turn off the current at the socket. When called away, detach the plug from the iron and set the iron up on its end or stand. Courtesy Edison Co.

An unadorned, formal combination of water and turf is often effective within an enclosure of clipped yew or even privet. The whole design in such cases should be distinctly geometrical—a matter of angles, circles and straight lines—as is evidenced in this English garden.

WATER GARDENS AND THEIR MAKING

England and U.S.A., 1920-24

There is no sort of garden more delightful than the water garden, and none which, contrary to the general opinion, is so easy to make or to maintain. Once you have constructed the pool and put in plants, your work in the water garden is at an end. You need only visit it each day and see what surprises it has in store for you. Water lilies, nympheas, water hyacinths, water poppies are some of the attractive plants you can grow in your pool. The different varieties of iris are also appropriate, as well as our own wild cardinal flower (Lobelia cardinalis). The hardy bamboos reach a considerable height and act as a windbreak

This guest house and boulder garden are part of the property of Mrs. Emma Flower Taylor, of Watertown, New York. The pool nearest the cottage is stocked with trout. Above it is a lily pool, below one for swimming.

From the middle of the rock and water garden is a glimpse of the main house through a rustic arch. All the rocks were hauled in and set in place—none was here originally. W. Maredydd Harrison, landscape architect.

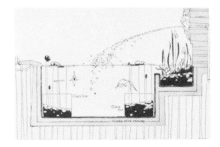

In making a pool, glass or wooden boxes to hold the soil in the bottom permit the easy shifting of plants. Varying depths will allow wider range of planting.

This circular pool is lined with a "waterproof" concrete mixture reinforced with woven wire. Inlet and outlet pipes insure proper water level maintenance.

In this garden of G.S. Van Gilder in Knoxville, Tennessee, a tall pottery jar stands at each end of the lily pool. The curves of these jars afford a pleasant relief to the straight lines of the pool's rim and the precision of the lattice at the far end.

This circular garden is set with a rose-rimmed pool from which flagstone paths lead in four directions—to the house, tennis court, arbor and lawn. A jet marks the center. The plan, below left, indicates its secluded character, with the tall and robust enclosure of shrubs. C.S. LeSure, landscape architect.

. . . A water garden needs no weeding; no cultivation, no care. And there is a fascination in seeing each bud, as it is formed, rise upward through the water, and each faded blossom sink back to the depths again—in seeing the actual working of the lily and other plants. From no other form of gardening is it possible to obtain such rapid and profitable returns . . .

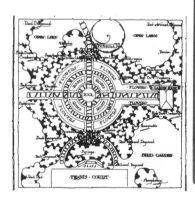

Above left: In this city garden an outdoor living room has been created by the protecting rear fence and the pavement around the pool. Note the simple changes of levels that give variation to this plot. Many city properties present about the same problem, and this plan, above, would solve them admirably. Landscape architect Elizabeth Leonard Strang designed this garden for Mrs. Jay Clark, Jr. of Worcester, Massachusetts.

Left: A knowledge of design and love for flowers can combine to make the city backyard a pleasant place. Here, looking from the pool toward the house you see the planting on each side of the turf panel and the happy handling of the porch, basement lattice and visitor's stairs. The trellis is pale green.

MODERNIST BATHROOMS AND BEDROOMS

Paris, New York, Long Island, 1927, 1928, 1929

The striking wall decorations of this bathroom are not painted in oils but executed in that great medium of the Renaissance— fresco. The dado is marbleized and finished at the top to represent a shelf. This delightful bathtub niche is in the Paris apartment of Mrs. Selma Lewisohn and was painted by Gardner Hale.

The brilliant color characteristic of Empire decoration is found in this bath-dressing room where the background offers a study in contrasts. The walls are white with black marbleized pilasters. A jade green ceiling and black and white floor complete the design scheme.

Here is another view of the bath-dressing room, left. The curtains are old gold satin lined with deep blue and a gold and blue striped satin covers the chaise longue. This bath-dressing room is in the New York apartment of Mrs. Seton Porter. McMillen, Inc., decorators.

The back of this bathroom niche is gold mirror with painted Chinoiserie decorations. Wallpaper has a cream ground figured in blues and greens. Wood trim is red and gold lacquer. In the Long Island residence of Colonel H.H. Rogers. McMillen Inc., decorators; John Russell Pope, architect.

Built-in details, so practical a feature of modernist decoration abroad, should be more widely adopted in this country where space is at a premium. The outstanding note in this room in a New York apartment is the built-in bed with its graceful arched opening and window at the foot. Lucian Bernhard, decorator.

The alcove of this studio contains a built-in bed covered in gray velvet. The ceiling of this niche is finished in silver leaf and lights are concealed behind a molding, also used to hold three vases of fragile bright blue glass—a vivid color note against the gleaming background. Lucian Bernhard, decorator.

1930/s

LIVING
WITH
MODERNISM

This decade saw the acceptance of modernism. What had seemed rigorous, architectural, or mechanistic took on a new functional purity in these years of social and economic austerity. The modernist look evolved into a more graceful style, enhanced by the use of lacquer, mirror, and cork, Scandinavian designers influenced cabinetmakers with their use of blond, laminated, and bent woods. The supply of more industrial materials, including aluminum and plastics, created a new group of experts, industrial designers—such as Gilbert Rohde and Donald Deskey, who designed the furniture for the Radio City Music Hall in New York. As a counterpoint to the more austere modern styles, Victorian and Baroque revivals were stimulated by Hollywood glamour productions, and the Williamsburg restoration in Virginia inspired a new popularity in Colonial design. Architectural innovations were presented at the Berlin Exposition of 1931, where the more mature work of Bauhaus artists such as Walter Gropius, Marcel Breuer and Ludwig Mies van der Rohe was displayed to a large public, paralleling the progressive architectural ideas of Le Corbusier in France. The interior design of two great European ocean liners, the *Bremen* and the *Normandie,* expressed vividly the preocupations of the decade—the remembrance of things extravagant, combined with a sure knowledge of the stringencies to come.

*The Executive Lounge of the Ford Exposition
at the 1939 New York World's Fair.
Designed by Walter Dorwin Teague, the color scheme is
moss green and pale tan. The furniture, designed
by Mr. Teague, is of pickled rift oak. A panel of rawhide
with squares of gold moldings is above the gold mirror
fireplace, and is flanked by curved
lighted recesses filled with white hydrangeas.*

Above: *The living room, with a view of the wall opposite the fireplace, painted white. The large couch is upholstered in geranium red velvet, with bookcases in niches either side. The bookcases are white lacquer with red lacquer linings to match the couch, and the books complete the color scheme.*

Below: *The fireplace wall is white; the fireplace white marble. The niches are covered with white leather, and the couch upholstered in white leather. The white velvet cushion has a red stripe. The legs of the two comfortable leather seats built in the niches are made of transparent glass.*

LATEST DEVELOPMENTS IN MODERN DESIGN

U.S.A., and England, 1933-1935

The problems that confronted the architect, Joseph Urban, when he came to decorate the New York apartment of Katherine Brush were many. As the only light was from two tall north windows, a coldness had to be overcome. So Mr. Urban closed off the east and south corners, developing the latter into a bright, airy glass pavilion where the sun streams through orange and yellow chiffon curtains. Round mirrors on opposite walls are the real architectural element of the room. A silver head by Josef Hoffmann of Vienna embellishes one of the bookcases, and a centerpiece of silver by Dagobert Peche, another famous Viennese, adorns the mantel. The carpet in the room is black, with a few large squares of red. Along the shelves which line the sides of the right-angle sofa before the fireplace gayly hued book bindings weave a brilliant tapestry of color. White leather upholsters the sofa, and zebra striped cushions provide accent. To be happily livable a room should both express the thoughts of the designer who controls the scheme and makes the room artistic and should contain furniture and articles cherished by the owner. With commendable skill Mr. Urban has used Miss Brush's treasured possessions in his scheme.

Something new under the sun–Donald Deskey hobnobbing with the Celestial Empire! Result: Chinese-modern furniture–a new conception combining the forthrightness of today with the curves, the color, the quirks of that glamorous style from the Far East.

Walls in this dining room are pale larkspur blue, the rug deeper blue and the curtains silvery satin with crystal tiebacks. The furniture painted white, with chair seats in deeper delphinium blue, is brilliant against the subtle background.

England sends the dramatic group designed by Arundell Clarke, the English decorator. Pieces are black and white lacquer with a smart absence of ornament. Plates, black and platinum bands, glasses, opaque white bases; Arundell Clarke. Napkins; Mosse; vases; Rena Rosenthal.

A modern living room in a bachelor's apartment, decorated in the new bright blue–lavish use of mirrored and colored glass, and rough textures in curtain and upholstery fabrics. Raymond Loewy was the consultant; furniture designed and executed by Cummings and Engbert.

This is a glimpse of Paul T. Frankl's apartment. Two marked changes are evident in this new modernism—much of the furniture is now built-in and new materials are employed. A broad band of cork as an extended fireplace mantel gives the studio a horizontal character. Sofa and chair frames are also covered in cork. Among the newer tenets of the modernist is the abandonment of grotesque angles and the substitution of the curve. The former lacked charm; the curve is beginning to bring an air of grace into our contemporary rooms. The old-fashioned word ''cozy'' is rarely associated with modern decoration; in fact, much of this contemporary decoration would seem to avoid that atmosphere as though it were the plague. Yet a modern room can be cozy. And this comfortable spirit is found in the apartment of Paul T. Frankl.

In this man's realm, created by Paul Frankl for Hubert C. Winan's New York apartment, not even a fingerprint of the so-called feminine touch is apparent in these two views of the living room.

The jungle painting over the sofa dominates the color scheme—a blend of beige, gray, and brown interspersed with reds and black. Rough and unusually textured fabrics give character to the neutral colors.

A TWENTIETH ANNIVERSARY IN MODERNISM

New York City, 1934, 1935

In the past twenty years the room layout and size of apartments has definitely changed, and the change has affected their furnishing and decoration. Our rooms are much less cluttered with useless objects, and simplicity of line makes for restfulness and utility. In 1917, Paul T. Frankl, fresh from schools in Paris, Munich, and Berlin, made his first efforts to gain a hearing here for the modern taste. Today we congratulate him on his anniversary in modernism, by spreading on these pages his most recent designs.

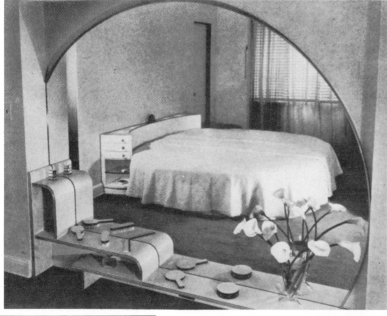

Top: *In the apartment of Roger Wolfe Kahn, by Paul T. Frankl, the corner sofa creates a corner where there is no corner and thereby gives an architectural feeling to the living room. Soft cork is used to cover the wood frame, and the upholstery of the couch is natural colored lapin cloth. The walls are covered in light beige Japanese grass cloth put up in blocks. The cork table has a mirror that is supported by glass rods.*
Above left: *Mrs. Kahn's bedroom is done in shades of white, with accents of pale blue. Modern air conditioning makes it possible to use white even in cities with dust-laden air. The circular bed is reflected, in this picture, in a mirror that carries out the curves of the room.*
Above right: *In this black and white entrance foyer, long mirrors are lighted from pedestals below. One decorative pattern picture is set flat on the wall. The only other design activity in the space is in the zebra cloth.*
Right: *In Mr. Kahn's comfortable living room, the fireplace mantel is painted black, and so are the leather arms of the deep, low, inviting chairs. Their seats and backs are covered with an astrachan material. The low table is reflected in gunmetal mirrors.*

AN ENGLISH RESIDENCE DESIGNED BY TWO NEW YORK MODERNISTS

Darlington, Devon, England, 1934

Such a typically British name as High Cross Hill, Darlington, Devon, conjures up pictures of a typical English manor, overgrown with ivy and mellowed by age, but in reality it is the name and address of the steel and concrete modern house presented here—the residence of Mr. W.B. Curry, designed by the American architects, Howe & Lescaze.

Opposite page, top: *A view of the house as seen from the east, with the entrance front at the right, and landscape with trees behind.*
Opposite page, bottom: *The living room, with grand piano, as seen from the dining room.*
This page, from top: *Beginning in upper corner of the page and working down, pictures show: Terrace corner, living room left, dining room right. South side, living room ahead, study at left. Southwest corner, guest bedrooms above garage. North facade showing principal entrance. Kitchen, with west windows. Living room, stairs at right to dining room; doorway opposite to hall and entrance. Study, at southeast corner of the house.*

Bear Run, Pennsylvania. Frank Lloyd Wright, architect

Woodbridge, Connecticut. William Lescaze, architect

Whipsnade, England. Tecton, architects

Los Angeles, California. Raphael Soriano, designer

In the style of Crete. Harvey Stevenson, architect

Modified Georgian style. Frank J. Forster, architect

126

HOMES OF TODAY: MODERN DESIGN INVOLVING NEW MATERIALS AND TECHNIQUES, IS GAINING POPULARITY

Danbury, Connecticut. A. Lawrence Kocher, Gerhard Ziegler, architects

Poissy-sur-Seine, France. Le Corbusier, architect

Regency up-to-date. James W. O'Connor, architect

Denver, Colorado. Burnham Hoyt, architect

Midwest modern. Boyd Hill, architect

U.S.A., and Europe, 1933, 1935, 1937, 1938

127

THE BERLIN APARTMENT OF A GREAT MODERNIST

Berlin, 1933

In Berlin's smart Königin Augusta-strasse is one of the most successful modern apartments in that city. It is the home of Professor Fritz August Breuhaus, who has executed such interesting commissions as the interiors of Germany's famous liner, "Bremen," and more recently, the cabins of the new super-zeppelin which is to supersede the "Graf Zeppelin."

The dining room ceiling is cream, walls are of grayish pink, the curtains are dull blue and the glass curtains net. The table is of dark mahogany inlaid with modern designs of ivory and brass . . . All furniture designed by Professor Breuhaus.

The living room is a combination of coral, gold, yellowish gray, and dull reds and greens. The walls are covered with a hand-woven gold and mauve fabric, with matching curtains. Primitive African sculpture mingles with daring modern paintings.

Above: *Drawing room colors are canary yellow, light blue, biscuit, and pink. Here too, Oriental art blends with modern furniture.*

Below: *This is the hallway of Professor Fritz August Breuhaus's Berlin apartment. A large mirror hangs on the right-hand wall.*

In Madame Breuhaus's bedroom, walls and ceiling are in shades of tan. Tan rugs are on the floor. The closets are particularly interesting; across one side of the room are sliding panels of Japanese silk, giving access to about 20 feet of well-lighted space. Furniture is painted apple green. . . .

THE COMING AND GOING OF TIDES OF TASTE

BY RICHARDSON WRIGHT

U.S.A., and Europe, 1934

Dictionaries, with their canny way of being on both sides of the fence at once, define taste as the capacity for discernment, which can be either good or bad and can affect everything from morals to furniture. As a fashionable word, taste seems to have come into smart usage in that English era of luxury and dirt, the 18th century. At that time the capacity for good taste in personal surroundings apparently was restricted to the upper classes—a sort of Heaven-dispatched talent—and rarely did it filter down to people of less ambitious circumstances.

Somewhat of that same connotation of taste has been prevalent here. While England still looks to the Court and the Quality as monitors of taste on many matters, one does not, in this country, expect the White House to set the style in matters artistic. The contemporary Washington dynasty, for instance, cannot be said to have changed the style of the chairs in which we sit or the color of our walls. In fact, the present rage for social readjustments has put taste pretty far into the background. It remains for creative artists—decorators, architects, and designers—to set the styles. And the styles, if we judge them by the pictures shown in newspapers and magazines, are not selected because of the good taste they display, but because they are news. Novelty is the aim of our machine age, and novelties are now crowding so fast upon each other that the average person is very apt to be utterly bewildered by them.

Because an article or a design is new does not, by any means, assure that it is in good taste. Nor does the slavish repetition of traditional design make it good taste for today. We no longer are following exactly the yardstick set up by Winckelmann a century or more ago. That eminent archeologist and arbiter of taste stated solemnly, "Imitation of the Ancients is the shortest way to perfection in the fine arts." Nevertheless there is constant evidence, to be found in furniture, fabric, and wallpaper designs alike, that taste is playing safe by taking the short-cut to Classical styles. For those to whom the impersonal and untraditional Modernism does not appeal, these reflections of the past are a safe harbor in which to keep one's taste.

During the past thirty-four years in which House & Garden has pursued its course, many tides of taste have been discernible. Each in its time was proclaimed good, and then eventually faded from popular favor to be supplanted by something new. We have seen the remaining vestiges of the Italian influence, a rise and fall of popularity in Spanish furnishings, the coming and acceptance of French Provincial and its descent into banality, the sturdy nationalism that persistently keeps alive a demand for Early American and Georgian architecture and furniture. We have seen vigor give way to grace and grace give way to fantasy and fantasy finally ditched by blunt and functional Modernism. And in the short course it has run, we have watched Modernism take account of its own weaknesses and repent of its brash boastings. Onto this crowded canvas of thirty-four years have also appeared several exotics and anachronisms — in Chicago a short-lived flair for the William Morris craftsman and flower-spattered style, in New York a dip into German rural baroque, in other sections a hoydenish flirtation with peasant designs and Victorian, and everywhere the appearance of the home bar and game room.

About the only old style that we haven't seen revived in these three and a half decades, except for the architecture of churches and colleges, is the Gothic. England in Victoria's time had a rush of Gothic to the head. It fairly wallowed in Gothic insincerities. Of the many calamities that Heaven can well spare us, we sincerely pray that no one begins to make Gothic popular again. Its ultimate descent was in those country cottages and furniture and monstrosities covered with jig-saw work, which delighted people in the General Grant era, that darkest of dark ages in all the history of taste.

At the present moment the situation in furniture and decoration is this "you pays your money and you takes your choice." Nevertheless some definite tendencies are discernible. Classical Modernism is still enjoying a vigorous popularity and promises to be a long-lived taste. The English 18th-century, Sheraton and Chippendale especially, is coming back with reassured strength. Both of these styles follow the Winckelmann advice—they are, to a greater or lesser degree, imitations of the Ancients and as such are the shortest way to perfection.

The improvement in Modernism is another story. It has ceased shouting about its functionalism—a gross word anyhow—and is attaining some of the grace that the early examples sorely lacked. Especially in its use and combinations of colors it is giving rooms a fresh and stimulating air. Its furniture has now gauged itself to the capacity of machines without sacrificing beauty. This evolution of Modernism, however, was to be expected. It is inherent in Modern taste to change and to gradually adapt itself—and Modern design is so swiftly adapting itself to the widespread desire for grace and beauty that more and more people are now accepting this style whole-heartedly.

There is also, today, a marked tendency to make the home gayer. This is not necessarily in the prevalence of game rooms, but in the general color schemes of all the rooms of the house. We have safely passed out of the era of mousy pastel shades and are enjoying strong, pure color and combinations of colors that would have shocked our grandparents. Shocking grandparents is one of the delightful habits of each new age. It is youth's shout of freedom. Whenever a new style appears, it is bound to shock someone. Indeed every coming and going of taste has been accompanied by its own particular shock, and the best test of the vitality of your taste is how easily you take the jolt.

Opposite page: *In this exciting circular setting—combination studio-library—Katharine Brush writes her alluring tales, California redwood burl with German silver moldings and green leather wainscot welted in black. Chairs are black satin corded in green, the desk redwood burl with green leather top. Carpet is green and black. The architect was Joseph Urban; Irvin L. Scott, associate.*

NOW YOU CAN ACTUALLY LIVE IN A HOUSE OF GLASS

Chicago, 1933

America's first glass house, revolutionary in design and construction, is creating excitement at the big fair in Chicago. Of glass and steel, this circular "House of Tomorrow" is built around a spiral column that encloses the electrical, plumbing, and air-conditioning systems. No need to worry about curious neighbors in this glass house—new type aluminum-finished Venetian blinds deflect infra-red rays and keep the room dark and cool. There are roller shades that pull up from floor and, also, soft draw curtains. No windows open, the air-conditioning system keeps the atmosphere fresh as a day in June. Century Homes; George Fred Keck was the architect.

Top: *View of the glass house, showing three floors, garage, and extensive terraces.*
Center: *The circular stairway winds around a central steel column from ground to top-most terrace. Walls are lacquered gray, steps in gray rubber tile.*
Bottom: *Floor plans, showing glass circles around a steel axis. The ground floor contains airplane hanger and garage; hall, heating and cooling unit room, laundry facilities, and recreation room. On the second floor are the combination living-dining room, kitchen, bedrooms, bath, and terrace. The sunroom, circular and surrounded by an observation terrace, constitutes the third floor.*

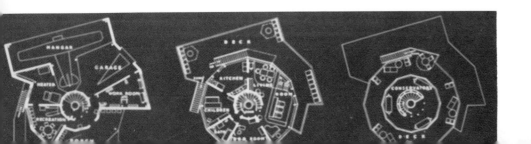

GLASS HORIZONS

New York City, 1939

Within the past few years all the brave new worlds have been full of glass houses. Glass has become a symbol associated in our minds with progress, Utopia and the sleek and cleanly future. These glass designs appeared at the New York World's Fair.

Left: *Max Ingrand's mirror mural in the Ford dining room by Walter Dorwin Teague. The mural, on fifteen panels of glass, is etched and sandblasted on the reverse, painted in golds and grays, then mirrored.*
Below: *High-tension plate glass doors without frames make their first appearance in the Ford Exposition executive lounge, also designed by Teague.*

THE WESTERN WORLD'S FAIR

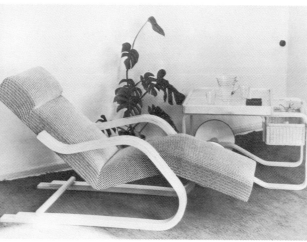

San Francisco, 1939

Like a magic city raised from the ocean's floor, the Golden Gate Exposition stands on man-made "Treasure Island" in the middle of San Francisco Bay. The Decorative Arts section, directed by Dorothy Liebes, noted designer of textiles, is one of the outstanding features of the Fair. . . . There are rooms by well-known American designers and decorators. The Indian and Hawaiian exhibits are significant in the field as are the rooms by such foreign designers as Le Corbusier, Aalto, Lurçat, Malmsten and Dunand.

Above left: *A group by Californian artists: the hand-woven rug is by Elizabeth Jennings; wooden tray and glass container by Amberg-Hirth; figure by Brents Carlton.*
Above right: *Designed along unusual lines, this compact tea-wagon and comfortable lounging chair from New Furniture, Inc., in the Aalto room.*
Below left: *"The Girl of the Rainbow" is one of the many unusual groups of sculpture. This work is by O.C. Malmquist.*
Below right: *A group in cast stone by Helen Burton, who with her sister, Esther, executed several interesting compositions for the Fair.*

ALUMINUM NOW STEPS OUT OF THE FRYING PAN INTO THE FIREPLACE

Top left: *Mantel with grate, fender, coal scuttle, shovel of aluminum. Last three, Kantack. Mantel, grate, H.A. Bame. Urns, flowers, Gerard.* Lower left: *Lacquer and aluminum tray, Rena Rosenthal. Bouillon cup, Mrs. Ehrich. Other accessories, Russel Wright.*

Above: *Among game-room accessories a sophisticated scheme of black and silver is achieved in a portable bar with black linoleum top and sides of aluminum. On the latter an alternate mat and polished finish produces an interesting striped effect. From Berri.*

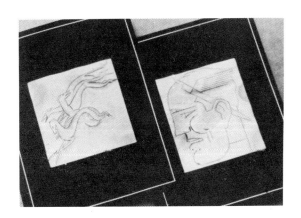

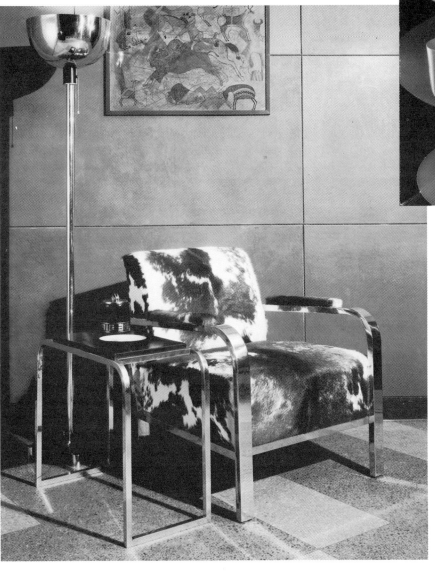

Top left: *Etched aluminum framed in black leather covers modern portfolios.* Lower left: *Aluminum and calf armchair; table and lamp of aluminum and Formica—men's lounge, Radio City Music Hall, Donald Deskey, designer. Tobacco jar, Rena Rosenthal.*

Top right: *Aluminum tumblers and steins, aluminum and wood trays, Russel Wright.* Lower right: *Aluminum wallpaper depicts history of tobacco in smoking room of Radio City Music Hall. Paper, formica, and aluminum table designed by Deskey. Vase, Gerard.*

Europe and U.S.A., 1933

MODERNISM IN THE WESTCHESTER HILLS

Mount Kisco, New York, 1935

A modern design, executed in modern materials and furnished with the most recent equipment, the Richard H. Mandel house is built of cinder concrete masonry units covered with Portland cement stucco. Its floors are reinforced concrete and the roof is of concrete slabs on steel joists. The house was designed by the architect Edward Stone, with Donald Deskey co-designer and decorator. The top floor of the house contains bedrooms and children's rooms, the second floor contains living room, library, dining room, kitchen, and a squash court. The ground floor holds entrance hall, barroom, office, and three-car garage, with storage space.

Top: *The exterior of this modern house, a fireproof structure with flat planes on a hilltop.*
Right: *The hall, with white and light cream walls and a window of white hollow glass brick. The floor is dark brown cork, stair carpet brown, and the stair rail aluminum.*

The dining room has flat white curved walls with vacuum glass bricks and a black terrazzo floor. The rug is a shaggy, hand-woven geometrical design in cocoa brown and chartreuse. White Cellophane in diagonal weave makes the curtains. Chairs are chromium and emerald leather. An especially designed table is in white lacquer and chromium with an etched glass center and lighting beneath.

In this living room the view's the thing. The color scheme is beige and white with occasional brown and yellow spots. Draperies are a rough-textured beige linen with a diagonal brown stripe. This same fabric has been used for the curtain that separates the living room from the library. The rug is café au lait. On the sofa is a brown, white, and yellow plaid and on the chairs a pale cream ribbed fabric.

One of the bedrooms has three walls painted chalk white and the fourth, behind the bed, light sapphire blue. The floor is cream linoleum with a blue rubber border. A flat mantel of white marble is surrounded by mirrors. The furniture is rubbed maple and white lacquer.

CONTEMPORARY IDEALS IN AN $11,500 HOUSE

U.S.A., 1935

The site of this house is a lot 75 feet wide and 125 feet deep, sloping toward the south from the road. The garage, entrance, service quarters, and kitchen are arranged along the north side of the house, leaving the south side, with its sunny garden and wide vistas over the sloping terrain, free for lounging, dining, recreation, and sleeping quarters. Dining, living room, porch, and terraces extend across the entire width of the lot, at a level slightly above the garden, insuring the view. The space can be opened up for large gatherings. The dining room end may be separated from the living room by a sliding curtain. The south wall of the dining-living room is principally glass, inviting the eye to explore the country outside. The picture window is framed by planting on either side. This welcome touch of green is repeated along the windows of both the master's and children's sleeping rooms. Adjacent to the living room, the covered porch—which may be either screened or glazed—flows out to the terrace and offers opportunity for indoor games or lounging. The southern façade is stucco, the remainder is redwood grooved siding. The architects for this modern, air-conditioned "Ideal" house were J. André Fouilhoux and Don E. Hatch.

Top: *Entrance façade, showing garage (with door closed), entrance, and the expense of glass that light the stair hall.*
Above left: *A section through the house showing how it is fitted to the sloping site.*
Right: *Broad windows, porches, and inviting terraces of the ideal modern house create no emphatic line of demarcation between the indoors and out–as demonstrated here.*
Below right: *Plans show how convenience and economy are secured without loss of space.*

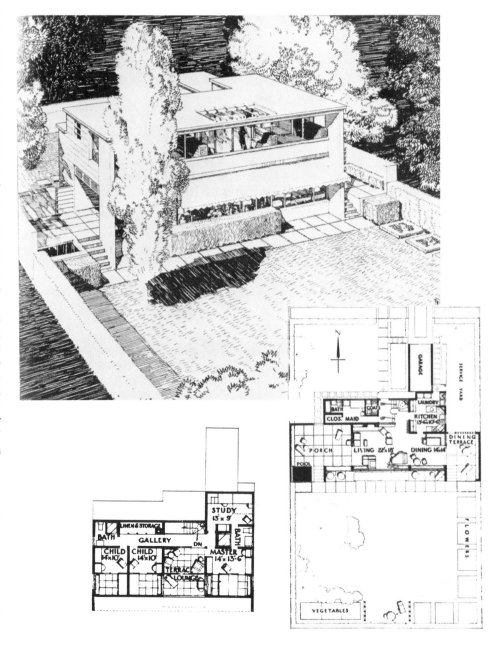

INTRODUCING THE PREFABRICATED HOUSE

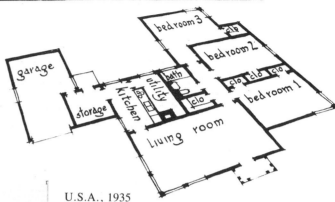

U.S.A., 1935

Ever since steel has been seriously considered for houses, the home that would be entirely factory fabricated, shipped knock-down to a site and then assembled rather than constructed, has been on the way. Now the idea has become a reality, and any one of a series of six houses, two of which are shown here, may be ordered from catalogue. . . . A most interesting feature of this prefabricated house project is the purchasing plan. It is expected that the houses now offered will range in price from $3,800 to $9,900, these figures to cover everything having to do with the complete erection of the house, not including, of course, plot and landscaping. A financing plan is contemplated whereby no down payment will be required and the house paid for over a period of fifteen years through a stated monthly sum, which for the smallest house would be in the neighborhood of $38. The six houses now offered range in size from three rooms, kitchen and bath, to nine rooms, kitchen and two baths . . . Each house is an interesting example of modern design and is thoroughly durable, fireproof, and termite-proof. Adequate insulation is provided against heat, cold, and sound. The development of this "whole house" problem was worked out by Houses, Inc., of which Robert W. McLaughlin, architect, is head.

Top and top right: *One of the smaller prefabricated houses and floor plan, as designed by the architect, Robert W. McLaughlin.*
Left: *The two story type, is as practical as the smaller, one-story design. For beach and country summer homes the convenience factor makes the prefabricated house especially desirable.*

A DECORATOR DOES AN APARTMENT
TO SUIT HERSELF

New York City, 1935

If decorators had mirrors for personalities, changing their reflections with succeeding clients, all decorative schemes would approach perfection. In each and every room there would be that complete harmony of setting and spirit that invest the background created by a decorator for herself, with results as happy as in the New York apartment of Mrs. Archibald Manning Brown, shown here. Mrs. Brown is president of McMillen, Inc., whose charming interiors have frequently appeared in House & Garden. In arranging her own

apartment she has combined both French and English features of the 18th and early 19th centuries with most effective results. In the green and white dining room, opposite page, French Directoire chairs fraternize with an English Regency table. There is no carpet on the green and white marble floor. Curtains are white taffeta with an emerald Empire border. In the living room above, most of the furniture is Louis XVI, while the rug, an Aubusson, follows the early Empire trend of design. The upholstery fabrics are damask and moire.

INTERESTING DESIGNER ROOMS

New York City, 1933, 1934

This is a hotel room transformed by the clever hand of one who knows the fundamental principles of governing his art—William M. Odom, President of the New York School of Fine and Applied Art. Its salient feature is the ingenious way he used the existing walls and furniture, with the addition of a few pieces of his own, and without making any structural changes to achieve the result.

Above: *To start with, a commonplace hotel room with cream-colored walls and a mixture of chairs covered in a variety of unimaginative materials. Transformed into this serene scheme by means of a coat of gray-white paint, a window treatment in the same cool tone, slip covers of white damask and dull brown satin, and the addition of a few fine pieces of furniture, bibelots, and many flowers.*

Left: *To complement the conventional hotel furniture, two French chairs were added, as well as the fine old French screen of eight panels, which is placed across the entire end of the room. As the fireplace did not function, and was merely an ornamental feature, it was completely ignored in the clever arrangement of chairs and tables and one is practically unconscious of its existence when in the room; there is a writing corner, a piano in the bay, with armchairs and a sofa, and overstuffed and straight chairs nearby. Opposite is the table holding lamps, flowers, books–the type of commodious table that should be in every living room. Owner and decorator, William M. Odom.*

Elsie de Wolfe designed this room in the New York home of J. Robert Rubin. This is Mrs. Rubin's bedroom, with a canopied bed of quilted blue satin; the same satin, with a quilted border, is found in the curtains. Engraved mirror is used to line the walls and cover closet doors, as well as in the triangular wall appliqués. The chandelier is of crystal and blue glass.

The oval breakfast room, also decorated by Elsie de Wolfe for Mr. and Mrs. Rubin, is paneled in cream incised lacquer with brown decorations by Robert Pichenot. An oyster color rug with a seal brown rim covers the floor of Versailles parquet and a marbleized edge. Curtains are silver gray satin and embroidered chenille. Lighting is effected by mirror-backed vitrines . . .

Above: *This white drawing room in the New York home of Mr. and Mrs. Harrison Williams was established by the choice of furnishings of Mrs. Williams and the decorator, Syrie Maugham. From the orange and blue of the Isaphan rug rise walls of white. The portrait of Mrs. Williams is by Savely Sorine.*

Left: *Some of the furniture in the Williamses' home is covered with white brocade and some is upholstered in white silk with delicate pastel embroidery. The brocade curtains are white. The crystal chandelier is from Waterford.*

NEW
AMERICAN
INTERIORS

New York City and Glencoe,
Illinois, 1934, 1935, 1939

These rooms are the work of the American designers Elsie de Wolfe, Joseph B. Platt, Billy Baldwin, Mrs. William C. Langley and Mrs. Thomas L. Robinson of Ysel, Inc., and architect Samuel A. Marx. Also shown is a room from the recent Fine Arts Exposition, the comprehensive display of modern industrial design at the Metropolitan Museum of Art in New York City.

Above: *As a contrast to the murk, clamor, and confusion of New York, the walls of the living room in the apartment of Joseph B. Platt are a serene white. Some of the furniture is painted white and the upholstery of the large lounge at one end is white also. The curtains are pale chartreuse, the same tone of fabric being used on some of the chairs. Two Chinese Chippendale étagères hang over the sofa.*

Below: *In the dining room of the home of Samuel A. Marx, architect, at Glencoe, Illinois, the walls are in eggshell white enamel. Hangings are a glazed chintz in acid green and deep brown over green striped window shades. The same colors are in the Aubusson rug. Italian Empire chairs in walnut burl with green leather seats accompany a Biedermeyer table and sideborad.*

Opposite page, top left: *Elsie de Wolfe designed this glittering modern dining room inspired by 18th-century Venice. Gray walls broken by mirrored niches, silver cloth curtains, white, gray, and aubergine floor, crystal and mirror mantel. The gray lacquer table is inlaid with mirror strips. From the Fine Arts Exposition at the Metropolitan Museum. New York.*

Opposite page, top right: *In the entrance foyer of the New York apartment owned and decorated by William W. Baldwin of Ruby Ross Wood, Inc., a little white leather commode, stamped with golden honey bees and the black initials BB (for Billy Baldwin). One chair wears black velvet, one a blue leather cushion.*

Opposite page, bottom: *Two views of Mr. Victor Emanuel's dining room in his New York apartment, showing the two small tables for informal dining, which are put together on more important occasions, and the sideboard with indirect lighting concealed in the columnar supports. The decorations are by the firm of Ysel, Inc.*

Behind the guest house is a formal evergreen garden. Because of the cold winters of upper Connecticut, the design is carried out with low, clipped American arborvitae instead of the more tender boxwood. A sheared hedge of tall American arborvitae encloses the garden. In spring the center beds are filled with white tulips, followed by white Canterbury Bells and then by white petunias for late summer. The architect for Mrs. Arnold Whitridge was Frederick R. King.

RETURN
TO
FORMALITY

The garden of Mrs. Arnold Whitridge is one more indication that the tide in garden design is turning to formality. In a sense, it is a return to old forms that once were popular before the Romantic Era insisted on gardens copying nature's informality. In the rose garden at right, a large circular reflecting pool is fringed on one side by sprays of the white climbing rose, Snowflake. Marian Coffin was the landscape architect for this garden in the old-fashioned manner.

Above: *A view of the formal evergreen garden is commanded from the guest house, showing its two main circular beds and the other forms that correspond with them. Essentially a green and white garden, the beds provide the white and the others are left unplanted. Between the beds well-kept turf forms the flooring, a sophisticated and frankly old-fashioned decoration laid down on a flat area as a contrast to the ruggedness of the hills that encircle the property–and it supplies color all year.*

Below: *The locations of the main house and guest house are seen in this view of the perennial garden, the latter being on the right. The crosspath of this garden leads to an iris garden and pergola. Here the general flower color scheme includes blue, white, and yellow in beds close to the hedges; and pale pink, blue, and white in the beds that flank a broad grass center panel. Steps lead here from the rose garden, right.*

Above: *This view shows the long middle path of the rose garden, which breaks at the pool and continues on to the farther terminus. Here again the design is formal, the beds being edged with low arborvitae and filled with hybrid teas, polyanthas, and floribundas for massed color effect. This rose garden is reminiscent of those found in the early 19th-century France and in Victorian England.*

Salisbury, Connecticut, 1939

DIVERSIONS WITH DAVY JONES

St. Louis, Missouri, 1935

Like the amazing contraptions in a Jules Verne story, the recreation room in the Marion L.J. Lambert St. Louis home sits at the bottom of a tropic sea visible, as through glass, beyond the walls. The sea floor is Mr. Lambert's cellar–submarine scenery painted by Chris Olsen. H. Clifford Burroughs, decorator.

Left: *The scene through the porthole in the ship's door that leads to the game rooms.*
Below: *Before and after views–a small card room adjoins the recreation room, its walls lined with fabric for the hanging of sporting pictures and bordered with white rope. Card motifs decorate the linoleum floor.*

Three views of the Lambert recreation room appear on this page—one taken before the cellar went amphibian. To put the surrounding sea-life at ease, all the furniture is wholeheartedly nautical. A soft, green and blue cushion on a built-in seat that conceals game closets along one wall harmonizes with the water colors outside. Smaller cushions are disguised as life preservers and ships' bumpers done in rakish blue and white. Ships' wheels are the backs of chairs in which guests steer their way to fun. The dark blue linoleum floor is punctuated with salty emblems and at the ceiling's edge the lighting system is concealed by a valance of draped fish nets trimmed with wooden and glass ball floats. This system is a special three-color device designed to make one feel completely submerged by producing the effect of sunlight filtered through water. An automatic switch alters the play of light to produce daybreak, midday, and twilight as the angel fish see them. Additional lights over gaming table.

1940/s

The movement of many of Europe's finest artists, architects, and craftsmen to the United States during this decade caused an infusion of talent that internationalized design. In particular, the members of the Bauhaus, teaching and practicing in America, spread their views to local art and architecture centers, invoking their principles of architectural primacy over design to an increasingly receptive audience. Philip Johnson, for instance, a longtime admirer and exponent of Mies van der Rohe, created his own house of glass that reflected the intellectual purity of the Bauhaus school. Utility was a watchword for this wartime decade. More and more ersatz materials, created by wartime conditions, were developed and utilized by designers, prefiguring the explosion of industrial materials in the next decade. In reaction, there was also a revival of more traditional and eclectic looks borrowed from Greece, China, England, Italy, and France. This was part of an attempt to bring back a feeling of romance to 40s living.

LIVING WITH INTERNATIONAL DESIGN

The Barcelona chair, designed by Ludwig Mies van der Rohe, the German-born American architect. "Architecture is the will of an epoch translated into space," he wrote in the early Twenties. During the Thirties Mies was Director of Architecture in Illinois Institute of Technology in Chicago, where he worked on a new campus. When completed, it consisted of 19 buildings, making it the largest executed example of group planning by a major living architect. The house in the background, which floats on eight columns, was designed by Mies for Dr. Edith Farnsworth in Fox River, Illinois.

A CROSS-SECTION OF DESIGNERS AND CHARACTERISTIC EXAMPLES OF THEIR WORK

U.S.A., 1949

ROBSJOHN-GIBBINGS

A highly vocal designer with an aversion to ostentation in any form. Mr. Robsjohn-Gibbings today is a prime champion of straightforward American furniture design. Two debunking bestsellers (*Goodbye, Mr. Chippendale* and *Mona Lisa's Mustache*) are both vigorous statements of his firm convictions. *Above:* A new coffee table, low and large, and an occasional chair made by Widdicomb. *Below:* Robsjohn-Gibbings sheltered by raincoat, symbol of his ideal house.

DOROTHY LIEBES

The effervescent high-priestess of the hand loom whose superb textures, fresh colors and new materials (for Goodall) initiated a revolution in machine-weaving techniques was born in California, where she has a studio that acts as a magnet for talent. *Above:* In "Golden Gate" Dorothy Liebes (now in New York) translates her feeling for texture into a bamboo-design wallpaper, made by United. *Below:* Weaver Liebes, A.I.D., A.I.A, with her spools of many-colored thread.

ISAMU NOGUCHI

Born in Los Angeles, this vigorous, multifaceted designer spent his childhood in Japan. At 14 he came back to America, where he won a Guggenheim fellowship. Later he studied sculpture with Brancusi in Paris. *Above:* Palette-shaped dining table and stools were planned for a small space and are made by the Herman Miller Furniture Company. *Below:* The sculptor-designer, Isamu Noguchi is currently working on an object he likes to describe as "a structure in space."

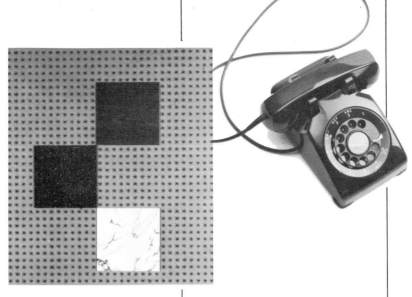

FLORENCE KNOLL

The capable director of the Knoll Planning Unit is an architect in her own right. She graduated from the Armour Institute, studied under Mies van der Rohe, worked at the Architectural Association in London and has been on the staffs of Breuer, Gropius and Bayer. She has won two A.I.D. awards for furniture design. *Above:* Blond wood stacking stool has bent metal legs. Made by Knoll Associates. *Below:* Mrs. Knoll and her dog.

JOSEPH B. PLATT

An alumnus of the Parsons School of Design, The Condé Nast Publications, Inc., Butterick Publishing Co. and Marshall Field, this versatile designer has had his own industrial and interior design office, since 1938. *Above:* ''Authority Line'' fabric wall covering (background) and ''Santile'' welded vinyl flooring tiles. Both, Interchemical Corp. *Below:* Mr. Platt, A.I.A., S.I.D., seated on Platt-designed wooden folding chair, by Brower.

HENRY DREYFUSS

At 18, this urbane New Yorker was designing stage settings. At 25 he became an industrial designer (everything from Big Ben alarm clocks to the 20th Century for the New York Central Railroad). *Above:* Appearance-design of new telephone carried out by Dreyfus—developed by Bell Telephone Laboratories, will be made by Western electric Co. *Below:* Dreyfus, S.I.D, ponders the five facets of industrial design.

DORIS AND LESLIE TILLETT

Inveterate travelers, London-born Leslie met and married New Yorker Doris in Mexico. So dedicated are they to creating perfect materials, they work their designs directly on cloth, have their own private mill to make them. Their designs are born at their finger tips. *Above:* ''Grain in Squares,'' a cotton as smooth and bright as a polished parquet floor, made by D.D. & Leslie Tillett. *Below:* The Tilletts and a square of wood.

MARION V. DORN

Though born and educated in California (Phi Beta Kappa, Stanford University), she has made her career as a designer of textiles, wallpapers, in England and in the U.S. Poised and purposeful, she is guided in her designing by elegance, taste and logic. *Above:* "Cameo" wallpaper, example of classicism, made by Katzenbach & Warren. *Below:* Designer Dorn and classic theme: an antique Italian cameo cut into a shell.

WILLIAM PAHLMANN

A confirmed trail blazer, this mobile-minded designer from Texas is currently concerned with furniture-on-wheels. He won wide recognition for rooms created for Lord & Taylor, now heads his own firm, and is decorating the Bonwit Teller shops. His designs are aimed to reconcile and blend modern living with tradition. *Above:* Mobile table in the Momentum design by Contempo. On it, Dumont's new Rumson television cabinet. *Below:* Pahlmann, A.I.D., and an Etruscan wheel.

RAYMOND LOEWY

This debonair gentleman from Paris heads the largest industrial design firm in the world. Transportation, product designing and packaging are three of his principal concerns. Although he is a graduate engineer, he started his career as a fashion illustrator, designed his first car in 1929. America, France and England have given him honors and awards. *Above:* Sleek Frigidaire electric range has two ovens. *Below:* Streamlined designer Loewy, S.I.D. has given new, simpler shapes to everything from locomotives to kitchen ranges.

VERA NEUMANN

Connecticut is her birth state, though her training, like her sensitive transcriptions from nature, stems from the Vienna Workshop. With her husband she designs and prints fabrics and wallpapers, working from the object themselves to achieve a photographic directness of line and quality. *Above:* "Jack-in-the-Pulpit" chintz and wallpaper are both sold by F. Schumacher. *Below:* The fields furnish Mrs. Neumann with countless elements for fresh wallpaper and fabric designs.

PAUL McCOBB

Always fascinated by design, he went A.W.O.L. frequently as a small boy in Massachusettes, could always be found in the nearest museum. He made his start painting scenery, worked for stores in Boston and New York as display manager, for manufacturers, is now a consultant for Modernage, Raymor, Burlington Mills, Multiplex. Proportion dominates all his designs. *Above:* McCobb armchair with free-form arm in proportion to today's living. By Custom-craft, Inc. *Below:* McCobb demonstrates the relation between space and design.

TAMMIS KEEFE

In her work as a designer, this Los Angeles-born New Yorker studied at Chouinard Art Institute. She sketches, paints and pursues her work as a freelance designer of materials. She conceives of design as growing from the nature of the cloth, not as being an arbitrary overlay. *Above:* "Collector's Item," myriad butterflies on a bright chintz made by Cyrus Clark Company, Inc. *Below:* Miss Keefe with a simple, familiar object: the pineapple, which is traditionally a symbol of hospitality.

JENS RISOM

Born in Copenhagen and schooled in design in Denmark, he decided a decade ago that America offered the scope he needs for his work. In 1939 he joined the staff of Dan Cooper. Two years later, after touring the U.S.A. to learn about its life and architecture, he opened his own establishment, mainly devoted to furniture design. *Above:* A table suited to modern life is graceful in design and soundly made by Jens Risom Design, Inc. *Below:* Risom broods over design, material and construction of chair in process of design.

EDWARD J. WORMLEY

From his Illinois roots (born in Oswego, trained at Chicago's Art Institute, first job: designing for Marshall Field in Chicago) has grown a national reputation. He is now designing Dunbar's furniture, created Drexel's original Precedent furniture and is a consultant to Lightolier. He has designed showrooms and stores, headed the O.P.A. furniture unit during the war. *Above:* Cantilevered desk designed by Wormley, made by Dunbar. *Below:* Wormley, A.D.I., A.I.D., with a tree root, one of nature's profusion of designs.

TIME MELLOWS THIS MODERN HOUSE

TEN YEARS' EXPERIENCE WITH OUR OWN HOUSE

BY WALTER AND ISE GROPIUS

Lincoln, Massachusetts, 1949

A great deal of the charm of old houses is due to the mellowing effect of time and of their well-established gardens. . . . The appearance of our own house has changed within ten years because the landscaping and gardens have had time to grow up to our original plan. The house is opened up to take in a part of the surrounding area and extends beyond its enclosing walls; it reaches out with "tentacles" of trellis, low walls, and planting designed to delineate the outdoor living spaces and make them a part of the over-all composition. The large window walls are a most desirable asset, we have found. They establish the outdoor-indoor relation of our living space throughout the year. They provide a view of a natural stage on which the dramatic events of nature entertain us from morning to evening, summer and winter. There is nothing like watching a blizzard through 12-foot-wide glass panes while sitting cozily at the dining table. . . . The inside drain for the flat roof works perfectly. It is warmed by indoor temperature and cannot freeze.

Top left: *1938—just when Mr. and Mrs. Gropius moved in, before time had mellowed this modern house.*
Top right: *1948—What a decade has done for the appearance of the house. Landscaping and garden have developed well.*
Above: *The roof deck, open to the sky, is perfect for summer night parties—like the house, it is planned to make a picture.*
Right: *The spiral staircase to the roof-deck and to the Gropius's daughter's room proved very practical as the children could enter directly without tracking through the house.*

The floor plan of the house was designed for freedom of motion from one room to another and to the out-of-doors. Throughout the years the house has responded well to almost every need of our family. The kitchen and service areas were designed to be run by a maid, but we have discovered that a servantless household is more to our liking. . . . We moved into our house a few days before the great hurricane of September, 1938, which put it to a severe test right away. The porch screen was torn and part of the trellis loosened, but everything else, including the large glass panes, remained intact. The flat roof was not affected, although nearby pitched roofs wire damaged.

A GLASS HOUSE DESIGNED BY PHILIP C. JOHNSON

New Canaan, Connecticut, 1949

Despite the technological wonders of the 20th century, the idea of living in a glass house still astonishes most people. And residents of Fairfield County have not yet recovered from their astonishment at the glass house that Philip C. Johnson recently designed and built for himself in New Canaan. Mr. Johnson, who is Director of the Department of Architecture and Design at the Museum of Modern Art, takes it all quite calmly . . . The house, inside, is one large room arranged for simple yet formal living, without sacrificing elegance. His interest in architecture being scholarly as well as creative, he feels no compunction about looking backward for inspiration. Thus his house, despite its originality, conveys a sense of historic continuity. It rises from the ground as formally as any Georgian mansion, yet it is the example par excellence of the contemporary ''bring the outdoors indoors'' theory. It is as elegant as the *Petit Trianon,* yet conforms to the exigencies of living in one room. . . .

Above: *The house, with its massive brick cylinder, rides across the horizon like a ship. It is made of plate glass, structural steel and brick, built on a plateau partially surrounded by trees, with a fine view.*

Right: *The guest house, part of the larger plan of the House, is made of brick, contrasting with the glass of the main house. A grass-planted area separates them.*

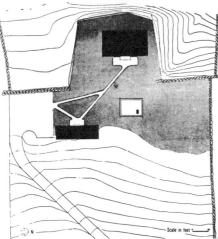

The glass house is one of
three related rectangles in a
carefully planned arrangement of
topography and architecture.
The others are the brick guest house
and a sanded base for sculpture
not yet installed. Mr. Johnson
regards the two houses as parts of
a larger house —the enclosed grass-planted
area in which they are placed.
This area has been deliberately
cultivated to contrast with the casualness
of its natural surroundings.

The protection provided by the trees was a determining factor in Philip C. Johnson's choice of glass; that, and the magnificent view over ridge after ridge of Connecticut hills. The result is a truly original building of timeless elegance and classic simplicity, as well as a conclusive demonstration of the fact that modern building techniques have come of age. . . . Sybaritic in his tastes, Mr. Johnson has surrounded himself with an ordered array of art objects and museum-piece furniture. They are part of a setting as rich as the painting attributed to Poussin that stands on an easel beside the conversation group. Constant waxing has already given the dark red brick floor, the fireplace cylinder, and the walnut cabinets a patina that belies their age. The furniture by Mies van der Rohe was acquired by Mr. Johnson in 1930, and he moves it from house to house as anybody else might move precious antiques . . . The bedroom lamps with steel bases are by Van Nessen; the wrought iron candelabrum that lights the living area at night was designed by Mr. Johnson.

Above: *This glass-walled room, 56 by 32 by 10 feet 6 inches high, contains living, dining and kitchen areas, Mr. Johnson's bedroom area, and bath. The furniture was designed by the contemporary architect, Mies van der Rohe, the rollicking papier mâché girls by Elie Nadelman.*

Opposite page, clockwise from top: *This conversation group, with a superb view of the Connecticut hills, is defined by the boundaries of a white wool rug. The "Barcelona" chairs and stool are chromium steel and natural pigskin; the couch of steel and rosewood is upholstered in black nylon; the table holding a plaster sculpture by the Swiss, Giacometti, is glass and steel. The living area at night is illuminated by candles and concealed spotlights. The floor plan of the house is spacious and efficient. The bedroom, opening on to green lawns, has a quilt of bottle-green raw silk; the desk is covered in black leather, the chair in natural calfskin. The screens are natural colored pandanus cloth, which run on tracks along all four walls and can be pulled to enclose the entire house. The open kitchen has work surface of black linoleum; the kitchen, when closed, is sheathed in walnut cabinets.*

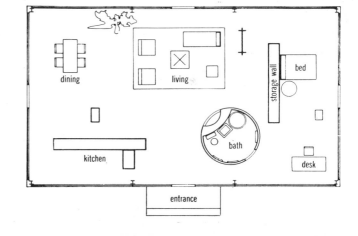

dining

living

storage wall

bed

kitchen

bath

desk

entrance

A STEEL HOUSE WITH A SUAVE FINISH

San Fernando Valley, California, 1949

In this Richard Neutra-designed house of steel and aluminum, Ayn Rand wrote *The Fountainhead*. When she first arrived in America, Russian-born Ayn Rand stood spellbound before Manhattan's steel-sprung skyscrapers. Later, in California, she chose to live and write in an all-steel house, elemental in form, dynamic in color. Surrounded by flowering shrubs and exotic trees, the house inside is peacock blue. Ayn Rand believes that a man, like a building, should embody a central idea, a single truth . . . In her San Fernando Valley house, designed for sun, steel, and sky, Ayn Rand's pattern for living is crystal-clear.

Above: *First impression of the house from outside the entrance gate is the surprising quality of aluminum-covered steel walls, satin-hued against the dark green trees, immaculately cropped lawns, blue skies. Second surprise: geometric forms dramatically reflected in the curving moat, broken by water reeds, hedgerows, ever-changing shadows of clouds above.*
Left: *Inside the 8-foot curved wall is this sunny patio. Planned as an ''open to the sky'' part of the living room, it is terrazzo-paved in black Belgian marble. Here Ayn Rand and her husband, Frank O'Connor, relax and entertain their San Fernando Valley friends.*
Opposite page: *Looking across the dining table to the fireplace corner of the living room. Giant philodendron make an arresting pattern against the the balcony wall. Gladiolus enrich a polished table, echo the colors of the interior. Ayn Rand's secretary uses the north gallery as an ''office.'' Miss Rand's private study, on the first floor, opens onto a glass-partitioned patio, a superb view of flowers, foothills, mountains. In cold months the south gallery is a winter garden housing delicate plants, in summer it is an airy sun deck.*

Right: *The porte-cochere from the house looks out toward the highway. Here the moat ends, flowing under the little bridge to the corner of the bright steel fence. Massed evergreens border the water areas, giving depth and shade. An ingenious feature: the sprinkler system, which, at a touch, cools the circular walls of the outdoor patio during hot, dry weather.*

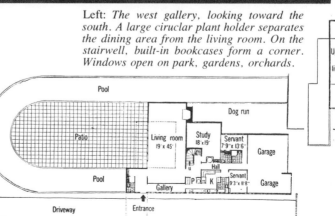

Below: *Floor plan, show-ing windows the length and width of the master bedroom, which frame the Sierras, but Polaroid glass eliminates glare. The garage roof, designed to mirror skies and trees, is a copper-lined pool where tropical fish float among water lilies.*

Left: *The west gallery, looking toward the south. A large ciruclar plant holder separates the dining area from the living room. On the stairwell, built-in bookcases form a corner. Windows open on park, gardens, orchards.*

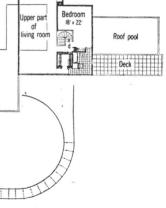

Pool

Gallery

Upper part of living room

Bedroom 18' x 22'

Roof pool

Deck

Pool

Dog run

Patio

Living room 19' x 45'

Study 18' x 19'

Servant 7'-9" x 13'-6"

Garage

Hall

Pool

Gallery

P K

Servant 9'-3" x 11'-8"

Garage

Driveway

Entrance

Pool

THIS
RANCH HOUSE
LIVES
AS WELL AS
IT LOOKS

Above: *The dining room is separate but enjoys a view of the living room fireplace. On the opposite side it opens to a screened dining terrace. Built-in birch buffet provides storage. Ebony-topped maple table and green leather chairs were designed by Mr. Belluschi.*
Left: *Slender columns of rough fir support the eaves of the concrete-paved terrace.*

Yamhill, Oregon, 1949

When Mr. and Mrs. Percy Lee Menefee, whose house is shown here, catalogued their requirements for their architect, they wished to capitalize on the beautiful site with terraces and large windows, which would make their small valley a part of their rooms throughout the year. Pietro Belluschi, their architect, was delighted with this forthright approach; he believes that a house should make a very personal yet thoroughly adaptable background for good living. "The form," he says, "developed naturally through an understanding of the region." As a result, the house seems to have grown right out of the land. Low, horizontal lines, walls of weathered fir, blend into the landscape. Rain dictated the pitch of the roofs, the width of the eaves, the covered outdoor passages to every part of the house. The rooms themselves make use of the outdoors by taking in generous areas through walls of glass; and the sense of distance dispels the gloom of wet days. Mr. Belluschi placed the guest house on the far side of the central court away from the main part of the house. . . .

Opposite page, top: The roof extends out over the terrace, protects the windows from rain and glare; glass walls achieve openness and light.
Top right: In the entrance court, only a low plant bed divides the two patios. The living room adds depth with a glimpse of the view through its parallel walls of glass.
Right: In rainy weather, the fireplace wall becomes the focal point of the living room. The copper hood, with its relief by Fred Littman, is both decorative and heat-dispensing and the wide, raised hearth brings the fire closer to eye level. The colors, planned by Mr. Belluschi, are keyed to the surrounding landscape; deep brown, daffodil yellow, golden tan and a range of greens blend with the natural tones of native woods used throughout.

ITALY
LOOKS AHEAD

BY MARYA MANNES

Italy, 1947

What you see here is the evidence of a great vitality. Italy has had a hard and bitter war, however self-imposed, which has laid waste much of her country, much of her heritage of art; destroyed innumerable homes, impoverished innumerable people and brought the usual chaotic aftermath. In spite of this. Italy is at work. Her people are not only rebuilding towns and bridges, they are looking forward creatively. They are making new things with new ideas. With every material obstruction, they are laying cornerstones of a new and better Italy. . . . There has been time for the great anonymous army of Italian artisans to produce decorative and useful objects. I would like in this age of self-advertisement to stress the word "anonymous," for in it lies the strength of Italian art. It is no accident that in the past it has produced a Giotto, a Leonardo, a Michelangelo, a Donatello; these giants grew out of a tradition of artisanship in which child-apprentices learned to mix paint, to prepare clay, to chisel stone, and to carve wood. The Italian hand is a fruitful hand, and much of the wisdom and tranquility of the Italian peasant and workman derives from the deep satisfaction of producing with these hands a completed object, be it a shoe or a chair. . . . Much of the credit for reviving this tradition goes to two individuals in

particular—architect Galassi in Rome, and Ponti in Milan. One woman, English-born Vera Lombardi, is also responsible for a fresh stimulation of artisanship. Galassi has an establishment in the Villa Giulia (on the periphery of Rome), where some of the best artisans and artists in Italy are engaged in producing mosaics, ceramics, metal, and woodwork for decorative and architectural purposes. . . . Architect Gio Ponti in Milan directs the same kind of production on a smaller scale and with lesser talents. He scours the country each year to find the best artisans and proceeds to channel their particular talents into new forms. Mrs. Lombardi's work is on a much less ambitious and more practical scale. . . . This traffic of ideas and products can only be for the best. Italy, emerging from the dust and disintegration of war by virtue of her people's extraordinary vitality, is again able to show us the enduring values of craftsmanship and individual vision.

Above: *Designed by Banfi, Belgioioso, Peressutti & Rogers, this interesting storage wall makes a decorative asset out of glass and china cabinets. Light swings on a wooden arm.*
Left: *Box spring and mattresses are covered in striped ticking; string curtain. Note off-center placing of Baroque sculpture.*

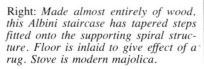

Right: *Made almost entirely of wood, this Albini staircase has tapered steps fitted onto the supporting spiral structure. Floor is inlaid to give effect of a rug. Stove is modern majolica.*

Tempestini's sculptured wood cocktail table

Architect Franco Albini uses a painting on a swivel device to separate his living room from the dining alcove. Chief point in this room is a suspension bookcase with glass shelves steadied by a diagonal wooden strut, shown at left.

Tempestini's captain's chair

Tempestini's leather lounge chair

Glass table by Canella, Fontana & Radici

Left: *A new way to hang a painting—a thin shaft running from floor to ceiling supports an adjustable light and serves as a picture easel in the library study of architect Ignazio Gardella of Milan.*

Right: *Everything is within easy arm's reach in this combination work-table and bookcase file. Alternating open and closed sections, popular with Italy's modern architects, add to the interest. Banfi, Belgioioso, Peressutti, Rogers.*

Left: *Linoleum-faced sliding shelf is a blackboard for phone numbers. Latis.*

TASTE IN
OUR TIME

U.S.A., 1947

Here is a cross section of contemporary taste. We do not suggest that you will want to copy these rooms, because you are probably as much of an individualist as the designers who created them. You will take from them whatever is appropriate to your own way of life; color schemes, arrangements, and use of accessories. They were created by top-flight designers and are a tribute to their skill.

Opposite page: *The marble mantel is Venetian; the lacquer screen, Korean; the Directoire chandelier, French; the modern, textured fabrics, American, in the New York living room of William Baldwin of Ruby Ross Wood, Inc. This is a sophisticated blending of styles from many lands in a two-room apartment.*
Right: *In San Francisco, Richard Gump's dining room, designed by him, typifies still another blending of styles. The background is modern; Ming altar pieces on the long side table; Han-inspired screen design; a head sculptured in Cambodia in the 11th century.*

Above: *Against whitewashed brick and white, woven-wood curtains, black wrought-iron chairs, table and an Alexander Calder mobile trace their Spencerian outlines. This is the dining room of Mrs. Francis L. White's New York house, remodeled by Harold Sterner, architect, decorated by Elsie McNeill, Inc.*
Left: *New York decorator Frederick P. Victoria collected antique furniture for his house in New Lebanon, built in 1778. The chair, under a Louis XVI sand toy, is by Duncan Phyfe; the table is a Hepplewhite traveling case. Eighteenth century English brackets have original Bristol glass globes.*

Above: *T.H. Robsjohn-Gibbings designed this bleached-oak desk and chair for Mr. and Mrs. John Rawlings. Desk top is glass; chair strapped with ash-gray leather. Paintings by Rufino Tamayo; Tang horse head.*

Above: *For Mr. and Mrs. Philip Isles's New York apartment, designer George Stacey uses baroque chairs in Venetian red velvet, and ruby glass, against walls of turquoise blue, to create a room of great style.*

Taste in decoration is a sense of fitness and proportion, of balance and beauty. It is with taste in American decoration today that these pages are concerned. The broad outlines are here. For more than a score of years, American decoration has followed the classic tradition of the 18th century in England, America, and France, while developing a modern style of its own. What has been happening in recent years is a blending of all styles. We have borrowed beauty from Greece and Rome, from England and France, from Italy and China, from everywhere and every time, and woven out of it a bright new pattern. It is hardly surprising that what we have done in terms of people, we have also accomplished in terms of things. The American taste, like the American citizen, is recognizably American. It is a mosaic of parts composed into a picture as personal and unmistakable as our skyscrapers and red barns, our movie palaces and Cape cod houses.

Opposite page, below left: *For Mr. and Mrs. Harold K. Guinzburg, decorators Jones & Erwin turned the "back parlor" of a New York house into a new kind of dining room, with small tables arranged in various parts of the room. Here a red Victorian sofa, bold against a pink wall, is set off by a flowered red carpet.*

Opposite page, below far left: *Mrs. Juliana Force, Director of the Whitney Museum of American Art, has a living room whose white walls silhouette such diverse treasures as Portuguese figures flanking a window, a Pennsylvania Dutch primitive and four gilt eagles holding white globe chandeliers on gold ropes.*

Above right: *The proportions and decorations are perfect in this oval Adam reception room in the New York apartment of Mr. and Mrs. Carl J. Schmidlapp. Diane Tate and Marian Hall of New York were the decorators.*

Below right: *McMillen, Inc., of New York designed this distinguished room for Mrs. J.D. Wooster Lambert around mimosa murals by Charles Baskerville. In India Mr. Baskerville made the preliminary studies for these beautiful paintings, depicting 18th-century English milords entering the city of Jaipur. Chandelier and epergne are Waterford crystal.*

LIVE AS WELL
AS YOU LOOK

France, England, U.S.A., 1949

The women whose rooms you see here live and dress with taste. subservience to any given set of "rules." Just as they consult their dressmakers when they choose their clothes, they turn to their decorators when they plan their rooms. They neither look nor dress nor decorate alike. But all of them make equally great contributions to the charm and beauty of their respective worlds. They do in fact "live as well as they look."

Top left: In the living room of Mr. and Mrs. Lewis Lapham's house above San Francisco Bay, a Coromandel screen is teamed with a Jean Michel Frank lamp; a French Provincial table with an Oriental rug. Carnations in a dozen bright colors are massed in bowls everywhere. Honey-beige curtains hang against walls of the same tone. Frances Elkins, decorator.

Center Left: Mrs. James S. Bush of St. Louis has a living room decorated by McMillen, Inc., whose pale heather walls are played up by white accents. Dressmaker curtains emphasize the scale of the room. The handsome parquet floor sets off formal 18th-century furniture.

Bottom left: Bleached walnut accordion walls, banded in copper, lead into the bay off the library of Mr. and Mrs. William Goetz's house in Holmby Hills, California. Against the window, a Maillol bronze is impressive in a setting of soft colors and white . . . Designer William Haines of Beverly Hills decorated the house and designed the furniture.

Opposite page, top left: With the help of McMillen, Inc., Mrs. Pierre Bédard has created a primarily white and black room, punctuated by American Beauty red, which glows in this New York studio-living room. Under the window, the Bédards hang a frieze of engravings of Picasso ballet drawings.

Opposite page, top right: Bulbridge House in Wilton, England, the home of Lady Juliet Duff, is a compendium of superb furniture, paintings, and bibelots. In the drawing room, paintings by Mlle. Marguerite Gérard, Boilly, and a Lenoir portrait of Voltaire hang against pink and gold Regency wallpaper, immensely effective with the Louis XVI commode, the Napoleonic clock and the home-grown flowers. . . .

Opposite page, bottom left: Mrs. George Schlee's dining room, high above New York's East River, has panels of rare French Empire flocked wallpaper, copper service plates, and Chinese rice bowls, with massed fruits and flowers at the base of a tall crystal candelabrum.

Opposite page, bottom right: This small "office" in the Lopez-Willshaws' house at Neuilly is in the romantic style, its gray walls framed in bands of 19th-century wallpaper and hung with Mme. Lopez-Willshaw's collection of paintings of dogs from the same period. The mahogany Restoration furniture, the green and gilded chandelier are charming. Victor Grandpierre collaborated in the decoration.

TRAVELED CALIFORNIA DECORATOR FRANCES ELKINS BECAME HER OWN CLIENT WHEN SHE DESIGNED THIS HOUSE

Monterey, California, 1945

For her own house, Mrs. Elkins chose a typical Monterey dwelling built in the 1830s as the wedding gift of a Spanish don to his daughter. She has given its interior a cosmopolitan elegance, predominantly Gallic, yet indebted to China, England, and Italy for its individual flavor . . . Her deft way with color is echoed in her confident blending of periods. Chinese tapestries, an English horse painting by Sartorius, and Venetian prints hang on the living room walls; Louis XIII chairs and old Spanish portraits are equally at home in the spacious red-tiled entrance hall. This house, by a decorator for a decorator, has achieved great individuality and style.

Opposite page, left: *A fine old Directoire wallpaper with its background of brilliant blue, gives a feeling of airy space to the upstairs hall. Mrs. Elkins has cannily furthered the effect with masses of growing plants—banked in corners against the marbleized baseboards, tiered (in the foreground) on a library step table. California touch: redwood stair rail.*

Opposite page, bottom: *Unusual French Provincial chairs, Louis XV table against the wall; shelf holds turquoise porcelains.*

Above: *Front doorway, flanked by two old French stone dogs; clipped box, carefully planned beds of pink and red flowers in the garden.*

Right: *Unusual in arrangement, with many conversation groups, this living room has off-white walls, and a matching painted ceiling of boards as wide as those in the dark polished floors. The soft clear yellow of the old Chinese rugs echoes in the fabrics, accents are lapis blue and turquoise. California touch: old wine-taster's table to hold potiche and plants.*

Below left: *Mrs. Elkins's own room. The white bed has a shell-pink cover. Baseboards and mantel are marbleized slate gray. Ivory white chairs with red seats, against whitewashed walls and white string rug, have a strawberries-and-cream quality.*

Below right: *Brilliant turquoise porcelain in a bedroom contrasts with dark furniture and red and white toile de Jouy hangings.*

Old tenement houses   *Remodeled into the Yard*

AMSTER YARD

A SIGNIFICANT EXPERIMENT IN COMMUNITY LIVING

New York City, 1946

Amster Yard, a garden oasis in crowded New York, is a sign of the times and a blueprint for the future. James Amster, well-known New York decorator, grew up in a house in Boston with a yard; his nostalgia for it was the first motivation for Amster Yard. He missed the grass, the trees, the old houses; he searched a long time, not only for a house where he could live and have his decorating establishment, but for a group of houses that might be woven into a small community with a mutual yard. Collaborators in this venture were Harold Sterner, who was the architect for the Yard, and Ted Sandler, art director. It was a sorry batch of buildings that James Amster acquired one April afternoon in 1944: a tenement, a boarding house, half a dozen backyard shacks and a bit of blighted earth . . . The plan, which has now been realized, includes shop and apartment for Mr. Amster, a common room for conferences, exhibits, and parties, small house and offices for Harold Sterner, and a group of apartments. It is essential in so small a community, that neighbors know each other and have a bond of interest that makes it possible for them to live together amicably. The Yard,

dow moldings, the recessed book and curio shelves. The Yard is barely finished today, but it has had so many old details incorporated into it that already a feeling of age and stability distinguish it . . . flagged and grassy, is common ground where they are bound to meet almost daily. Each tenant (six live at the Yard) worked out, within the limits of floor space, features that he would like to have. Bedrooms face away from 49th Street, on which the Yard fronts, toward the quieter reaches of the garden. Kitchens are modern-small, but as bright as any rooms in the houses. Bath-dressing rooms are lined with closets, their doors set flush, swung on piano hinges. Closets and storage cupboards are scaled to each person's possessions. But where the talents of the collaborators show themselves most clearly is in the refinement of architectural detail: the restrained door and win-

Top right: Awning-covered gallery at one end of Amster Yard; the awning is metal, painted dark green and white. Doors in far walls are entrances to the conference room and Amster offices. The gallery and common room between Amster and Sterner offices is on two levels, with Dutch caryatids flanking the low dividing wall. Banquettes and settee are Louis XV. Country furniture, chiefly French Provincial, is shown in its own shop. One wall is finished in modern plywood, others are antique wood paneling with doors of pickled pine. The floor of the gallery is tiled.
Center right: The Amster living room, decorated in various shades of soft gray, takes its color scheme from the Utrillo that inspired much of the design and color of Amster Yard. The drawing room above the shop is shell-white with antique panels between windows. Tufted loveseat is Turkish, covered in emerald green lampas with pink and blue flowers. The master bedroom of the Amster apartment is entirely sand-beige, exactly matching the carved fruitwood headboard of the bed, originally an old Italian overdoor. The carpet is cedar-colored.
Bottom right: William Baldwin's living room at Amster Yard is a monochrome study in shiny pine-needle green, which is repeated in the foyer and the bedroom seen beyond; moldings are dull gold. The bedroom in the Baldwin apartment has a lettuce-green Directoire chaise-longue; Directoire bronze cherub sconces light a collection of obelisks on a marbleized mantel. Harold Sterner's living-room is furnished with a family collection of Victorian pieces, a Brussels carpet. The painting of Mrs. Sterner between the windows is by Mr. Sterner.
Left: The garden, looking like the South of France.

Awning-covered gallery

Amster living room

William Baldwin's living room

Gallery and common room　*French Provincial shop*

Drawing room over shop　*The master bedroom*

Bedroom in Baldwin apartment　*Harold Sterner's living-dining room*

I am afraid that when I have finished this composition on house decoration, there will be no stopping me. I may go on and rip off a thesis on the prophecies of the pyramids. Both subjects could equally acknowledge me their master.

My husband, the present Pvt. Alan Campbell, U.S.A., and I did our house in the country without the aid of any decorator and without any knowledge of the principles of decoration. I say "did," and the word looks secure and substantial, but it's a black lie. We do, and we must continue to do; for there is no past tense to the doing of a house. There is, for that matter, only the smallest, most grudging amount of the present; it is always going to be done, some day.

We planned the arrangement and furnishings of our house as a sort of tacit protest against the theory that if you live in the country you have to become Early Americans. We never formally said that was what we did, but it turned out that way. We didn't feel like Early Americans; we didn't even look like them. Quickly, I say that they must have been admirable people, though scarcely, I imagine, adorable.

We felt that we were gaited to our own times, and not theirs. We experienced only backaches from sitting on settles. We thrilled to no aesthetic joy on contemplating salt boxes. Our French poodle looked like a fool, lying on a hooked rug.

We caused talk. We even caused hard feelings. We bought our place in Bucks County, Pennsylvania, six years ago, when the invasion of New York literati was just beginning. There are no folk so jealous of countryside tradition as those who never before have lived below the twelfth story of a New York building. They moved into their beautiful Pennsylvania stone houses, and they kept their magazines in antique cradles, and they rested their cocktail glasses on cobblers' benches. They put their famous tongues in their somewhat less famous cheeks, and went in for the quaint.

Their walls were hung with representations of hydrocephalic little girls with scalloped pantalets and idiotic lambs, and their floors were spread with carpets that some farmer's wife, fifty years ago, must have hated the sight of, and saved her egg money to replace. Now, they can't really think such things are a delight to live with. Can they?

They found us vandals. In our dining-room, as in all other rooms of our house, we have fine, deeply recessed windows. We lined the sides and the tops of the recesses with sheets of mirror. The effect, I mean to us, is lovely; the orchard lies

DESTRUCTIVE DECORATION

WE DIDN'T KNOW ANYTHING ABOUT HOUSES, BUT WE KNEW WHAT WE DIDN'T LIKE

BY DOROTHY PARKER

Bucks County, Pennsylvania, 1942

Dorothy Parker in her garden.

beyond the dining-room, and its trees seem to stand up in the mirrors at the sides, and its boughs and leaves look down from the mirrors at the top. But this was regarded as desecration. "Those old windows," they cried. "Oh, how could you?" Well, we could and we did. And we love it.

Then there was the terrible day when they found that, on the outside of our house, we had painted the blinds, not tea-room blue, but Mediterranean pink. All shuddered, and several swooned. And then, when we cut down a clump of sickly, straggly maples so that we might have an uninterrupted view of dipping meadows and the hills of Jersey beyond—well, that did in even the hardest to die of the Fifty-second Street Thoreaus. Now only the natives speak to us. We feel all right.

We wanted our house comfortable and gay. That is all we knew of what we wanted. We went to Bucks County not because of any literary ambitions, but because we loved the gracious field, the Botticelli cedars, the fine, direct fieldstone houses, and the great, honorable barns.

When we bought our house (we call it Fox House, not, for heaven's sake, for any huntin' set reason, but because it had always belonged to a family named Fox, and when you went to describe it for purposes of direction, people would say, "Oh yes, you mean the Fox House," so we mean the Fox House), it was inhabited by a Lithuanian family, who didn't want anybody to buy it because they lived there rent-free.

The Lithuanian lady, in fact, went to such lengths to keep us out as to place across the front door threshold the body of a dead ground-hog. It was August weather, and the ground-hog had not too recently passed on. . . . In case the need ever comes up in your life, I present you with this, as a good system to keep out prospective buyers.

Anyway, we got the house. It was, and a blushing understatement, a mess. There was no cellar, and the floors were rotting into the ground. What was left of the floors was carpeted with dead chickens, not still corpses, not yet skeletons. I remember wondering if all the perfumes of Arabia would ever—but it's all right now.

We put in electricity and cellars and bathrooms and a well. I say all this quickly, but you should see these scars. We could not get a telephone. At least we could, but it would have cost three thousand dollars to bring it in, so we didn't. It sounds sweet and peaceful and sequestered to be without a telephone. It is a nuisance and a deprivation and a block, not to have one.

So—the curtain drops to indicate the passage of eight months—there we were, with our lovely, tapestry-colored fieldstone house, and our fine barn and our hundred-and-ten acres of farm land. The land is farmed; you feel so guilty if it lies idle, and we farm it in what the Government asks you to plant. Corn, not people's corn, but fodder corn, and oats and soybeans.

I cannot imagine where we would have been or what we would have done without Hiram, our farmer, and that his name is Hiram is just a dividend. He ploughs the fields, he harvests the crops, he feeds the dogs and cats, he takes care of the house plants when we are away, he watches the

Salute to the new style: "D. Parker Provincial." This is the fieldstone exterior of the house. Bright pink blinds, white iron lace, flowers, accent the original stone.

Ten shades of red in the living room—hugely becoming to guests.

In the dining room, Mexican glass lilies.

Jumbo red roses on the walls, iron tassels on the powder table.

Blueprints of the house for upstairs hall.

house and the garden and us. He paints and does carpentry and cures motor troubles.

Hiram and his family live in the barn, the upper part of which we had made into an apartment for them. And we were let loose on the house.

Both of us had been brought up in a mistaken school of decoration, the school that selects "good dirt colors" and avers that you never get tired of a neutral tint. Even then we knew they were wrong. We both felt rebelliously that the only colors of which you did not tire were the bright ones. We wanted our house crammed with color. We got it. From the strawberry wallpaper in the front hall to the Paris-green linings of the bookshelves in the workroom, we've got color.

The other thing we wanted was that the house should be our own. We got that, too. My husband did an upstairs hall wall with all the blue-prints of our house. There is no finer blue than their color, and he shellacked them after pasting, so they shine and last.

He also, whenever we needed something for some place in the house, made it. For instance, we wanted somewhere near the porch where we live through the summer afternoons and evenings, a sort of chest in which to keep bottles and glasses and ice-bucket and whatever. He made that with boards and nails and a saw, practical and roomy and exact, and then he painted it in flowers and scrolls. It is quite Swedish and yet at the same time it's Mexican with a pronounced touch of Chinese. All right. It's useful, it's comfortable, it's hospitable, it's pretty, it's for its own place and nobody else has anything like it.

I guess that chest is the symbol of what I mean by decoration.

Brody is the cat napping in the blue and white master bedroom.

179

HOW VARIETIES OF PAVING ARE AN ASSET TO LOOKS AND COMFORT

Below: *Thomas Church, landscape architect, marked the slight change in level of a fairly flat area by an arc of three steps laid in brick. It belongs to Mr. and Mrs. George Coleman at Pebble Beach, California.*

Below: *Thomas Church also designed this swimming pool terrace with curved brick steps leading to a rose garden. The paving in the rose garden is flagstone with brick bands to provide contrast.*

The landscape architect is finding how useful steps in a garden can prove. First, steps add importantly to garden design. Even where the slope is gentle, a short broad flight will relieve monotony. Second, steps make it pleasanter to get from one level to another. If there is considerable slope, they may be broken, as the stairs in your house are, by landings and turns, adding immeasurably to the charming arrangements you can make. The materials you choose, whether brick, native stone, or sod, depend primarily on the type of garden you happen to have. But if it is near the house, it is attractive for the architecture of the one to reflect the architecture of the other. The pictures here prove how varied steps can be. . . .

Opposite page, top left: *This courtyard, designed by landscape architect Umberto Innocenti for his garden in Roslyn, Long Island, is encompassed by walls made of old Charleston brick. As in Italian gardens, plants in pots keep it bright. On the brick paving around the old wellhead, summer furniture, painted leaf green and upholstered in yellow, is disposed informally.*

Opposite page, top right: *At Bayville, Long Island. Mr. and Mrs. Harrison Williams have created the atmosphere of a Chinese garden. A round pool forms the center of the willow garden. Flagstones form bridges and frame the pool. The garden is ringed with a Chinese Chippendale fence, painted willow green, and set against a planting of huge rhododendrons.*

Left: *Naumkeag, Miss Mabel Choate's place in Stockbridge, Massachusetts, was built in 1885 by a young architect, Stanford White. Simultaneously, the grounds were shaped and planted by Nathaniel Franklin Barrett, landscape architect, who deserves more renown than memory gives him. Finally, there was Mrs. Joseph H. Choate herself, Miss Choate's mother, a painter by training and a horticulturalist . . . In one of the loveliest gardens in the Berkshires, a tiny box hedge outlines the black glass pool and fountains.*

Below: *In the garden of Mr. and Mrs. J.D. Biggers at Toledo, Ohio, stone stairs lead from a walled flower garden up to an informal planting, where an irregular old Scotch pine arches over a wellhead.*

Below: *The picture window, an anticlaustrophobic architectural element, unifies indoors and out. This picture window is in the house of Mrs. S.T. Dickinson, Pasadena, California. Architect was Woodbridge Dickinson, Jr.*

Exterior of Le Noviciat, made of Caen stone, with a slate mansard. The gardens, adapted from Versailles, have eighteenth-century statues.

THE DECORATING ART OF LADY MENDL

182

Though based on historic documents, Villa Le Noviciat is no lifeless copy. Here is a house that fits its environs and at the same time meets the needs of modern living. Inside, Lady Mendl and Commandant Weiller have achieved that rare combination; period accuracy and warm livability. The living room is off white, pale green, and gold.

Center: *The bedroom of Villa de Noviciat is hung with 18th-century silk panels, giving period authenticity to the redecorated room.*
Right: *Modern murals of Montgolfier's balloon ascension, by the late Nicolas de Molas, decorate this bathroom, reflecting Commandant Weiller's interest in flying. The color scheme is soft red.*

New York City, 1941, and Versailles, 1949

The story of Lady Mendl, the former Elsie de Wolfe, is told in the homes she has made for herself and others. Each speaks eloquently of her ability to assemble the ingredients of beauty; each is a reflection of the woman herself whose simple philosophy "Never complain, never explain," is embroidered on the little blue pillow that accompanies her wherever she travels. For many years Lady Mendl lived in Paris where her husband was attaché to the British Embassy. When France fell in the present conflict she returned to New York. How she has decorated the living room in her suite at the St. Regis is shown here. Also shown on these pages is Villa Le Noviciat, designed by Patrice Bonnet, chief architect-in-residence of the Château de Versailles, for Commandant Paul-Louis Weiller, recently redecorated under Lady Mendl's supervision.

Opposite page, left: *Curtained in Venetian red, this area of Le Noviciat is used for outdoor dining. It has a brown and white marble floor. Eighteenth-century table is alabaster marquetry; the lamp crystal and bronze.*
Opposite page, far left: *The round library glows with touches of gilt and old bindings used as a decorative element. The rug is Samarkand; the sofa covering and curtains are of salmon taffeta.*

Above right: *In the living room of Lady Mendl's St. Regis suite, deep laurel green walls, white ceiling, panels of mirror and a white Aubusson rug make a dramatic setting for French and English antiques. The writing table is an Empire piece, handsomely ornamented with ormolu.*
Below right: *An ivory damask loveseat at one end of Lady Mendl's living room, with a Queen Anne secretary against the wall.*

Cornwall, England, 1947

It was an afternoon in late autumn, the first time I tried to find the house. October, November, the month itself escapes me. But in the West Country autumn can make herself a witch, and place a spell upon the walker. The trees were golden brown, the hydrangeas had massive heads still blue and untouched by flecks of wistful gray, and I would set forth at three of an afternoon with foolish notions of August still in my head. I will strike inland, I thought, and come back by way of the cliffs, and the sun will yet be high, or at worst touching the horizon beyond the western hills. Of course, I was still a newcomer to the district, a summer visitor, whose people had but lately, within the year, bought the old "Swiss Cottage," as the locals called it, which name, to us, had horrid associations with an Underground railway in the Finchley Road at home. We were not yet rooted. We were new folk from London. We walked as tourists walked, seeing what should be seen. So my sister and I, poring over an old guidebook, first came upon the name of Menabilly. What description the guidebook gave I cannot now remember, except that the house had been first built in the reign of Queen Elizabeth, that the grounds and woods had been in the last century famous for their beauty, and that the property had never changed hands from the time it came into being, but had passed down, in the male line, to the present owner. Three miles from the harbor, easy enough to find; but what about keepers, and gardeners, chauffeurs, and barking dogs?

My sister was not such an inveterate trespasser as myself. We asked advice. "You'll find no dogs at Menabilly, nor any keepers either," we were told. "The house is all shut up. The owner lives in Devon. But you'll have trouble in getting into the house. The drive is nearly three miles long, and overgrown."

But I for one was not to be deterred. The autumn colours had me betwitched before the start. So we set forth, my sister more reluctant, with a panting Pekinese held by a leash. We came to the lodge at four turnings, as we had been told, and opened the creaking iron gates with the false courage and appearance of bluff common to the trespasser. The lodge was deserted. No one peered at us from the windows. We slunk away down the drive, and were soon hidden by the trees. Is it really nigh on twenty years ago since I first walked that hidden drive and saw the beech trees, like the arches of a great cathedral, form a canopy above my head?

MENDABILLY— THE MOST BEAUTIFUL HOUSE I HAVE EVER SEEN

BY DAPHNE du MAURIER

Daphne du Maurier, whose house, Menabilly, is the setting, as "Manderley," for her novel, Rebecca.

I remember we did not talk, or if we did, we talked in whispers. That was the first effect the woods had upon both of us. The drive twisted and turned in a way that I described many years afterwards, when sitting at a desk in Alexandria looking out upon a hard glazed sky and dusty palm trees, but on that first autumnal afternoon, when the drive was new to us, it had the magic quality of a place hitherto untrodden, unexplored. I was Scott in the Antarctic. I was Cortez in the Andes. Or possibly I was none of these things, but was a trespasser in time. The woods were sleeping now, but who, I wondered, had ridden through them once? What hoofbeats had sounded and then died away? What carriage wheels had rolled and vanished? Doublet and hose. Boot and jerkin. Patch and powder. Stock and patent leather. Crinoline and bonnet. . . .

The trees grew taller and the shrubs more menacing. Yet still the drive led on, and never a house at the end of it. Suddenly my sister said, "It's after four . . . and the sun's gone." The Pekinese watched her, his pink tongue lolling. And then he stared into the bushes, pricking his ears at nothing. The first owl hooted. . . .

"I don't like it," said my sister firmly, "Let's go home."

"But the house," I said with longing, "we haven't seen the house."

She hesitated, and I dragged her on. But in an instant the day was gone from us. The drive was become a muddied path, leading to nowhere, and the shrubs, green no longer but a shrouding black, turned to fantastic shapes and sizes. There was not one owl now, but twenty. And through the dark trees, with a pale grin upon his face, came the first glimmer of the livid Hunter's moon. I knew that I was beaten. For that night only.

"All right," I said grudgingly, "we'll find the house another time."

And following the moon's light we struck out through the trees and came out upon the hillside. In the distance below us stretched the sea. Behind us the woods and the valley through which we had come. But nowhere was there a sign of a house. Nowhere at all.

"Perhaps," I thought to myself, "it is a house of secrets, and has no wish to be disturbed." But I knew I should not rest until I had found it.

If I remember rightly the weather broke after that day, and the autumn rains were upon us. Driving rain, day after day. And we, not yet become acclimatized to Cornish wind and weather packed up and returned to London for the winter. But I did not forget the woods of Menabilly, nor the house that waited. . . .

We came back again to Cornwall in the spring, and I was seized with a fever for fishing. I would be out in a boat most days, with a line in the water, and it did not matter much what came on the end of it, whether it would be seaweed or a dead crab, as long as I could sit on the thwart of a boat and hold a line and watch the sea. The boatmen sculled off the little bay called Pridmouth, and as I looked at the land beyond and saw the massive trees climbing from the valley to the hill, the shape of it all seemed familiar.

"What's up there, in the trees?" I said.

"That's Menabilly," came the answer, "but you can't see the house from the shore. It's away up yonder. I've never been there myself." I felt a bite on my line at that moment and said no more. But the lure of Menability was upon me once again.

Next morning I did a thing I had never done before, nor ever did again, except once in the desert, where to see sunrise is the peak of all experience. In short, I rose at 5 A.M. I pulled across the harbour in my pram, walked through the sleeping town, and climbed out upon the cliffs just as the sun himself climbed out of Pont Hill behind me. The sea was glass. The air was soft and misty warm. And the only other creature out of bed was a fisherman, hauling crab-pots, at the harbour mouth, it gave me a fine feeling of conceit to be up before the world. My feet in sand-shoes seemed like wings. I came down to Pridmouth Bay, passing the solitary cottage by the lake, and opening a small gate hard by, I saw a narrow path leading to the woods. Now, at last I had the day before me, and no owls, no moon, no shadows could turn me back.

I followed the path to the summit of the hill, and then emerging from the woods turned left, and found myself upon a high grass walk, with all the bay stretched out below me and the Gribben head beyond.

I paused, stung by the beauty of that first pink glow of sunrise on the water, but the path led on, and I would not be deterred. Then I saw them for the first time—the scarlet rhododendrons. Massive and high they reared above my head, shielding the entrance to a long smooth lawn. I was hard upon it now, the place I sought. Some instinct made me crawl softly through the wet grass to the foot of the shrubs. The morning mist was lifting, and the sun was coming up above the trees even as the moon had done last autumn. This time there was no owl; but blackbird, thrush, and robin greeting the summer day.

I edged my way on to the lawn, and there she stood. My house of secrets. My elusive Menability. . . .

The windows were shuttered fast, white and barred. Ivy covered the gray walls and threw tendrils round the windows. The house, like the world, was sleeping, too. But, later, when the sun was high, there would come no wreath of smoke from the chimneys. The shutters would not be thrown back, nor the doors unfastened. No voices would sound within those darkened rooms. Menability would sleep on, like the sleeping beauty of the fairy tale, until someone should come to wake her.

I watched her awhile in silence, and then became emboldened, and walked across the lawn and stood beneath the windows. The scarlet rhododendrons encircled her lawns, to south, to east, to west. Behind her, to the north, were the tall trees and the deep woods. She was a two-storied house, and with the ivy off her would have a classical austerity that her present shaggy covering denied her.

One of her 19th-century owners had taken away her small-paned windows and given her plate glass instead, and he had also built at her northern end an ugly wing that conformed ill with the rest of her.

I edged my way onto the lawn and there she stood—my elusive Menabilly . . .

But with all her faults, most obvious to the eye, she had a grace and charm that made me hers upon the instant. She was, or so it seemed to me, bathed in a strange mystery. She held a secret—not one, not two, but many—that she withheld from many people, but would give to one who loved her well.

As I sat on the edge of the lawn and stared at her I felt like many romantic foolish people have felt about the Sphinx. Here was a block of stone, even as the desert Sphinx, made by man for his own purpose—yet she had a personality that was hers alone, without the touch of human hand.

One family only had lived within her walls. One family who had given her life. They had been born there, they had loved, they had quarrelled, they had suffered, they had died. and out of these emotions she had woven a personality for herself, she had become what their thoughts and their desires had made her.

And now the story was ended. She lay there in her last sleep. Nothing remained now for her but to decay and die. . . . I cannot recollect now, how long I lay and stared at her. It was past noon perhaps when I came back to the living world. I was empty and light-headed, with no breakfast inside me. But the house possessed me from that day, even as a mistress holds her lover.

Ours was a strange relationship for fifteen years. I would put her from my mind for months at a time, and then, on coming again to Cornwall, I would wait a day or two, then visit her in secret.

Once again I would sit on the lawn and stare up at her windows. Sometimes I would find that the caretaker at the lodge, who came now and again to air the house, would leave a blind pulled back, showing a chink of space, so that by pressing my face to the window I could catch a glimpse of a room. There was one room—a dining room I judged, because of the long sideboard against the wall—that held my fancy most. Dark panels. A great fireplace. And on the walls the family portraits stared into the silence and the dust. Another room, once a library, judging by the books upon the shelves, had become a lumber-place, and in the centre of it stood a great dappled rockinghorse with scarlet nostrils. What little blue-sashed, romping children once bestrode his back? Where was the laughter gone? Where were the voices that had called along the passages?

One autumn evening I found a window unclasped in the ugly north wing at the back. It must have been intuition that made me bring my torch with me that day. I threw open the creaking window and climbed in. Dust. Dust everywhere. The silence of death. I flashed my torch on to the cobwebbed walls and walked the house. At last. I had imagined it so often. Here were the rooms, leading from one another, that I had pictured only from outside. Here was the staircase, and the faded crimson wall. There the long drawing-room with its shiny chintz sofas and chairs. And here the dining room a forgotten corkscrew still lying on the sideboard.

Suddenly the shadows became too many for me, and I turned and went back the way I came. Softly I closed the window behind me. And as I did so, from a broken pane on the floor above my head came a great white owl, who flapped his way into the woods and vanished. . . .

Some shred of convention still clinging to my nature turned me to respectability. I would not woo my love in secret. I wrote to the owner of the house and asked his permission to walk about his grounds. The request was granted. Now I could tread upon the lawns with a slip of paper in my pocket to show my good intentions, and no longer crawl, belly to the ground, like a slinking thief.

Little by little, too, I gleaned snatches of family history. There was the cavalier found beneath the buttress wall more than a hundred years ago. There were the 16th-century builders, merchants and traders; there were the Stuart royalists, who suffered for their king; the Tory landowners with their white wigs and their brood of children; the Victorian garden-lovers, with their rare plants and their shrubs.

I saw them all, in my mind's eye, down to the present owner, who could not love his home, and when I thought of him it was not of an elderly man, a respectable justice of the peace, but of a small boy orphaned at two years old, coming for his holidays in an Eton collar and tight black suit, watching his old grandfather with nervous doubtful eyes. The house of secrets. The house of stories.

In the year of '37, married by now, I found myself in Alexandria and because I was not happy in the glare of pseudo East, I shut my eyes and dreamt of Menabilly. The story that came of this was called *Rebecca,* and was based on nothing and on no one. Yet in a sense I cannot now explain, even to myself, far less to others, Menabilly was Manderley, and Manderley was Menabilly. They were the same. Yet they had no likeness. What might have been. . . . What could have been. . . . What in truth was not. . . .

"Rebecca" was written, but my house of secrets held her secret still. The war came, and my husband and I were now at Hythe, in Kent, and many miles from Cornwall. I remember a letter coming from my sister.

"By the way, there is to be a sale at Menabilly. Everythng to be sold up and the house just left to fall to bits. Do you want anything?"

Did I want anything? I wanted her, my house, I wanted every stick of furniture, from the Jacobean oak to the Victorian bamboo. But what was the use? The war had come. There was no future for man, woman, or child. And anyway, Menabilly was entailed. The house itself could not be sold. No, she was just a dream, and would die, as dreams die always.

In '43 changes of plans sent me back to Cornwall, with my three chldren. I had not visited Menabilly since the war began. No bombs had come her way yet she looked like a blitzed building. The windows were not shuttered now. The panes were broken. She had been left to die.

It was easy to climb now through the front windows. The house was stripped and bare. Dirty paper on the floor. Great fungus growths from the ceiling. Moisture everywhere, death and decay. I could scarcely see the soul of her for the despair. The mould was in her bones.

Odd, yet fearful, what a few years of total neglect can do to a house, as to a man, a woman. . . . Have you seen a man who has once been handsome and strong, go unshaven and unkempt? Have you seen a woman lovely in her youth, raddled beneath the eyes, her hair tousled and gray?

Sadder than either, more bitter and poignant, is a lonely house.

I returned to my rented cottage in an angry, obstinate mood. Something was dying, without hope of being saved. And I would not stand it. Yet there was nothing I could do. Nothing? There was one faint, ridiculous chance in a million. . . . I telephoned my lawyer and asked him to write to the owner of Menabilly and ask him to let the house to me for a term of years. "He won't consent for a moment," I said. "It's just a shot at random."

But the shot went home. . . . A week later my lawyer came to see me.

"By the way," he said, "I believe you will be able to rent Menabilly. But you must treat it as a whim, you know. The place is in a fearful state. I doubt if you can do more than camp out there occasionally." I stared at him in amazement. "You mean—he would consent?" I said. "Why, yes, I gather so," answered my lawyer.

Then it began. Not the Battle of Britain, not the attack upon the soft underbelly of Europe that my husband was helping to conduct from Africa, but my own private war to live in Menabilly by the time that winter came . . .

"You're mad . . . you're crazy . . . you can't do it . . . there's no heating . . . you'll get no servants . . . it's impossible!"

I stood in the dining room, surrounded by a little team of experts. There was the architect, the builder, the plumber, the electrician, and my lawyer, with a ruler in his hand, which he waved like a magic baton.

"I don't think it can be done . . ." And my answer always: "Please, please, see if it can be done."

The creeper cut from the windows. The windows mended. The men upon the roof mortaring the slates. The carpenter in the house, setting up the doors. The plumber in the well, measuring the water. The electrician on a ladder, wiring the walls. And the doors and windows open that had not been open for so long. The sun warming the cold dusty rooms. Fires of brushwood in the grates. And then the scrubbing of the floors that had felt neither brush nor mop for many years.

Relays of charwomen, with buckets and swabs. The house alive with men and women. Where did they come from? How did it happen? The whole thing was an impossibility in wartime. Yet it did happen. And the gods were on my side. Summer turned to autumn, autumn to December. And in December came the vans of furniture; and the goods and chattels I had stored at the beginning of the war and thought never to see again were placed like fairy things, about the rooms at Menabilly.

Like fairy things, I said and looking back, after living here two years, it is just that. A fairy tale. Even now I have to pinch myself to know that it is true. I belong to the house. The house belongs to me.

From the end of the lawn where I first saw her, that May morning, I stand and look upon her face. The ivy is stripped. Smoke curls from the chimneys. The windows are flung wide. The doors are open. My children come running from the house on to the lawn. The hydrangeas bloom for me. Clumps of them stand upon my piano.

Slowly, in a dream, I walk towards the house. It's wrong, I think, to love a block of stone like this, as one loves a person. It cannot last. It cannot endure. Perhaps it is the very insecurity of the love that makes the passion strong. Because she is not mine by right. The house is still entailed, and one day will belong to another . . .

I brush the thought aside. For this day, and for this night, she is mine.

And at midnight, when the children sleep, and all is hushed and still. I sit down at the piano and look at the panelled walls, and slowly, softly, with no one there to see, the house whispers her secrets, and the secrets turn to stories, and in strange and eerie fashion we are one, the house and I.

Right: *The drawing room from the hall door, looking toward my husband's study. The room is white, pale green and saffron. A tall chair, behind the bunch of chrysanthemums, came from the Continent, where it was made some time around 1800; the chair on the right is about 1810 and probably Dutch while the painted leather screen is Spanish.*

A painting of my father hangs in the oak-panelled, curving stair hall.

Below left: *The map in the oak-panelled library is of the Menabilly estate. Through the open door, you can see the nursery where the children's toys are lying.*
Below: *On my dressing table, once a spinet, are pictures of the children, Viburnum Tinus, and tortoise shell.*

Above: *A portrait in bronze of my father, my books bound in chocolate brown leather. My husband's Airborne badges are set in the wooden bookends. The plaque on the table is a National Book Award.*

LIVING
IN A
GLASS HOUSE

Just as in the decade after the First World War, a brilliant influx of new ideas and plans for living burst upon the world. The decade belonged to the architects. Their work was inspired by the industrial materials suddenly made available—glass, plastic, aluminum. Wrap-around glass houses, sunken living rooms, storage walls, were some of the innovations introduced by architects such as John Johansen, Eero Saarinen, Alexander Girard and Edward Durell Stone. Glass-skinned buildings changed the look of the landscape, just as space took on a new dimension with the dramatic space explorations initiated in 1957. The simple chair underwent a revolution in this decade—armless chairs, chairs made of fiberglass, chairs made of metal, and the famous chair designed by Charles Eames gave comfort a new expression. The Scandinavian influence, this time Danish Modern, also altered the shape of furniture, with designers such as Arne Jacobsen and Finn Juhl turning chairs and sofas into gravity-defying forms. In response to a growing interest in designer rooms, decorators were encouraged to give a more personal signature to interior design. The 50s might also be called the electronic decade. Television, hi-fi, and stereo presented a challenge to designers and allowed families to rediscover the joys of staying home.

1950/s

This trend-setting house in Houston, Texas,
has a living/dining area that rises two full stories, with towering
glass walls, dramatically lit by night. The plan is in two parts,
with the second floor planned for the owners' two children.
The house was designed by Preston M. Bolton and Howard Barnstone
for Mr. and Mrs. Gerald S. Gordon.

A GLASS SHELL THAT FLOATS IN THE AIR

Chicago, Illinois, 1952

Designed by architect Mies van der Rohe, this is one of the most uncompromising modern houses in existence. Basementless, atticless, suspended in air by steel columns, it is a single room, 54' by 28', entirely enclosed in glass. A partly cantilevered porch and a travertine

190

terrace add outdoor living space. Window walls provide a close communion with the outdoors. They also enlarge the interior visually. An ''open'' plan creates general spaciousness, allows the space to be used flexibly for entertaining, dining, sleeping. The use of wear-resistent building materials and automatic mechanical equipment is insurance that the house will work for its owner instead of the owner working for the house. Beyond these trend-setting characteristics, this is a house with a unique architectural spirit. The weekend home of Dr. Edith Farnsworth, it ''floats'' on a site overlooking woods near Chicago.

Glass walls on four sides catch maximum sun, light, enjoy wide-angled views of fields, woods, river. Four steel columns on the two longer sides of house (welded to steel frame of floor and roof) hold house 4' above ground for best view. Central core houses utilities.

Some five years ago, Dr. Edith Farnsworth decided she wanted a place in the country to relax from her professional duties. She wanted a house that would be esthetic in terms of today. She submitted her problem to Mies van der Rohe, the pioneering purist who wrote "architecture is the will of an epoch translated into space." The translation as expressed in Dr. Farnsworth's house is a structure of implacable calm, precise simplicity, and meticulous detail. It could not be built in any age but our own as its realization depends on today's building methods. It's a one-story, open-plan design. It has a utility core, replacing the basement, and storage walls, replacing the attic. It has glass walls for more sun, more view, more space.

Above: *Travertine terrace for outdoor living also serves as entrance. Cantilevered steps lead to porch, which provides a sheltered outdoor living area. Curtains veil glass walls of living area to maintain privacy, shut out night.*
Opposite page: *The porch (to be screened later) extends living space outdoors. It has the same white-painted steel frame, travertine floor, plaster ceiling, as indoors. The terrace below is suspended on steel posts like the house itself.*
Below left: *Floor plan, showing how spaciousness is attained through the simplest possible design. There are only four parts to this house—a glass-enclosed room, a central "core" to house utilities, an entrance porch, and a terrace. Kitchen equipment—two refrigerators, dishwasher, sink, waste disposal, two ranges—are fitted under a single counter.*
Below: *Utility core, organized as a control room, is center of structure. It houses furnace, warm-air heating ducts, flues, vents, water pipes, and drainage. Bathrooms, at either end of utility core, are enclosed by handsome panels of primavera wood. Kitchen cabinets run the length of the utility core, fireplace is on the other side of it. Wall projections at either end of utility core mark off living, dining, and sleeping areas.*

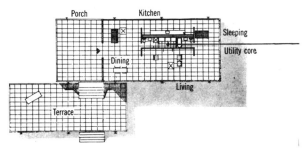

PAVILION LIVING IN MISSOURI

IN A SUBURB OF ST. LOUIS, A NEW KIND OF COOL, POOLSIDE LIVING HELPS THIS FAMILY ESCAPE THE HEAT OF THE CITY

Clayton, Missouri, 1953

Some people think you have to go miles away from home to escape summer heat and humidity. But this airy pavilion is just twenty minutes away from St. Louis. Chief requirements for owners Mr. and Mrs. Joseph Pulitzer, Jr., were a large, screened-in room and a swimming pool. Elaborating on this idea, architects Bernoudy-Mutrux designed a screened-in pavilion that catches the breezes and seems to draw coolness from a pool of water at its doorstep. It's an innovation in the suburbs of St. Louis, which are by tradition conservative, but the neighboring houses are out of sight beyond shade trees that form a natural boundary for the property. The roof of the pavilion looks as if it is suspended in mid-air, but is actually anchored to the site by angled steel columns; this kind of framework frees the walls and permits the use of sliding screens across the front of the living room and clerestory screens on the other three sides.

The idea of a screened-in room developed into a combination living and dining room with floor-to-ceiling screens that slide open to the concrete terrace and pool. Two large electric fans overhead help to circulate air from the clerestory openings, so the room remains cool as a cucumber all summer long. The only glass in the entire house is translucent glass in the north wall of the bedrooms, which during the winter can serve as storage rooms for valuable and vulnerable furniture. All the bedrooms are on the back of the house, plus a separate child's wing, which opens out onto a play yard equipped with a sandbox . . .

The living room and adjoining concrete terrace command a clear view of the pool, which turned out to have just about the same proportions as the living room. A lily pond was raised above the level of the terrace. Screened, sheltered by the wide overhang of the roof, the house is cool to live in as well as to

look at. Natural materials help to link it to the outdoors; cypress walls, cement floors, brick fireplace, woven-fiber rug. The open effect of the pavilion is intensified at night when candles of every size and shape are lighted indoors and out, white silk Japanese lanterns hung in trees, pool flooded with underwater lights, and a waterfall from the side of the pond produces soothing sound effects.

Right: Plan, showing how living-dining room opens outdoors to terrace and wide steps descending to pool.
Above: The terrace, with steps to pool. Indoors, air circulates freely. Canvas curtains can be drawn down during heavy rain. Circular lounging terrace at right, outlined by yew hedge, overlooks lily pond with bronze sculpture by Mary Callery. The dogwood, hydrangeas, and natural greenery add country flavor.
Opposite page, bottom: At night, firefly magic is performed by pool lights and candles both indoors and out.

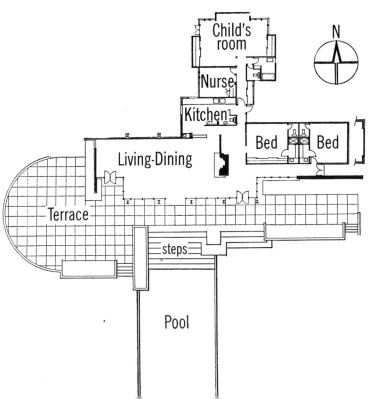

A NEW CONCEPT OF BEAUTY WITH DARING NEW USES OF SPACE, LIGHT, AND FINE MATERIALS

U.S.A., 1959

Although this house has borrowed liberally from the stuff that dreams are made of, it is not just a fantasy or a fine facade. Its true aim is to enrich the lives of the family dwelling in it, not merely to provide a rich background. What lifts the spirit here is the disposition of space and light, the easy alliance with nature outdoors, and the tranquillity of each part of the house. Designed by architects Eero Saarinen and Alexander Girard, with Kevin Roche as associate, the diverse arrangements of space give the house wonderful variety inside the 100-foot-long and 80-foot-wide rectangle. Entering the great central living area, which spreads to glass walls and loggias at north, south, and west, you feel 10 feet tall. Then, moving on to the smaller rooms at each corner of the house you gain a pleasant sense of seclusion and privacy. Bands of intersecting skylights pierce the roof and also border the outside walls. The result is a house alive with light. The framework of the house is steel, and all sixteen of the elegantly proportioned steel posts that support the roof are left unconcealed and finished in white enamel. . . .

Above: *House exterior, with concrete-block walls covered with richly grained black slate panels, forming a dark band around the house to add solidity to its appearance. Above the slate the massive, white, drum-like roof seems to float. The 10-foot-wide terrazzo terrace surrounding the house links all parts of it, enlarges the living, dining, and sitting loggias and forms a sort of Arabian Nights platform for the house.*

Opposite page, far right: *Loggia joins living room through wide, sliding windows. Water rains into reflecting pond from jets overhead. Skylights run length of roof.*

Left and opposite page, right: *Conversation center provides a cushioned raft of seating without blocking floor area or vista through window. Marble coping makes handy counter for ash trays, glasses. Padouk wood steps down are laminated with rubber for safety.*

The astonishing blend of exotic and native, ancient and modern, rich and austere that you find in the interior of this house has the quality of a painting. Yet in the ordinary sense, the house was not decorated at all. There are no color schemes, no matching of woods or fabrics. The style suggests no period. On the other hand, all the furnishings and accessories seem a part of the house. Everything from the major furniture to the smallest decorative detail was the responsibility of Alexander Girard, one of the architects. Because everything is good—that is, the best of its kind—everything goes happily together.

Above: *From the east loggia you can look across the reflecting pool into the living area with its recessed conversation center and 50-foot book/storage wall. Divider panel at left, covered with antique Kashmir shawl, screens main entrance.*

Below and opposite page: *50 continuous feet of storage and display of exotic objects are a dominant decorative element.*
From left to right: *Chinese birdcage: tiny Peruvian figures: black paper, flecked with gold and silver: antique Italian, Greek and Chinese ornaments: English antique brass box: Victorian flower montage: storage for camera equipment: French Provincial clock, Hopi Indian figures: Latin American religious figures: Venetian glass birds: Early American toys, 18th-century Austrian cabinet: East Indian gouaches and bronzes, Balinese carving: New Mexican crucifix and record player cabinet: Mexican candelabra: double doors conceal TV: Oriental lute: William Blake engraving: doorway to guest room.*

THE MODERN HOUSE IS A PERSONAL HOUSE

Connecticut, 1958

Modern houses, you often hear, are all the same. But, of course, they are not. A contemporary house can take any form the architect and owners wish to give it. It can be of glass and steel, furnished with molded chairs and decorated with spinning plastic mobiles. Or it can assume a rustic character, warmly embellished indoors with natural wood finishes. Modern can be many things. The house shown on these pages for instance, is notably contemporary in spirit; but what makes it outstanding are not its similarities to other modern houses, but

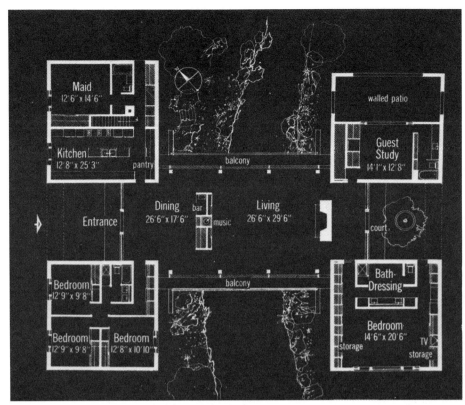

Of all this house's distinctive features, the most impressive is seen on approaching the site. Anchored on either side of a woodland stream, the house is an extraordinary bridge straddling the flowing water. The three arches over the bridged section are designed to suggest a sense of fluid motion, in contrast to the four flat-roofed wings branching from its corners (see plan). Glass walls on both sides not only give the 47-foot living-dining area the open effect of a bridge but also allow the owners to enjoy a view of the brook, its pools and falls, both upstream and down. In fair weather, they can sit outside on balconies running the width of the bridge. Each of the four wings is a distinct zone with direct access to the living-dining bridge. Each has its own bath, and the walls of these wings, in contrast to the bridge, are largely solid for privacy.

Below: The H-shaped house is formed by junction of the four wings and the arched living-dining bridge, which spans the stream. Open sections in roof are above entrance at left, rear courtyard between master bedroom-guest wings, and the walled guest room patio.
Opposite page, bottom: The rear entrance is approached through a courtyard. It is defined by roof section with thick cornice running between two wings. Exterior walls of all four wings are finished in pink stucco. These walls carry a pattern of geometric figures in bas-relief designed by the architect.

rather its striking differences. . . . The plan, designed by architect John Johansen, is unusual, consisting of four perfectly square structural units, each of which intersects with a corner of the central living-dining area. Two are bedroom units, another a guest suite and the fourth a kitchen-service area. Inside, vaulted and gilded ceiling sections, *opposite page,* are evidence of its departure from conventional design. Landscape architect: James Fanning; interior decorator, Katherine Hartshorne, A.I.D.

NEW VIEW FOR AN OLD HOUSE ON TELEGRAPH HILL

San Francisco, California, 1956

These are views of designer-importer Lowell Groves's remodeled top-floor apartment in a narrow old two-story house on Telegraph Hill. Until architect Roy Starbird and Mr. Groves went to work, the upper floor was a cramped railroad-type flat, with no view. Now front walls of glass and a deck, *opposite page,* open it to the hills and bay. The simple scheme is a perfect setting for Mr. Groves's fine Eastern antiques. Of particular interest are the vertically striped navy and white blinds to draw over window walls at night, an accent of color in the living/dining room . . .

Bottom right: *Plan of the renovated story.*
Above and right: *Dark woods and brass furniture trim stand out against white walls. Textured beige silk, natural linen, and navy blue tweed are the upholstery fabrics. Bare oak flooring creates coolness, plants and striped shades add a colonial atmosphere. The uninterrupted view through the living area to the deck enhances the fine collection of art and antiques.*

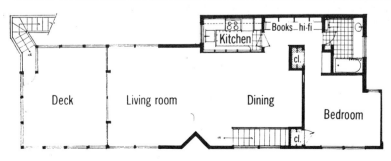

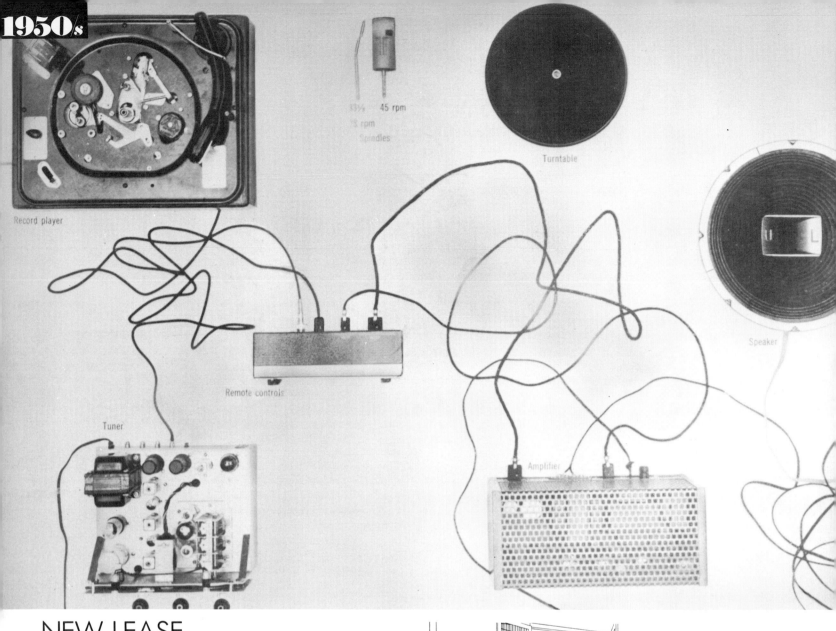

Record player

Spindles
33⅓ 45 rpm
78 rpm

Turntable

Remote controls

Tuner

Speaker

Amplifier

NEW LEASE
ON LISTENING
AND LOOKING

U.S.A., 1951

High fidelity is the key to the new lease on listening, which is spreading rapidly across the U.S.A. Young people particularly have "discovered" high fidelity. By the thousands they are learning about it, assembling and expanding their home music systems. The reasons? You don't have to be a licensed electrician to assemble a home music system for high-fidelity reproduction. What are the units? A tuner, a record player, an amplifier, and a speaker . . . a reliable combination of high-fidelity units will cost you about $175—but you can easily spend more if you want to. . . . You can assemble them yourself, and install them in cabinets or in a wall. As your interest increases you may want to add remote-control tuners, television, or a tape recorder. . . . However, this is an advanced stage; as a novice you are more likely to

be bewildered by the wide choice of tuners, amplifiers and speakers available, and by a new specialized vocabulary. For this reason House & Garden invited technical help from the editor and associate editor of Audio Engineering magazine, C.G. McProud and Harrie K. Richardson, two tolerant authorities in a highly controversial field. Our joint efforts produced a chart of high-fidelity units that work well together for you to enjoy at home.

Radio and phonograph built into the wall, with sliding panel. Designer, Ted Sandler.

In a dividing wall, the television chassis revolves to face the living room, above, *and dining room,* right.

In this two-way cabinet, there is space for radio, record player, speaker, storage for books and dishes.

This table holds record player and tuner. The speaker has floor-to-ceiling baffle.

In a library wall, equipment has been built in behind doors that match the paneling.

In sectional cabinets, there are a tape recorder, record player, radio, storage space, a speaker.

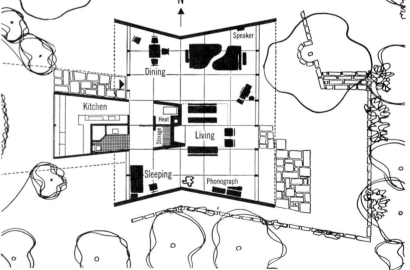

A television set, a record player, a radio, and a tape recorder— these are the Alladin's lamps of the 20th century, a magic-making quartet. Not many of us can afford to buy them all at once, most of us acquire them in a rather haphazard order; but whichever way they come, it is wise to have a plan for placing them if you are not to end up with a room that looks like a radio shop. House & Garden's "sound wall," for instance, (see drawings on opposite page) is an attractive arrangement of shelves, drawers and cupboards that takes care of the present and anticipates the future.

Above left: *This house was designed for Mrs. Dorothy Roosevelt of Birmingham, Michigan, a pianist who likes to give informal musicals for as many as 75 people. Designed by architect Edward P. Elliott, it has V-shaped walls and roof for acoustics. The performing end of the room has two grand pianos. Mounted on the wall behind them is the speaker of the record player. The player is concealed in a cabinet.* Above: *A well-ordered room, approximately 39 by 26 feet, takes care of Mrs. Roosevelt's musical and living requirements (cooking excepted). The fireplace, furnace, and storage unit in the center of the house divide sleeping, living, and dining areas. Flared walls help acoustics. . .*

THE VERY PERSONAL ART OF DECORATING

U.S.A., 1951, 1957

JOSEPH B. PLATT, *New York designer by prac-*
tice, is a country gentlemen by choice. With his wife, cookbook author June Platt, he commutes weekends from the pace of the city to the peace of Little Compton, Rhode Island. Their small, shingled house looks westward over peaceful New England meadows. The simple color scheme (white walls dark-stained floors, low-key colors in wood and fabrics) was designed to give a feeling of space and elegance. In the dining room, above, early American dining furniture, a patchwork quilt (used under glass on cocktail table) mingle with English tiles, a Louis XIV mirror, to give a personal feel to the room.

MELANIE KAHANE, *the New York designer,*
makes the most of a tiny room, opposite page, by settling on a unified color scheme: black, white and nasturtium. Black plus white plus color is an old team, but a new trend—Melanie Kahane uses black and white as staccato accents for French Provincial furniture. A black ceiling serves to tranquilize the room. By putting a four-poster bed on a platform, building the ceiling down, she achieves the effect of a French Provincial lit clos, demonstrating how happily a black and white color scheme can combine with many different kinds of furniture. Time-tested in a variety of historic styles, black-and-white takes its place with ease in today's decoration.

U.S.A., 1958–1959

BILLY BALDWIN *of Baldwin & Martin, Inc., transformed an old summer house for Mr. and Mrs. Lloyd Hilton Smith, opposite page. Existing furniture was brought up to date with bright paint and fabrics. Victorian camel-back armchairs became accents. Rosewood frames are painted white and set off with green cotton damask seat pads. White lacquer and brass coffee tables are modern Chinese. Sofas are covered with a brilliant French cotton print.*

WARD BENNETT *revived the conversation pool as the oldest and friendliest kind of social group, above. The pool is added on to an old house, with the floor raised a step above hearth level, then carpeted and cushioned. Filled with light from a strip in the floor, the travertine hearth has a magic glow as you sit around it on mattresses with your feet on the hearth, or stretch out beach fashion on rattan backrests, with ashtrays beside you.*

SYRIE MAUGHAM, *ex-wife of the author*
Somerset Maugham, is famous for her all-white rooms, full of texture and white-painted furniture, and wonderful style, which she brings to houses in England and America. In this Lake Forest hall, she uses flowers for color and pattern. Hybrid lilacs and tulips are reflected in the mirror, with antique wallpaper behind.

LADY MENDL, *born Elsie de Wolfe, changed the liv-ing habits of a generation of Americans. The library of the Villa Trianon, her French house, exemplifies her predilection for French 18th-century furniture, rich fabrics, and wood paneling. Her flair for individual touches is seen in the mirror above the mantel, fronted with potted flowers, enhanced by draped silk and concealed lighting.*

U.S.A., 1950–1959

MALLORY-TILLIS *give the dining room of Mr.*
and Mrs. Monroe Hess a new vista with hot and cool color. Matchstick blinds and silk shantung curtains form a simple backdrop. A mirrored wall reflects the bright orange trim on the closet, table pedestal and orange-covered cushions, contrasting with the cool white walls and floor, green plants.

T.H. ROBSJOHN-GIBBINGS
creates serenity in the New York duplex apartment of Mr. and Mrs. Jerome Kandell. The living room has creamy Italian marble floors; walls painted the palest gold, curtains and upholstery in shades of old gold and bright gold, add warmth. The conversation group is underlined by a sand-colored rug the shape of an L, and outsized ottomans.

DOROTHY DRAPER *has lavished her imprint on houses, hotels, hospitals, and night clubs from New York to Brazil. In her New York apartment living room, she has covered chairs with chintz of the cabbage rose pattern that has long since become her trademark; heaped logs in an ordinary bushel basket because it is a good size. White and gold liven the antiques.*

WILLIAM PAHLMANN *uses books to enhance Margaret Cousins's living room. The simplest kind of open shelves hanging from a white wall allow the books themselves to dominate one end of a room furnished with a rich mixture of styles. Shelves are covered with tortoiseshell paper to match the tortoiseshell leather of the spool chairs and painted finish of the sofa frame.*

JAMES AMSTER *conceals storage in this dining room he designed for a busy host. The handsome façade of the sideboard has lined drawers for flatware; space below holds serving pieces, trays, round tablecloths on rollers to keep them uncreased. Shirred fabric on the bookcase doors conceals wine and coctail glasses, ice buckets, shakers, and other bar equipment.*

MICHAEL TAYLOR *brings tradition up to date by painting English chinoiserie pieces—both the fourposter beds and the benches—a crisp white. The sheer bedspreads and the matching hangings soften the overall look of the room, while the bright green seat cushions on the pair of matching benches add the necessary sharp accents.*

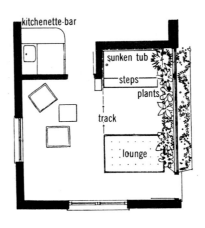

kitchenette-bar

sunken tub

steps

plants

track

lounge

THE NEW HEALTH ROOM — BUILD THE OUTDOORS RIGHT INTO YOUR KITCHEN OR BATH

Rumson, New Jersey, 1954

The room shown on this page is a new kind of room. Its purpose is health and relaxation, in an atmosphere at once modern and reminiscent of old Pompeii. It is an exercise center and bathing pavilion, a room for basking in the sun or under a sun lamp. Designed by architect C.L. De Sina for Mr. and Mrs. M.C. Guarino of Rumson, New Jersey, one side, overlooking a flagstone terrace and rose garden, is built like a modern greenhouse, with a glass wall and ceiling to admit sun all day long. Beneath it is a sunken window garden. Otherwise, it is a marble hall with rose marble walls and floor of travertine . . . Bathing is a luxurious affair in the big (4-by-6-foot) sunken Roman tub, into which one descends two steps. When the tub is not in use, it is hidden beneath a comfortable day-bed whose lightweight aluminum frame is mounted on ball bearings so that it can be easily moved about

the room or out onto the terrace. . . . In addition to its glamorous atmosphere, this health room is equipped with an exercise mat and bicycle, and a small kitchenette-bar. The outdoor-feel kitchen, *opposite page,* has a charcoal grill, skylight and window wall, framing the garden view. It's as though you were out-of-doors while working in your kitchen.

Above: *Plan of the health room.*
Left: *Sunken tub, with view through window wall to terrace and rose garden, and sun streaming in.*
Top: *For sunbathing and relaxing, daybed on rollers is pushed over tub—slipcovered in a shantung plastic material impervious to steam and water.*
Opposite page: *Kitchen, designed by architect Thornton M. Abell, with interior by Jane F. Ullman, showing barbecue grill, with revolving baffle, tiled counter, with translucent sliding panel that functions as a pass-through into the dining area. Glass wall and skylight provide light and view of nature.*

SISSINGHURST

BY V. SACKVILLE-WEST

IN THE RUINS OF A
TUDOR CASTLE,
V. SACKVILLE-WEST,
THE AUTHOR,
AND HER HUSBAND,
HAROLD NICOLSON,
WRITER AND DIPLOMAT,
HAVE EVOKED A
SERIES OF CHARMING
GARDENS AND ALLÉES

Right: In the ruins of a Tudor castle, V. Sackville-West, the author, and her husband, Harold Nicolson, writer and diplomat, have evoked a series of charming gardens and allées. In the castle courtyard, tall yews cast cool shadows on sun-baked stone, sprawling rosemary at right.
Opposite page: Brilliant Eremurus (foxtail lilies) rise from the Kentish soil like flowering swords, standing vigilant before Sissinghurst Castle's ancient tower.

Sissinghurst, England, 1950

The thing to remember about this garden is that nineteen years ago, in 1930, there was *no* garden. The place had been on the market for three years since the death of the last farmer-owner; the buildings were occupied by farm-laborers; and the slum-like effect, produced by both man and Nature, was squalid to a degree. There was nothing but a dreadful mess of old chicken house and wire chicken runs, broken down spike fences, rubbish dumps where cottagers had piled their tins, their bottles, their rusty ironmongery and their broken crockery for perhaps half a century, old cabbage stalks and a tangle of weeds everywhere. Brambles grew in wild profusion; bindweed wreathed its way into every support; ground elder made a green carpet; docks and nettles flourished; couch grass sprouted; half the fruit trees in the orchard were dead; the ones that remained alive were growing in the coarsest grass; the moat was silted up and so invaded by reeds and bulrushes that the water was almost invisible; paths there were none, save of trodden mud. But it had its charm. It was the Sleeping Beauty's castle with a vengeance, if you liked to see it with a romantic eye; but if you also looked at it with a realistic eye you saw that Nature run wild was not quite so romantic as you had originally thought, and entailed a great deal of tidying up.

It took three years to clear away the rubbish, three solid years, employing only an old man and his son who also had other jobs to do. Neither of them was a gardener; they were just casual labor. It was not until 1933 that any serious planting could be undertaken, but this was perhaps as well, because during those three impatient years we had time to become familiar with the "feel" of the place—a very important advantage that the professional garden designer, abruptly called in, is seldom able to enjoy. A hundred times we changed our minds, but as we changed them only on paper no harm was done and no expense incurred. Of course we longed to start planting the hedges, which were to be the skeleton of the garden, its bones, its anatomy, but had we been able to do so in those early days I am sure we should have planted them in the wrong place. Even as it was, we made some mistakes; the yew walk is too narrow, and I stuck a *Paulownia imperialis* into the middle of a future flowerbed, where it is becoming too imperial, and is now rapidly attaining the dimensions of a forest tree. I have not the heart to cut it down, although I know I ought to.

It was not an easy garden to design. We had so very little to go on. There were no existent hedges, except rubbishy ones, which just demanded to be grubbed out, and no old trees, such as a cedar, or a mulberry, which one might reasonably have expected to find in so ancient a site and which would have provided a starting point here and there. It is true that we had some guiding lines in the old walls of pink Tudor brick, and God forbid that I should be so ungrateful to those, for they are in many ways the making of the garden, but after the charming haphazard fashion of Tudor builders (who presumably had no professional architect to draw plans for them) none of the lines seemed to be at right angles to one another, but shot off most inconveniently in odd directions. It looked all right from ground-level, but once you had climbed the tower and looked down upon the whole layout as though you were seeing it from an airplane, you discovered that everything was at sixes and sevens. The tower wasn't opposite the main entrance; the courtyard wasn't rectangular, as you thought, but coffin-shaped; the moat wall ran away at an oblique angle from everything else; the moat followed an even more inexplicable angle. It required great ingenuity to overcome those problems, but fortunately my husband Harold Nicolson (who might well have made his career as an architect or a garden-designer instead of a diplomatist, politician, and author) possessed enough ingenuity, and also enough large paper sheets ruled into squares, to grapple with these difficulties.

The result is, I think, entirely successful. He has contrived in the most ingeni-

215

ous way, as you may appreciate from the accompanying photographs, to produce a design that combines formality with informality. He has managed to get long vistas over and over again, in a relatively small space. This makes the garden look far larger than in fact it is. He has also managed to make vistas meet at the queerest angles, a condition particularly apparent in the placement of the classical statue behind the old moat; that statue is visible from the steps of the tower, and also from the seat at the end of the moat walk. This vista took some thinking out, I can tell you. I had the smaller part, for Harold Nicolson did the designing, and I did the planting. We made a good combination in this way: I could not possibly have drawn out the architectural lines of the garden, and he couldn't possibly have planted it up, because he doesn't know half as much about plants as I do. This is not saying much, for I know very little, but he knows even less. But he does know how to draw the axis between one viewpoint and another and that is something I could never have accomplished. To sum up, I think I have succeeded in making the garden pretty with my flowers, but the real credit is due to him, who drew its lines so well and so firmly that it can still be regarded with pleasure even in the winter months when all my flowers have vanished.

Having paid this tribute to Harold Nicolson, I must go back to some details about the making of this garden and what we grow in it. We found it, as I have said, in a dreadful mess. The only thing we found of any interest was an old Gallica rose, then unknown to cultivation, which is now listed as Gallica var. Sissinghurst Castle at 10 shillings a plant, by Messers.

Hilling of Chobham, to whom I gave some runners. Miss Nancy Lindsay, who is an expert on such matters, says that my old rose is Gallica Tour des Maures, a great rarity . . . that is as may be. I don't know whether this shrubby, woody old rose I found romping here is of any interest at all. I know only that it is fun and interesting to find anything growing on any old site, because you never know what it may turn out to be. This is the way in which many old plants are forgotten and then rediscovered, whether it is an old rose, or an old primrose, or an old double wallflower or an old double Sweet William, or what. Apart from that, there was nothing, unless you count a hoary quince tree, which certainly is a lovely sight in spring with its flat, pinkish-white blossoms and its heavy golden fruit in autumn; in the intervening months it now has a clematis scrambling all over it, clothing it in purple. The most urgent thing to do was to plant hedges. We were extravagant over this, and planted yew, and have never regretted it. Everybody told us it took at least a century to make a good yew hedge, but the photograph of the yew walk will, I think, disprove this: it is now only sixteen years old, a mere adolescent, and at the end where the ground slopes and it has been allowed to grow up in order to maintain the top-level, it is 16 feet high. This should be heartening to those who plant yew. We did nothing particular to encourage it; we did not souse it with bullock's blood or anything like that; but we did put in very young plants, what the nurserymen call 1½ feet to 2 feet, which look more like the head of a birch-broom dotted along a line that like anything that promised to become solid hedge. We did this partly from motives of economy but also because I am a firm believer in young plants that have not had time to get settled in their ways. The percentage of loss is far smaller. In fact I don't believe we lost a single one; and when they do ''get away,'' in the gardener's phrase, they go ahead without check and far more vigorously. But it does demand a lot of patience, and for year our garden looked like a nursery garden with rows and rows of little Christmas trees for sale.

Similarly, we planted some acacia. They looked like walking-sticks stuck in the ground. I paid about tuppence each for them, from a nursery in France, and true they were not more than 12 inches high. Twelve naked little inches of a miniature walking-stick. Today they are large and

Left: *Windblown poplars are silhouetted against the sky. In the foreground, the old moat, with the classical statue creating a perfect vista from the tower.*
Opposite page: *Seen from the Sissinghurst tower are evergreen yew hedges planted to be ''the skeleton of the garden, its bones, its anatomy. . . .'' in the words of author V. Sackville-West.*

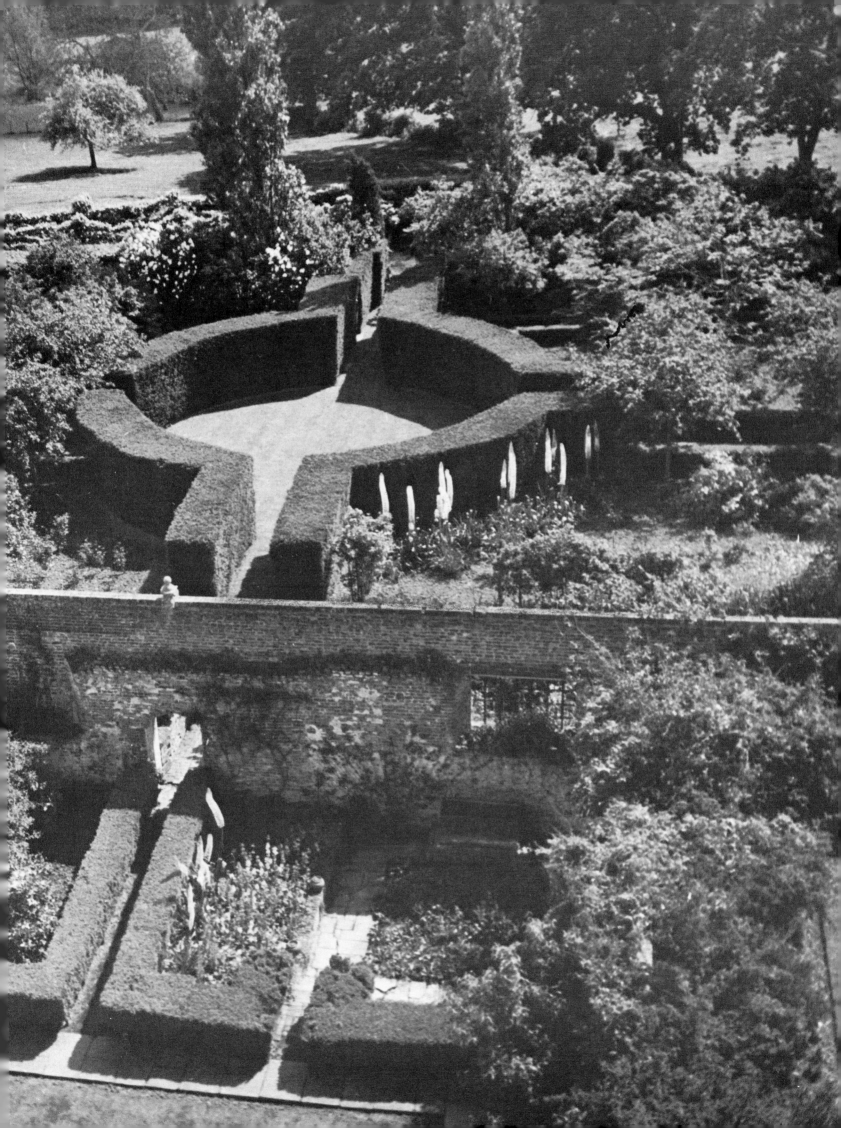

graceful trees, 20 to 30 feet high at a modest estimate, drooping their sweet-scented tassels of flower in June. A good tuppeny worth.

The only exception were the four big yews in the courtyard. Here we did take a risk. We found them in a nurseryman's garden, to which they had just been transplanted from Penshurst churchyard. The parishioners of Penshurst apparently thought them too gloomy and threw them out. They were old trees, but they were just what the courtyard at Sissinghurst demanded and we chanced it. We were justified: they all survived, and they now look as though they have been there forever. We did take some trouble over these; we sank drainage-pipes down to their roots, and poured bullock's blood into them. I used to absent myself while this unpleasant operation was taking place; but I now feel that the five pounds the four trees cost me was a fiver well expended.

In the same nurseryman's garden I found an old rose growing against the office wall. It was a very deep red, fading to purple, with the strongest rose scent that ever a rose had. They were rather contemptuous of it; didn't even know its name; hadn't even bothered to propagate it. They said I could have the old plant if I liked to risk moving it. I risked it; it bore the move; and has turned out to be Souvenir du Docteur Jamain, a climbing hybrid perpetual almost lost to cultivation. It strikes easily from cuttings, and now has a lot of children, both in my own garden and at Messrs. Hillings, at a price.

All this was great fun, but we had to get on with the hedges. We planted hornbeam where we couldn't afford yew; and we also planted an avenue of young limes in a rough place and left them to look after themselves. The result of this can be seen in the photograph showing the pleached walk with a statue looking down it. It is now the spring garden. Primroses and polyanthus in a carpet of color grow

beneath bushes of golden forsythia, with many bulbs of narcissus, *Scilla,* grape hyacinth and the like. It is prolonged and finished off by a huge expanse of colored primrose and polyantha growing beneath old nut trees of Kentish cob and filberts. At the end of all this is the herb garden, which always seems to allure visitors, no doubt because it is a secret sentimental little place. "Old World charm" is the phrase I always expect to hear; and nine times out of ten I get it. But, less romantically, the herb garden does supply very useful things to the kitchen.

How shall I sum up this garden, that has been made in so short a time, and yet looks so matured it might have been here for as long as the old Tudor house round which it has been made? This may sound sentimental, but it is very true. One needs years of patience to make a garden; one needs deeply to love it, in order to keep that patience. One needs optimism and foresight. One has to wait. One has to work hard oneself, sometimes as I worked hard, manually, during the war years, cutting all those hedges with shears in my spare time, I hated those hedges, when I looked at my blistered hands; but at the same time I still felt that it had been worthwhile planting them. They were the whole pattern and design and anatomy of the garden; and, as such, were worth any trouble I was willing to take.

The rest of the garden just went wild during the war years. We had begun to get it tidy, and then it reverted to the wildness in which we had found it in 1930. We could not cope with it at all. Now it is better. We have spent three years since the war ended in eradicating the weeds and getting things back into some sort of order. It was like starting at scratch again, and I must record my gratitude to my admirable gardener, John Vass, who returned to us after an adventurous career in the R.A.F., and whose keenness, intelligence, energy and devotion have gone far toward making the garden what it is.

This page, from top: Narrow path walled by sixteen-year-old yews; fragrant thyme creeps between well-worn flagstones; three-tiered hedge above the garden seat; Mr. and Mrs. Nicolson (Miss Sackville-West), with the pleached limes that make an allée.
Opposite page: The allée is full grown, graced by a classic statue overlooking a vista of green serenity.

DIAGRAM SHOWS THE THREE LEVELS OF THE HOUSE

Above: *The Hellers, who are avid gardeners, wanted the landscaping for their house to be typically Floridian. Accordingly, architect Polevitzky limited the lawn areas, using sand and gravel instead. Planting its native sea grasses, cacti, sea grape, palm and melaleuca trees. Water from the swimming pool drains into the fish pond, makes a decorative disposal system. The freshwater pool is above ground.*

WRAPPED IN A PLASTIC SCREEN

Miami, Florida, 1950

Ever since the first Roman built his house around an atrium (patio) and faced a peristyle (porch) to the view, outdoor living has followed the same basic pattern. In Florida, where oranges and outdoor living are equally big business, architects have been seeking new and better ways to make the famous sunshine and sea breeze an integral part of houses. This one, built for Mr. and Mrs. Michael Heller on one of the causeway islands in Miami, reverses the usual approach: instead of opening the rooms to the outdoors, architect Igor Polevitzky has screened off 20 by 76 feet of land and created varying degrees of shelter inside. The raised swimming pool welcomes sun

and breeze through walls and ceiling of plastic screening. For shade, the deck adds a roof made of sheets of asbestos-cement: for privacy, rail-high canvas panels. The Hellers can live outdoors at least 350 days of the year; so their living room is small, has one wall of sliding glass toward the garden near the stairs. Bedrooms are completely enclosed, and have slatted jalousied windows for privacy and ventilation. Because they run the house without servants, they chose materials that require little care—wooden columns are treated with plastic preservative. Windows are aluminum alloy. Everything resists salt air. The diagram, *opposite page, bottom,* shows that within its screened outer walls, the design comprises a two-story house and above-ground swimming pool. A center stair connects the three levels: 1) ground-floor living room, kitchen, and master bedroom; 2) mid-level pool; 3) second-story deck and cabana-guest room. Within the mosquito-proof envelope, doors and windows may be left open at all times; wide eaves of the second-story roof act as a shield against rain. As screens do not catch the wind, hurricanes do no harm.

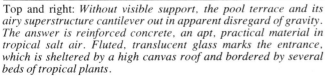

Top and right: *Without visible support, the pool terrace and its airy superstructure cantilever out in apparent disregard of gravity. The answer is reinforced concrete, an apt, practical material in tropical salt air. Fluted, translucent glass marks the entrance, which is sheltered by a high canvas roof and bordered by several beds of tropical plants.*

Above: *From the deck you look down on the pool through branches of a bucida tree rooted in the entrance garden below. Paradoxically, the pool is both indoors and out. The taut structure of webbed steel beams and wood columns ties it in with the house; yet sun streams in, breeze sweeps through, and trees (planted outside against west glare), add a foliage wall. Pale green screening makes it hard to see in, but yields a view of Biscayne Bay.*
Right: *The pool, with its enclose of plastic screening, is like another room.*

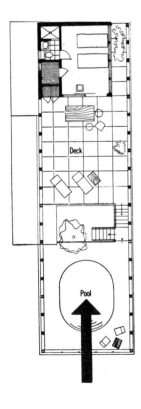

LIVING WITH ART

1960/s

The spread of affluence throughout society changed the look of interior design, as did mass production. It was a decade of personal expression—and what better way to express yourself than by what hangs on your walls? Art, formerly the private interest of a privileged few, was embraced by millions, who responded immediately to the unconventional canvases and experimental abstractions of the New York School, one of the most important movements in post-war modern art. Prints, silk screens, and posters made art accessible to everyone and created a new collectors' market for younger artists. Rooms were built around art; houses looked like sculpture. As a counterpoint to this stripped-down look, there was an explosion of elaborately upholstered furniture. In a revival of the plush, overstuffed Victorian taste, designers created large, richly upholstered sofas and chairs, banquettes, over-sized pieces to luxuriate in. New technological advances in construction gave people machines for living. Houses emerged from the earth, soared to the sky.

This is the living room at "Four Winds," in Palm Beach, Florida, showing the collection of J. Patrick Lannan. A huge painting by Nicholas Krushenick almost dwarfs the python-covered sofa and Italian chairs below it. Its vivid colors are reflected in the brass around the mosaic top of a coffee table. Mr. Lannan's furniture and wall color set off the art, yet stand on their own.

ART EVERYWHERE YOU LOOK

New York City, 1969

When collector S. I. Newhouse, Jr., asked William Baldwin to decorate an apartment for him around the paintings and sculptures he loves, his requirements were "comfortable furniture, but nothing with too strong a personality of its own." His collection has grown and changed—it was young when the decoration was finished—but the simple, livable settings Mr. Baldwin created have proved as hospitable to paintings as to people. The living room is a white shell decorated in a satisfying but visually undemanding blend of natural textures—a pale straw rug, loose covers of beige cotton on comfortable sofas, suede ottomans, beige-striped cotton blinds. The excitement for the eye is in the art: the spring-green shafts of a Caro sculpture, a Morris Louis on the opposite wall. An aquamarine glowing cube-of-concentric-cubes by Leroy Lamis floats on the light from its pedestal beside the arched opening to the hall—and to more planes of paintings—another Morris Louis, a Paul Feeley. Over the arch hangs a dense and secretive Clyfford Still and beside it a soaring, open Frankenthaler. A brilliant Kenneth Noland flares above a black-and-white Jackson Pollock. And all around the room small sculptures add their own kind of riches: the David Smith behind the sofa, the Ruth Vollmer on the coffee table, a Mark Di Suvero on the table under the Louis, an Isaac Witkin on the floor beneath it. None of the art is spotlighted; Mr. Newhouse enjoys the difference he sees in each work as the light in the room changes.

Below: *Mr. Newhouse has hung two enormous canvases—a Jules Olitski and a Kenneth No-land chevron—in his tiny game-and-guest room. Their vitality transforms the room and makes its dimensions irrelevant. The comfortable black leather chair and the black and green tweed sofa blend quietly into the green-clad flor and walls. A golden gleam is provided by the Morio Shinoda metal sculpture on the chair-side table.*

New York City, 1969

LIVING WITH ART

BY JOHN RUSSELL

It is as natural for the collector to think that he has re-invented collecting as it is for the lover to think that he has re-invented love. When he looks at what he has on the wall, all precedents are annulled, all parallels invalid; he is the non-pareil, here and now. Waiting for the lights to change at the corner of Madison and Fifty-seventh, he looks at his great predecessors as if through the butt end of a telescope. Distantly, and very small, he sees Charles I of England in touch with his agents in Venice, Catherine the Great of Russia in correspondence with Diderot about her latest acquisitions, Cardinal Mazarin promenading a favored visitor through his private picture gallery, and the brothers Goncourt holding court in their *grenier d'Auteuil*—an upper room in a leafy suburb of Paris, where top-class drawings by Watteau and Fragonard shared the honors with a pioneer collection of Japanese prints. He envies none of them. They and their collections are dead. He and his are alive, and collecting in his case may take—no, has already taken—a completely new turn.

It has and it hasn't, of course. It is perfectly true that no one has ever before housed in the name of art anything quite like a 40-foot horizontal stripe painting by Kenneth Noland, or a big-scale light-piece by Dan Flavin, or one of Robert Morris's hanging felt sculptures. These would disconcert Mariette, put Augustus of Saxony off his food, and make Sir Richard Wallace run for cover to that inmost room in his house where Titian's "Venus and Andromeda" hang over the bath. A collection of work done in the late 1960s does not so much rival the great collections of the past as propose new standards of validity. It tends, also, to domineer. It drives out earlier work. When Professor William Rubin hung great American paintings of the Nineteen Fifties and Sixties in his re-constituted loft on lower Broadway, they blasted everything else off the wall. Only the Egyptian grammar, so dauntingly displayed on its lectern, was left to argue the case for interests of an earlier date.

It is also true that certain kinds of new art are like very clever children who won't go into the next room to play. They want to stay and be admired. In this category come all varieties of motorized art and everything that has to do with computerized light and sound, holograms, laser beams, built-in telephone bells, tapes of Ethel Merman, ancient radios that scramble six programs at once, and imitations of streetsigns, traffic lights, and illuminated storefronts. All these clamor for our attention in a way that earlier art disdained to do, and they do undoubtedly give a new twist to the phrase "Living with art." Living with art gets to be like living with an iguana: either a privileged situation or an ordeal, according to one's point of view.

This is, as I see it, the only respect in which any genuine break with the past has occurred. A private collector who was bright enough, for instance, to acquire Rauschenberg's "Oracle" would find himself committed to what is in effect a department of the performing arts. He has something in common with the man who buys a Bernini, in that the component parts of "Oracle" are sculptures, which form-up with an effect of unforgettable forlorn grandeur. But he has quite as much in comon with a hypothetical tyrant of taste who would like to make captive house guests of the Julliard Quartet and force them to play all night and all day. "Oracle" is a sculpture-for-sound that only comes completely to life when each of its component pieces is honking, braying, tooting, haranguing, and spewing out static.

This is bound up, also, with something that is widespread among younger artists of consequence: the wish, that is to say, to produce "art that doesn't look like art" and to do it with "materials that don't have too much art history in them." This ambition is often thwarted by the rapidity with which both art and art history can adjust to the new: the sculptures of Caro in the S.I. Newhouse apartment, and of Grosvenor in the J. Patrick Lannan house, have already an old-masterly look. They have settled down. And wide-minded visitors to these two collections may find themselves reminded of conjunctions which, at the time, seemed no less daring: the combinaton, for instance, of panel-paintings by Duccio with Louis XVI furniture in the Park Avenue apartment of Mrs. John D. Rockefeller. Quality is what counts: where it is present in sufficient strength there is no such thing as incongruity.

Perhaps there is a divide, however. It separates those who try to do "the same, only better," from those whose object is a completely new lifestyle. When Stavros Niarchos bought the Hotel de Chanaleilles in Paris in 1956, he bought a dilapidated folly that had been allowed to go quietly into decay. In no time at all Mr. and Mrs. Niarchos gave it the kind of high gloss that in the 18th century would have been beyond the reach of even unlimited wealth. To this they added paintings from El Greco and Goya to Cézanne and Rouault, a silver dinner service from Berkeley Castle, a silver-gilt toilet set that had belonged to the Empress Josephine, and a Savonnerie carpet that Louis XV is thought to have given to his father-in-law, Stanislas Leczinski. That is one way of "living with art," and I doubt if there was a time in history at which it could be done quite so expeditiously.

The other way is quite different. Let me epitomize it with the following composite and quite imaginary apartment. A far extreme from the super-polite Hotel de Chanaleilles, it is a disused gymnasium in the East Village. Punch ball and parallel bars have been left as they were beneath a high, glassed, and vaulted roof. Changing rooms have been equipped with communal baths of Japanese design. A large scrap metal sculpture by John Chamberlain perches like the Winged Victory of Samothrace on a cornice that was put up in 1885 and has mysteriously survived to this day. The great bare waxed floor is empty, but a flotilla of tortoise-like pieces by Robert Breer crawls to and fro across its length and breadth. The 7-foot-high Open-E-Ze bag is by Alex Hay. The contents of the picture gallery are changed continuously; this week a combine-painting by Rauschenberg is back from the restorer, who has given it the kind of attention Uccello's frescoes got in Florence in the early 1950s. The invisible barrier that in earlier apartments separated art from life is nowhere to be seen, or sensed, and indeed it does not exist. Art is there to be lived with, not looked at. It is not an alternative to life but a part of it. It is not a background, and not a foreground, it is a part of a continuum. And it is present as a source of energy and not as a medal for being alert, or for being rich, or for having a sense of acquisition. "Living with art" used to mean giving the electric circuits of society just as much extra voltage as they would bear. Today, if it means anything, it means severing those circuits at the source with a very sharp knife and starting again with the miniaturized equipment that belongs to the late 1960s and to no previous time.

Every available square inch of wall in Mr. Newhouse's living room is tapestried with paintings; every vantage point offers a change of perspective, a fresh juxtaposition to enchant the eye: Barnett Newman's "The Word" over the fireplace, Anthony Caro's green steel structure slashing up to the Alexander Liberman on the ceiling, a Max Bill marble nestling on the hearth, two small Snelsons on a pair of tables flanking the fireplace.

Powerful paintings dominate the dark-walled bedroom in Mr. Newhouse's apartment. William Baldwin's design for the master bedroom is a beige and brown cave. But the brown velvet paper that clothes walls and ceiling also creates a marvelous background for art. "You don't have to limit yourself to white walls to enjoy painting and sculpture," Mr. Newhouse remarks. "Any solid color makes a satisfying backdrop."

Right: *In the bedroom, the view from the bed takes in a huge, mysterious Mark Rothko, a black and white Barnett Newman lithograph, a darkly luminous Morris Louis and a Paul Feeley sculpture to the right of the Rothko.*
Below: *Another Rothko hangs over the bed and a Julius Bissier over each table lamp.*

"COMFORT, RICH COLOR, AND THE THINGS WE LOVE"

New York City, 1969

To step inside Mr. and Mrs. Oscar de la Renta's Manhattan duplex is to leave the hubbub of the city street somewhere in the past. Now you are in another world, deeply comfortable, intensely personal, silent as a whisper. A world two people of fashion—he the designer, she an editor of *Vogue*—have created for themselves and their guests. "Our philosophy is comfort—comfort in everything. We think you should be able to sit everywhere. Really sink down, with lots of pillows for your back, places to put your drink down, your feet up." To accomplish this aura of total comfort they followed to the last detail one simple rule: everything in abundance. Every room has two layers of carpeting, thickly upholstered furniture, profusions of pillows, collections crowding tabletops, a rich concentration of color, and pattern upon pattern upon pattern—all put together with the sure skill of two people with absolute self-assurance and a great sense of style. Inspired by their collection of Chinese porcelains, they turned the dining room, *left* and *top,* just off the garden into a fantasy of blue and white; leopardy-print fabric shirred across the glass ceiling and covering all the furniture; walls of tile-patterned paper; a geometric needlepoint rug harlequinading on white wall-to-wall carpeting; the myriad patterns and shapes of the porcelains themselves. "We found some of our nicest things in New York: the two big plates on the wall, the carpet balls (for an English game), the deer—not blue, but Chinese and we love him." Across the room, the round dining table, in a spill of skirt that cascades onto the floor, fills the L of a built-in banquette bolstered with three rows of squashy pillows. "Here is where we love to entertain friends for dinner, or have Sunday lunches together when the garden is blooming."

Left: *Along one wall of the dining room, a glorious mélange of blue and white porcelains holding their splendid own against the sparkle of mirror on the wall and on the table.*
This page, top: *Bamboo chairs pull up to the round dining table for dinner parties.*
Center: *In the bedroom, delicate petit-point pillows look delicious on the flowered loveseat.*
Below: *Over the bed in its white-framed alcove, a painting by Michaud.*

233

"We think every room should have a color of its own," say the de la Rentas. "In French we call it a *camaieu*—a family of shades ranging from just off-white to very very deep." In the living room the *camaieu* began with the pale beige sculptured paneling that came with the apartment. Then they added a complex of furniture drenched in the natural colors and textures of earth and wood: two big cushiony sofas, a patterned rug spread on top of chocolate carpeting, wicker baskets holding potted orchids in full exotic bloom—and a mirrored end wall that doubles the whole room. "Rooms saturated with a single color make collecting exciting. Wherever in the world we go we are always wandering through the shops. If we see a marble egg we say, oh lct's buy that for the beige room." Already the tables abound with the de la Rentas' inexhaustible collection of treasures. On the coffee table is a big eighteenth-century Sicilian jewel case of tortoise shell inlaid with mother-of-pearl. On the other table are two of the twelve columns Napoleon is said to have presented to his twelve generals. "The atmosphere, we think, is the most important thing about a room. It should be a room people are happy to be in, a room that promotes relaxation and good conversation, a room that lives. We both admire flowers because they add so much to a room—they make it come alive."

Opposite page: *In the living room, the linen sofa is covered with pillows of Balinese batik.*
Left: *A profusion of patterns, singular bond between a room of cordial browns and fresh blues.*
Above: *Viewed across the tortoiseshell box on the coffee table, the suede sofa is covered with leopard velvet pillows. The paintings above the sofas are by the de la Rentas' friend, Feito, enhancing the room's colors.*

Below: *In the smoldering-red study, the sofa and armchairs are cheek-to-cheek, the two big mirrors face-to-face. With its glossy red paneling and luxurious upholstery, this is the de la Rentas' favorite room for their hours at home. "When we have no guests we are never downstairs. We even have our dinner in the study." Everything in the intimate little room is designed for comfort, relaxation . . .*

ART
INDOORS
AND OUT

Palm Beach, Florida, 1969

This is the collection of J. Patrick Lannan at "Four Winds," Palm Beach. Look in front of you, art is there. Look behind you, it is there. Look overhead, underfoot, out the window, art is there. And the range of art at "Four Winds" is tremendous: from ancient Japanese clay figures to contemporary American works, from wall-to-wall canvases to small drawings, from enormous sculptures to small masks. All are mixed with a free hand and each work seems to be placed almost casually. Yet each (you conclude, after studying it) is exactly where it should be. Repeatedly, as you walk around the lawns and gardens you catch sight of powerful sculpture, counterpoint to trees and planting. The only place where art is arranged in formal gallery style is a wing of the house devoted to the collection of the Lannan Foundation . . . Indoors, the art hangs or stands against architectural backgrounds in the British Colonial tradition, and much of the furniture is antique.

Top right: *In a guest room, against a background of lacquered black walls, paintings by Robert Goodnough and Nicholas Krushenick.*
Top left: *Peter Forakis sculpture under a spreading ficus.*
Center right: *By the pool, dramatic cantilevered sculpture by Robert Grosvenor.*
Center left: *Well-filled gallery in the bedroom hall, including a canvas by Kenneth Noland.*
Far right: *In the light-filled living room, vivid contrasts—Japanese Haniwa figures versus contemporary sculpture, Mayan pottery versus modern suede-covered sofas. Standing in the window bay, a copper-plated iron sculpture by Julius Schmidt. To the right (around the room) hang a painting by Philip Roeber, a Neil Williams, a Kenneth Noland, and floating overhead, a Robert Goodnough.*
Near right: *In one of the rooms devoted to the collection of the Lannan Foundation, even the furniture is art—two chairs and a table by the Mexican sculptor. Pedro Friedeberg.*
Bottom right: *View from one of the windows of a work in painted steel by Kosso Eloul.*

In the marble-paved loggia of "Four Winds," your eye meets art wherever you turn. The corners of the loggia—both furnished identically with glass, steel, and leather-covered furniture—are dominated by a series of ten vivid panels by painter-sculptor Peter Forakis, and under each glass coffee table is an area rug that serves as a "canvas" for a painting by Horia Damian. A bronze by John Storrs stands guard over this corner.

THE WHITE FIREHOUSE

Left: *White duck portières drape the old engine entrance to the firehouse.*

San Francisco, California, 1967

John Dickinson, a young San Franciscan designer of furniture and interiors and an accomplished draftsman, lives with his three cats in an old firehouse. The picturesque structure with its bell tower and gingerbread dates back to 1893 . . . Mr. Dickinson has set up his office in the rear of the building; his living room, bedroom and bath on the second floor; his dining room and kitchen in the old cookhouse at the rear of the back garden—and furnished and decorated them in a style peculiarly his own. White, etched with black and warmed by natural wood tones, predominates in almost every room. He mixes good antiques with dressed-up junk, beautifully made furniture of his own design with valueless artifacts of another day . . . He has a flair for taming ornate Victorian and Art Nouveau until they seem the epitome of simplicity. Trompe l'oeil decoration is one of his passions, and what he can't buy he does himself. White is his favorite color because of its infinite variety. "Every shade of white lives happily with every other shade," he explains. "What is handsomer than blue-white with creamy-white?" Although his favorite furniture period is nineteenth century, he doesn't confine himself exclusively to the Victorian. "I'd get stale. To me, a room should be a mishmash of things you can't live without."

The dining-sitting room with Napoleonic officer's bed and ferry-boat chairs.

Mr. Dickinson's bed, which he designed, is mottled in faux bois *tiger bamboo.*

Around the pine table of Mr. Dickinson's own design, French iron garden chairs. The table is set with white earthenware, stainless steel.

238

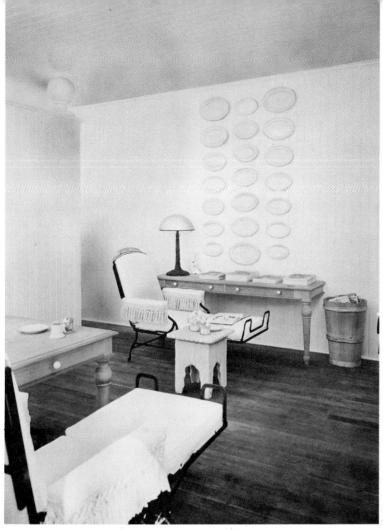

A collection of old ironstone platters above a Dickinson-designed console.

Dining table lamp, with bronze Art Nouveau tree trunk for its base.

Trompe l'oeil townhouse armoire, complete with lamp in window.

A sheaf of garden tools, enameled white, and Italian vineyard hamper.

THE TOTAL TOWNHOUSE

New York City, 1969

Manhattan's newest example of a townhouse, recreated from the bones of an 1870 coach house, is the suave steel and glass residence designed by architect Paul Rudolph. Behind its sleek façade, a low hallway leads into a soaring glass-walled room 27 feet high. The entire rear of the house is a floor-to-roof greenhouse, three walls of which are lined with 8-foot high mirrors. The living room's towering loftiness is dramatically contrasted with the snugness of a dining room tucked under a 7-foot high ceiling. Carpeted stairs lead to a mezzanine sitting room suspended over the dining room. The stair landing stretches along the wall, and at the far end, cantilevered treads climb to a platform that leads to an upper door in the greenhouse wall, which can be opened to circulate fresh air.

Top left: *Sleek façade of Mr. Rudolph's house.*
Top right: *Low-ceilinged dining area, with table of laminated clear plastic 3-inch cubes.*
Right: *Opposite the sitting room, but on a higher level, are guest bedroom and bath, which can be closed off by sliding doors. A 5-foot-wide, wall-hugging bridge (see section, below,) connects them to the billiard-room level in the front part of the 3-story house.*
Opposite page: *From the sitting room mezzanine one looks across the living room toward the spectacular three-story greenhouse. The mirrored coffee table is 6 feet square. Black slate paves the entire first floor.*

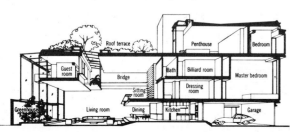

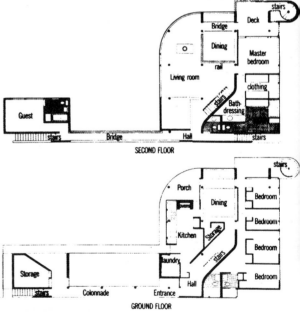

TOP FLOOR

SECOND FLOOR

GROUND FLOOR

Long Island, New York, 1969

"A HOUSE THAT SETS US FREE"

For Ellin and Renny Saltzman, their crisply modern house is a machine for living that sets them free every weekend. During the week, they work in a world of fashion and furniture—she's a topflight fashion consultant and he's a well-known interior designer. Their days speed by in New York City, but, for their children, they wanted a country house for weekends and holidays. They chose architect Richard Meier to design it, and he created for them a construction in both time and space—it unfolds completely only as you walk around it. "Our city apartment is quite formal, and one I've lived in since childhood," says Mrs. Saltzman. "We bought everything new for this house, so that I came to it like a bride."

Above: *Plan of the three-story house: top floor mostly air space–a mezzanine for children's play; second level for living room and master bedroom; ground level for children's rooms, dining room and kitchen.* Left: *Exterior, showing three stories and colonnade to guest house/storage.*

"Before we went to see Richard Meier, we made notes of everything we'd ever wanted in a house," says Mrs. Saltzman. "Small bedrooms so the children would be out and into the sunshine. Several exits to the outdoors. Loads of closets to hold clothes . . ." The Saltzmans also wanted: "Easy-to-care-for things like self-cleaning ovens and permanently finished floors. Wash-basins built 42 inches high so you don't have to bend double. A kitchen big enough to breakfast in as well as a dining room where we could seat fourteen. We know that might not sound like casual entertaining, but the best food in the world is nothing if you have to balance it on your lap." "At times the house has such purity it seems almost spiritual," says Mrs. Saltzman. "But if for no other reason, I would feel good about it because the children so adore it. Everyone, whether on the first or tenth visit, likes to wander around. Guests relax almost visibly and act at home."

Top: *Another view of the house, like a white cubistic cluster rising on a three-acre plan of sea-air tousled grass.*
Above: *At night, the house seems like the superstructure of a luxury cruise ship. From the top deck, miles of ocean and shoreline can be seen. Inside, superbly engineered lighting washes the walls with even brightness. The spiral staircase leads up to both the top and master bedroom decks without carrying traffic through the house.*

In the Saltzmans' Richard Meier-designed house, nine steel supports allowed great freedom in placing interior walls. These white columns, the freestanding fireplace, and dark stained floors seem a garden of abstractions. The railed bridge spans the 25-foot-high dining room, and leads to a sun deck off the master bedroom. Like a ship, there are decks on the two top floors, connected by a spiral staircase. "There is always room, no matter how many we invite," say the Saltzmans. Yet at the same time, "There is always a corner where you can be private."

Left and opposite page: *The two-story living room, showing areas for conversation, games, reading, stargazing. At the end of the plushly upholstered built-in couch, white lacquered cabinets conceal music system and bar.*
Above: *The 20-by-40 foot pool is set away from the house to mute the splashing and shouting. Fenced and surrounded by a wide paved terrace, it becomes a separate entertaining and barbecue area.*
Below: *In the dining room, to maximize the view, furnishings are held to a pair of paintings, eight chairs covered in glove leather and an expandable Formica-covered table.*

A ROMANTIC HOUSE OF SUNLIT ARCHES

Winnetka, Illinois, 1966

Beautiful and enormously alive, this house was designed by I.W. Colburn for Mr. and Mrs. Robert E. Brooker, employing the archmotifs he has made his trademark. . . . Built around a domed atrium, the Brookers' house is a snow-white pavilion of painted brick embraced on four sides with a perfectly symmetrical loggia of arches topped with arched finials of interlaced masonry. The house is built in 20-foot sqare bays, four wide, thrcc dccp. Although the plan and form are basically simple, the handling of the materials—brick, plaster, terrazzo, adroitly effects elegance and richness.

Above: *At the rear of the house, the white gravel ''lawn'' gives way to a flagstone-paved square enclosed by a low brick wall, boxwood hedges, and an ornamental border of black gravel inset with squares of white gravel. A true parterre, this is the Brookers' garden-and-terrace. All the flowers are potted.*
Below left: *The front of the house is like the back and differs from the sides in the number of arches. (There are sixteen at front and back, twelve on each side.) At 20-foot intervals around the perimeter, the bays are marked off by 2-foot-square supporting pillars with honeycomb finials . . . This stylish setting is made even more so by a little allée of trees that leads from the road to a gravel turnaround with two slim columns topped by bronze birds sculpted by Sylvia Shaw Judson.*

Light is a tangible element of the design. An atrium dome bathes the center of the house with sunlight, and light through the arches that girdle the house permeates the rooms. Each of the square bays that make up the plan, *below right,* is either a main room or a composite of smaller, related rooms. Slightly smaller than a bay, the study is a continuation of the living room, just as the dining court is an alfresco continuation of the dining room. Master bedroom, bath and two dressing rooms (adding up to two bays) are secluded in a quiet corner at the rear of the house; kitchen at the front. Interior designer, Louise Runnells.

Above: *In summer, the Brookers dine almost nightly in their court, between walls thick with bittersweet . . . Mrs. Brooker can seat sixteen indoors in the dining room, with the help of a black lacquer top that extends the marble-topped table almost to the size of the rug. Party space is doubled by the dining room's adjoining courtyard. On cool nights, electric heaters take off the chill, and the court becomes a charming room in candlelight.*
Below left: *Beyond the atrium's indoor garden is the living room, which is a bay-and-a-quarter long, with white velvet sofas and the Brookers' round-the-world furniture collection.*
Below right: *The atrium's third arm is the dining room, where a marble and steel table gleams in the company of Regency chairs, a Japanese screen, and an antique Agra rug.*

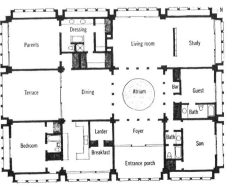

Rectangular plan, showing atrium framed by 16 arches.

HOUSE OF OUR TIME LATTICED WITH LIGHT

Maryland, 1969

As simple and stalwart in construction as a country barn, yet marvelously diverse in design, this is a house truly of the present. Designed by Moore/Turnbull and Rurik Ekstrom, architects, and built a year ago on a three-quarter-acre lot in Maryland for Dr. and Mrs. Stanley Tempchin, the 4,000-square-foot structure is unmistakably NOW—a kinetic juggling of light, levels, shapes. In the nave-like central gallery—the major element of the house—four interior walls pierced with irregularly shaped cutouts rise as high as 24 feet to create a tower of light: an inner sanctum. Throughout the house, ten skylights capture the sight of treetops, sun, clouds, stars. . . . The spine of the house is the gallery, which soars to the roof indoors, and connects house and garage outdoors. The plan disposes major rooms on either side of the gallery but lops off corners and juts out in bays so no two rooms are alike . . . The house is surrounded by decks and patios.

Right: *View of the gallery from the library, at the highest level of the house, up into the treetops, down toward the entry's "slate rug," then through the open front door to the roofed outside gallery that stretches 51 feet to the garage—later to become a guest house.*
Far right: *The view down to the tree trunks behind the house encompasses the snug paneled upper and lower libraries and white living room.*
Top: *At the front of the house, broad stairs of railroad ties ascend to the gallery. Beyond, the terrace off the kitchen backed up by a tool shed, shaded by oak trees. Beyond the parapet of the deck off the living room, a paved patio and the garage. Landscape architects, Thurmond Donovan Associates.*

9 ROOMS IN SEARCH OF A VIEW

At the push of a button,
the house revolves

Wilton, Connecticut, 1969

Oon a pastoral hillside, a breathtaking house perches amid breathtaking scenery. Resembling a giant glass-and-steel spaceship, it creates a stir—at the press of a button, all nine rooms of the house spin around, reorienting to any point of the compass. It was a simple love of nature that prompted the design of this imaginative house that architect Richard Foster created for his own family. They couldn't decide which marvelous view they liked best—so Mr. Foster came up with this carousel house. It consists of a circular series of pie-shaped rooms that revolve around a stairway core enclosed in a fixed pedestal . . . (See plan below.)

Left: From a single spot in their living room, the Fosters can enjoy with push-button ease any moment of the delightful 360-degree panorama that surrounds their revolving, glass-walled castle in the air.
Top left: Revolving on its stationary pedestal at night, lights on the round stone terrace shine up on the cedar-shingled pedestal and front door. To the left, granite stairs lead to court and garage.
Top right: The living room, the central control center for the spaceship-house. Painting next to the fireplace is by Marcelo Bonevardi. Walls are carpeted.

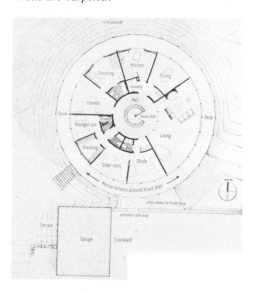

NEW ADVENTURES IN LIVING

U.S.A., 1960–1968

Left: This house on Long Island Sound, Connecticut, is built on a platform among the rocks by the beach. Architect, Ulrich Franzen.
Above: Walls that look like modern paintings become a practical living space in Chestnut Hill, Pennsylvania. Architect, Louis Kahn.

At the foot of a cliff in La Jolla, California, a spectacular round house is the guest house of the Samuel H. Bells. A perfect circle 30 feet in diameter, its roof and walls are poured concrete. An electric tram takes you there. Architects, Dale Naegle and Associates.

Above: A new version of the contemporary style was used for Mr. and Mrs. Harold L. Light's house outside Portland, Oregon. It is made up of shingles and bays, with a pyramid-roofed living room, situated on a gently sloping site. Architects, Donald Blair and Saul Zaik.

Architectural exuberance crowns these soaring rectangles and brings to astonished life this house designed for Mr. and Mrs. Arthur W. Milam on Ponte Vedra Beach, Florida. It shows an unfettered pattern of trellised walls and light indoors and out. Architect, Paul Rudolph.

Strangely beautiful, this monolithic house in Westport, Connecticut, rises above the shore as an inspiration to the beholder. Some find its rough-textured walls fortress-like; others see in its overlapping forms the sheltering construction of a seashell. Architect, John M. Johansen.

The Herbert Monts's house in New York State is a rectangular structure of steel, aluminum and glass, with a plate steel roof that hovers over the one-story building like a great folded wing. The terrace façade is almost all glass. Architect, Stanley Salzman of Edelman and Salzman.

This contemporary two-story house in Cambridge, Massachusetts, is based on a New England barn, enlivened by bays and skylights, and by whole sections of walls opened up with sliding doors and fixed panes of glass. In front, a swimming pool. Architect and owner, Hugh Stubbins.

A serene composition of stuccoed planes, rich wood paneling, sweeping panes of glass in this house in Chestnut Hill, Pennsylvania, geometry assumes a warm and human aspect, and at the same time the art of living acquires an exciting new dimension. Architect, Louis Kahn.

Soaring pillars of lime concrete block that resemble a formal row of columns give classic dignity to this house belonging to Mr. and Mrs. Frederick A. Deering at Casey Key, Sarasota, Florida. Solid and sturdy, the rear façade faces the beach. Architect, Paul Rudolph.

Wanderers through the purlieus of East Hampton, Long Island, are wide-eyed when they come upon Round House, Jack Lenor Larsen's year-round retreat, inspired by an African compound. There are three houses—main house, guest house, and studio—nestling near a man-made lake. The main house and adjacent studio are built in poured concrete, weathered in a Congolese design, by Masahiko Yamamoto. The terrace painted by Gerald Pierce. Architect, Robert Hays Rosenberg of Rosenberg and Futterman.

This umbrella house belonging to Mr. and Mrs. Frank S. Wyle, in North Fork, California, is sited on a 3,200-acre virgin tract of land. Indigenous woods were used—oak, cedar, redwood. The two-story living room has a glass wall. Architect, John L. Rex of Honnold and Rex.

A pergola and man-made terraces—one built like a Mayan pyramid—link this house in Fairfield, Connecticut, to its deep woodland site. A cluster of skylighted towers, plus windows and decks, take advantage of the view and bring in daylight. Architect, Edward Larrabee Barnes.

This villa, with its twin glass-gabled roofs, its trellised terraces, its pale sand-colored concrete brilliant against the blue sky, is part of the New Seabury development between Chatham and Hyannis, Massachusetts. The framework of the house consists of fifteen pavilion-like bays, each 15 feet square, constructed of prefabricated concrete posts and beams. Other ready-made parts are roof and floor panels. The bays can be enclosed with the wall panels to form rooms, or left as panels of glass—flexible space. Architect, Robert Damora.

A HOUSE
OF
SIX PAVILIONS

Cap Bénat, St. Tropez, France, 1967

High on a Riviera promontory sits a house that, seen from the sea, looks like a tiny village clustered under a great undulating sail. Designed by the American architect Philip Johnson for M. and Mme. Eric Boissonnas, it is a summer and weekend house planned for intensive use. It consists of six pavilions of which five are enclosed to form the village. The sixth is open but roofed by the ''sail'' and the entire complex is arranged around two courtyards (see plan below). Two of the pavilions are guest houses, the other four comprise the main house. . . . They are strung out in spearlike formation that points out to sea like a ship's prow, thus presenting to the biting Mistral wind only the narrow edge of the complex. All are heated for winter.

Opposite page, top: *Outdoor living room, open to the sea.* Left: *Open pavilion with canopy-like roof; paved with black slate blocks, polished.* Top left: *The columns supporting the canopy roof are of heavily textured concrete. Most of the furniture, inside and out, was brought from Denmark.* Top right: *In the living room is a prefabricated fireplace for chilly nights, and three walls of glass to embrace the magnificient view.*

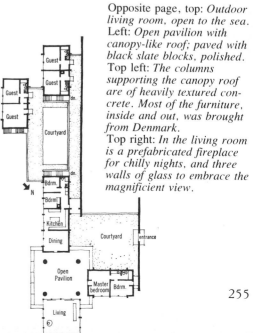

255

APARTMENT FILLED WITH SILVER AND WHITE

Milan, Italy, 1968

The young Italian architect Vittorio Gregotti and his wife, Carmen, took the 260-year-old Palazzo Trivulzio in Milan—with its towering ceilings and sculptured plaster friezes, its tall doors, windows and balconies, and fired it with the ebullience of youth, using simple measures that could be adapted to any house anywhere. They filled the rooms with the shimmer of silver and white that has become the international signature of young design. They added the curves of Thonet chairs, the comfort of capacious sofas, and all the stray furniture and bibelots that continually seem to follow them home. In one great room they call the studio—a room they use as living room, dining room, and library—they merely washed the ancient ceiling and sprayed the walls white. But at one end, partially screening a balcony, they boldly erected a wall and sprayed it silver . . . To reach the balcony, they dragged in a salvaged iron spiral stairway and painted it more white. In front of the silver wall they placed a rattan chair, a curvilinear design by Mr. Gregotti, painted that silver, too. Everything in the house adds to the jubilant pulse that beats in time with the Gregottis' own—a living tempo that impels them to acquire their treasures on impulse, or spurred by admiration for their friends' work, or by faith in the architect's own talents. The furnishings throughout reflect the Gregottis' varied enthusiasms.

Opposite page: *At the library end of the studio, a fake silver wall and a nineteenth-century iron stairway lead up to a balcony lined with white-painted metal bookshelves. The fake wall is dramatized with a painting by Giosetta Fioroni.*
This page, above: *At the living-dining end of the studio, capacious sofas and Thonet chairs; a tall lamp designed by Alvar Aalto, an Andrea Cascella sculpture on the floor by the window; white walls; dried flowers everywhere.*

Below left: *In the vast bathroom, the utilitarian gleam of white fixtures against glossy deep purple walls. A splendid baroque Mexican mirror is orbited by a white-painted Thonet clothes tree, a bathroom stool (the gift of Finnish architect Alvar Aalto). Light fixture designed by Mr. Gregotti; Villon poster.*
Below right: *In the quiet white-walled bedroom ruled over by the large Genoese scrolled iron bed, two more of the architect's silver-painted chairs, echoing the silver of the overmantel mural, also painted by Giosetta Fioroni.*

ROMANTIC SUMMERS IN A WALLED TOWN

The David Hicks family
in the south of France

Roquebrune-sur-Argens, France, 1969

Halfway between Cannes and St. Tropez, the tiny medieval town of Roquebrune-sur-Argens, the picture-postcard kind of spot artists like to paint—and if they are incurable romantics like the designer David Hicks—to live in for six weeks of the summer and random weekends during the winter. He and his wife, Lady Pamela, and their three children, fly from London to Nice then drive along the seashore to their eighteenth-century summer house . . . Dated 1780, it has always been a townhouse. There is a little garden in the rear, but no outdoor space to soak up the sun in comfort. So the Hickses sought and found an annex, a much smaller structure, three minutes' walk away, that was once a basket weaver's atelier. Once the the property was acquired, its sizable garden gave way to a swimming pool bordered by enough terrace space to lunch on . . . ''Interior decoration,'' says David Hicks, ''is the art of achieving the maximum with the minimum.'' True to his credo, both the main house and pool house are marked by a refreshing lack of fussiness . . . Yet Mr. Hicks loves heterogeneity in the objects he collects and combines them with a free-and-easy skill . . .

Above left: *The playhouse, once a basket weaver's atelier, its big garden now turned into a swimming pool.*
Above right: *Main room in poolhouse, is both lounge and dining room. Open kitchen is lined up along one wall.*
Left: *The Hickses' balconied summer haven—their main house.*
Below center: *Three-dimensional accents in the main room of the poolhouse include such disparate elements as elegant columns from a razed London mansion and pottery from Vallauris—Picasso's old stamping ground. Bold black and white fabric covers the tables.*
Below right: *The library in the main house is both Mr. Hicks's study, and, in winter, a sitting room warmed by the red of a tweed-covered sofa. In an unconventional grouping, the sofa, two arm-chairs and a side chair form a ''frame'' around a tea table. A wall of books opposite holds thrillers and sober sources of reference.*
Opposite page, bottom, from left: *In the Hickses' own bedroom, the bed is at dead center—''cooler, pretier''—with a Directoire chair at each corner, a night table-cest at the head. In the parental bathroom, Mr. Hicks brought into play a favorite notion: a tub thrust into the center of the room like a porcelain peninsula and swagged like a bed with looped-up linen curtains. In a guest room, with rugged beams, colors are unexpectedly delicate. A country armoire offers jacket-length hanging space.*

In the main-house dining room, tile floor provides a small sea of soft color. Dining chairs of bent and woven wood come from the Dordogne (snapped up for $3 each). Bright color comes from apothecary bottles in Welsh dresser; a Danish plastic tray, lustrous as a plum; tablecloths made in Japan for the East Africa trade. Overhead a gleaming brass chandelier spreads its sinuous arms.

GREAT NEW DESIGN AND PLAN FOR A BATHROOM

New York City, 1969

Look-alike bathrooms are as extinct as the dodo bird, thank goodness. But are you ready for what's taking place? House & Garden believes that a bathroom should be one of the most exciting, with-it, uniquely personal places in the house—a room you like to be in and so good-looking that the moment you step into it, you're automatically beautiful. On these pages, you'll find new planning ideas and brand-new equipment splendid enough to make a plunge-and-perfume-mad Roman green with envy. Given plenty of room—plus the talents of designer Alberto Pinto—and you have a bedroom-bathroom magically dove-tailed into something very new indeed: a spa to sleep in and, with a sun lamp, to tan in. The tub is sunk into a raised platform that separates sleeping and dressing areas; twin lavatories are mounted on plastic bases near the platform steps. Designed for man and wife, the sleeping spa (see plan, opposite page) is divided into three basic areas: bed, tub, and lavatory space; two 5-by-5-foot cubicles—one for make-up; one for toilet and bidet; dressing room and storage space.

Above: *In this bathroom designed by Alberto Pinto, double bands of translucent plastic, lighted from behind, climb two walls and cross the ceiling. Above the bed, a light sculpture by Ronoldo Ferri. Eljer plumbing fixtures; Amtico carpet; Filon plastic panels; Cannon terrycloth.*

Below left: *Mirrored inner walls of 12-inch-square tiles visually enhance the illusion of space in the tiny toilet and make-up space. For light, yet complete privacy, the walls the rooms share with the bedroom are made of darkly translucent plastic on illuminated bands.*

Below center: *The leggy, glass-topped table and clear plastic chair fill the make-up room, but with no sense of crowding. Above the table, a mirror equipped with swiveling lights spotlight the face at strategic points during the make-up ritual that takes place here.*

Below right: *In the bedroom area, the sculpture-like bases of the two lavatories are separated by a partition of double-faced mirror. No countertops, but space enough for immediate needs. The giraffe-necked bottle holds a declaration of male independence—Fabergé's Brut.*

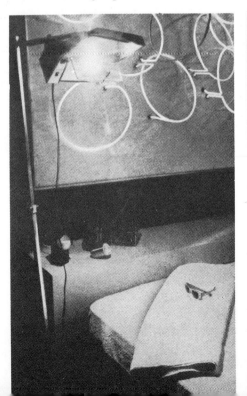

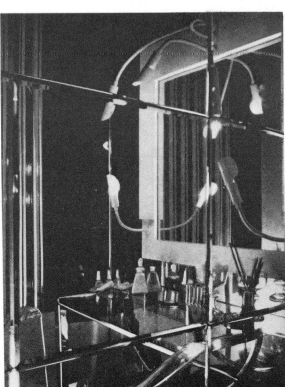

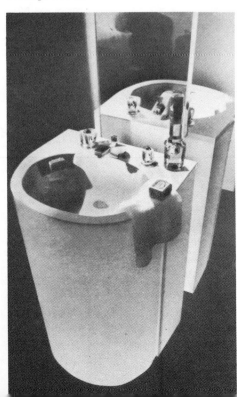

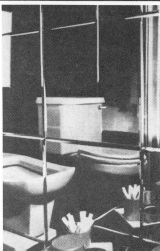

Above: *Sunk into a raised platform separating sleeping and dressing areas, is an elegant tub. Near the platform steps are twin lavatories mounted back to back on plastic bases lighted from within.*

Left: *The dressing room was designed as much for fun as for serious storage. (It is a mini-verson of the Cardin boutique at Bonwit Teller.) Clothes are hung in open lockers arranged around a terrycloth seat—a perch to watch family fashion shows.*

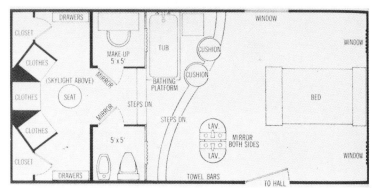

U.S.A., 1966

The best of today's swimming pools are so closely and subtly integrated with the design of the house or the landscape that it is not always easy to tell if a pool is meant for swimming or for visual adornment. Almost always the answer is: both. Some of the new pools are naturalistic, suggesting that a spring-fed pond has merely been channeled and tamed, as natural greenery is pruned and tamed, the better to enjoy it. Some pools are shaped as abstractly as cut gems and like gems seem to be the primary inspiration for their settings. Occasionally a pool is built within the confines of the house itself, where it adds its shimmer to the vistas from adjoining rooms. Other pools meander from indoors out, flowing under walls as serenely as quiet streams flow under bridges. And all are framed with terraces of meticulous masonry or grace by charming poolside structures that serve as engaging spots for entertaining.

Left: Roofed above, screened on three sides, and protected by the house on the fourth, the free-form pool in the Darrell Fleegers' house in Coconut Grove, Florida, is designed for all-weather swimming and easy maintenance. It is the chief ornament of a two-story, 20-foot-high veranda room that lies under the roof of the house itself. Designed by Darrell Fleeger.

Below: A deep-walled pool flows under a bridge in the Jerome Holts' house in Beverly Hills, California, and continues into the atrium of the house itself. Like the bridge, both the outdoor terrace and the atrium floor are made of highly polished terrazzo. Since air as well as water can enter under the bridge, all the rooms surrounding the atrium can be closed off in cool weather by means of sliding glass doors. The architect was Harold W. Lewis.

Opposite page: A delightful surprise is in store for first-time visitors to the Donald Sheffs' pool at Great Neck, New York—a table-top island emerging a few inches above the water level. Like the pool and surrounding terrace, the island is built of concrete, but faced with mica stone that blends naturally with the encircling greenery and flowers.

THE NEW LOOK OF SWIMMING POOLS

LIVING WITH NATURE

The rush to space-age technology was tempered by an equally powerful consciousness of the diminishing resources of a heavily populated planet. The wonders of computer-controlled electricity, plumbing, labor-saving devices, and leisure-time toys paved the way to a reassessment of natural wonders—of growing your own fruit and vegetables, and of surrounding yourself with the sweet-smelling things of nature. The urge to reacquaint the human spirit with nature was reflected in the houses built this decade; they had solar heating, indoor-outdoor rooms, greenhouse walls, spa baths, furniture made of natural woods and covered with naturally grown fabrics. There was an increased specialization of "purpose" or regional houses—people wanted desert houses, beach houses, ski lodges, weekend hideaways. A new spirit of back-to-the-land romance colored these years; a new look at tradition allowed a glass house to be filled with much-loved treasures. Quilts, Navajo blankets, Dhurrie rugs, and folk art became popular, inspiring a new interest in handcrafts of all kinds. A revival of interest in both Art Nouveau and Art Deco paralleled the overall feeling expressed in the

1970/s

decade that somehow it must be possible to retain the values of the past while appreciating the dramatic breakthroughs of the present.

The greenhouse center of a farmhouse in Pennsylvania designed by architect Paul Rudolph. A flying bridge at the far end connects living room with study.

A 20TH CENTURY FARMHOUSE WITH A GREENHOUSE CORE

Pennsylvania, 1973

It looks like a cliff or a floating rock with windows or maybe a spaceship, but it isn't. Designed by architect Paul Rudolph to perch assertively on top of the highest hill around in northeastern Pennsylvania, this is a farmhouse, headquarters of Stonewall Farms, where race horses are raised. It is also a greenhouse oriented to the light with cast stone-aggregate eyebrows on the south side for summer shade and shelter that still welcome in the lower sun of ice-bound eastern winters. And, an example of Mr. Rudolph's interest in modular housing—it is a collection of units that could have been—although wasn't—built elsewhere, trucked in for assembly . . .

Above: *Facing south, the bedroom, living room and guest rooms bathe in sunlight.*
Below: *The living room is stepped down, covered wall to wall with a mushroom carpeting . . . Each arm of the cross-shaped pit has its focus–Lowell Nesbitt's painting of grapes or the green marble-framed fireplace flanked by built-in bookcases. The greenhouse is nearby.*
Opposite page and bottom: *The greenhouse, divided into tropical and temperate sections, connects kitchen/living room and study/guest room. The master bedroom takes up the whole top unit. No curtains cut off magnificent views.*

FRESH COLOR AND A NEW LIFE FOR AN OLD HOUSE

Portofino, Italy, 1975

To remodel this landmark Italian farm-house so that it would be cool and airy and yet open to nature, architect Gae Aulenti glassed-in an open gallery at one end of the house to form a cave-like living room, *above,* and terraced an adjoining slope to make an enclosed garden, *left.*

An amphitheatre of flowers—a surprise and yet so sensible—for this old Italian villa garden. This small enclosure of warmth, fragrance and privacy invites everyone outdoors from earliest spring to the last golden drop of summer. No scouring wind can undo this garden's spring daffodils and tulips or summer cascades of lavender-pink ivy-leaved geraniums and passion vine. The rows of low sedums, succulents, and other plants are chosen to resist summer drought as well as wind. Although this garden is high above the Italian fishing village of Portofino, the idea and plants are suited to hot summers or dry climates anywhere: spiky aloes, red-flowering Dragon Blood, sedum, red echeveria (E. pulu-oliver), pink-petaled ice plant (Lampanthus, also known as Mesembryanthemum), a broad ribbon of golden gazania (G. ringens), lavender-blue ageratum. The terracing is sculptural land art; the planting is a kind of painting.

This page: *Colorful terraced garden, protected from wind.*
Opposite page from top: *Hill-top house, with enclosed garden, and arched living room windows. Dining room with black slate table, pink linens, centerpiece of red roses and cherries. Master bedroom opening to roof-top overlooking garden. Child's bedroom with step-up guest bed, built-in table.*

NATURE CAN BE A DECORATOR'S BEST FRIEND

San Francisco, California, 1973, 1978

"I learned long ago that nature, being an incurable romantic, can be a decorator's best friend, and she's mine,'' says interior designer Michael Taylor. In his own house, all the floors are paved with Yosemite slate laid like flagging. The azaleas, except for their tubs, are nature untouched and shuttle to and from the terrace, where they can look at the sea, have a little sun, then roll back indoors. What nature hasn't contributed, man has—for instance, the Chinese deer, *above*—Sung dynasty bronze.

Above: *In the guest room, the bed, designed by Michael Taylor and executed by Mimi London, is made of alder trees from Oregon. The bedside tables are cedar stumps with marble tops.*
Opposite page: *The strong rhythms in this living room came from colors and textures— nubby wicker against smooth leather, coarse cotton against shiny ceramic tile. Except for the yucca trees, everything pares down to a soft white. Special lighting designed by Michael Taylor and Russell MacMasters to spotlight art. Paintings by Morris Louis.*

TREASURES IN ART, OBJECTS, AND RUGS

California, 1974

Here's a house where the family's interests and travels did the decorating for them. The large, sunny, California house-on-several-floors gains its color and richness from a collection of contemporary art, beautiful patterned rugs, and a quantity of chests and screens and objects they found when they lived in the Far East. In the large living room on these two pages, neutral canvas-colored walls and big comfortable canvas-covered places to sit set the room up for color: a Japanese Namban screen, an English 19th-century mostly blue rug by William Morris, and contemporary pictures. All through the house, chests, boxes, art and other treasures are stacked one on other in a fresh adaptation of an Oriental idea.

Below: *In the living room, chaises longues, made from an English daybed split to make the pair, flank a fireplace. Leaning on each is a Claes Oldenburg drawing. On the mantel, two 19th-century gouaches and an Oldenburg lithograph.*
Opposite page and far left: *At the other end of the living room, a Japanese screen wraps around a red lacquered Chinese chest, a Chinese leather box, baskets, shells on top.*

A series of connecting sunporch-garden rooms wrap around the back of this California house that's two stories in front, and three in back. Overlooking a garden and pool, and one level above them, these latticed rooms follow the no-color theme. Big blocks of pattern stimulate the canvas-colored rooms, which are full of windows and plants. Large-scale art and objects take over the decorating, making this house a collector's paradise.

Below left: *The exterior of the house.*
Above: *In a corner of the sunporch, the space is filled with over-sized canvas-covered sofa and chair, Indian tables and bright batik pillows.*
Opposite page: *In another sunporch room, latticed walls frame huge light-filled windows. A kilim rug, a Chinese wedding chest and pots of flowers provide the brilliant color. The round table is covered in an over-sized canvas skirt, tucked under at the bottom.*

ROMANTIC PATTERN AND FABRIC

London, 1977

Furniture, fabrics, rag rugs and pillows designed by Tricia Guild fill a 4-story London house owned by the designer, creating a wonderfully romantic effect. To this personal mix, Tricia Guild has added treasures she found at flea markets and antique shops—old cane furniture, porcelain, century-old lace, and other fab-rics. She starts a room with a neutral background, like off-white walls and a beige matting floor, then fills it with the things she loves.

Above: *In the living room, a French park scene hangs above lace-covered table and baskets of flowers.*
Opposite page: *Tricia Guild's cool, green, fabric-covered bedroom, with lace as trim-ming everywhere—on pillows, tables, cur-tains, shades. The quilt-covered, French faux-bamboo bed and plump green quilted armchair were designed by Tricia Guild. Plants add a touch of living green.*

If a sermon on the uses of the past were required, any number of appropriate texts lie ready to hand. One thinks of Santayana's celebrated ''Those who forget the past are condemned to repeat it,'' and Maugham's ''Tradition is a guide and not a jailer,'' and best of all, Yeats's profound ''How but in custom and in ceremony are innocence and beauty born?'' Plenty of texts, in short, but it turns out that no sermon or preacher is required—the congregation is already convinced. Indeed, it has leapt from its prison of pews and for a good while now has been happily rummaging about in the big cobwebby attic of time past, raising clouds of dust, some of it golden, in pursuit of those souvenirs and emblems of custom and ceremony that we keep fearing we may have misplaced or thrown away, unaware that in most cases our neglect of them is precisely what has insured their preservation.

In regard to the life of the past, it appears that something as opportune as it was unexpected has happened, and it is this: that the nineteen-seventies are manifesting a greater interest in the usable past than the fifties and sixties ever did. Not in many decades, if ever, have we as a people so eagerly and wisely looked forward by dint of looking eagerly, wisely back. It is a feat that, as far as we know, only man among the animals is capable of performing, and when it succeeds, it enhances life as little else can. To dip one's hand into the river of life not at one place only but at a hundred is a form of immortality; it will not outwit death but it helps to outwit the infuriating brevity of life. By an instructive irony, this extension of life, this joyous mingling of past and present, has occurred at the very moment when many of our graybeards were sourly asserting that young folk nowadays were bent upon throwing every baby of past virtue out with the bath water of past evil. So much for the night thoughts of graybeards! The fact is that the babies are thriving, and the bath water . . . well, even the bath water tends to look more wholesome that it did.

One test of a generality is its least likely application; among those young whom we think of as farthest out and therefore most unregarding of the past we encounter, to our surprise, few of the conventional iconoclastic gestures of revolution. On the contrary, it is plain that they are attempting to create a new order out of

Opposite page: The living room of Mr. and Mrs. Charles Engelhard's house in Maine, decorated by the Engelhard's daughter, Mrs. Samuel Reed, and Mrs. Henry Parish II of Parish-Hadley. A special quilt, made exactly to measure, upholsters one of the sofas. The living room walls are covered with plain brown wrapping paper. Painting by Castro.

EMBRACING TRADITION

BY BRENDAN GILL

what amounts to the sacred materials of the old. They are laying claim to an inheritance that their parents and even their grandparents were inclined to spurn. It is not the elderly and timid but the young and bold who are prising open the battered, whale-backed trunks of yesterday and bedecking themselves with ancestral trophies. For them, the past is no mere grim minatory skeleton at the feast of life; it is a jolly companion and the best of teachers. We observe this playful transformation of past into present in the costumes of the young, in their songs, their politics, their so-called ''lifestyle.'' When a handsome young person approaches us along a street, it may be difficult at first to determine his or her sex behind the shining curls and the granny glasses and the melodious cinctures of beads and brass, but it is still more difficult to determine his or her place of origin: The smiling apparition is ablaze with hints of black Africa, the Moslem East, Christian Europe, Hindu India, Israel, and the American West. In styles of hair, the models for young men are the Union and Confederate soldiers of our Civil War.

There are fashions in traditions—what is a tradition, indeed, but a fashion that has lasted?—and it is obvious that certain traditions lend themselves much more readily to fashionable modifications than others do. In the case of clothing, a new material merges (silk from the East, nylon from DuPont), and fresh possibilities in dress instantly establish themselves. In the case of food, the potato, brought back from the New World, quickly alters the diet of Europe. In architecture, changes are notoriously slower—so slow that they are sometimes imperceptible to the very people who are engaged in bringing them about and who are seen long afterward to have opened the door of novelty by zealously seeking to keep it shut. Settlers in a new land, instead of responding to the importunate demands of a new climate, continue to honor the traditions of the land and climate they have left behind. It used to be thought that the steep roofs of 17th-century New England represented our ancestors' judicious resolution of the problem of heavy snow loads, but in fact the steep roofs were but an aping of the building practices they had been accustomed to in counties in England where

snow is rare. (Moreover, when for a time in the 19th century flat roofs became the rage in New England, no one appears to have given a second thought to snow. As the late Lord Raglan never tired of pointing out, what is customary and what is practical have no necessary connection with each other; and custom always carries the day.) After the forest itself, what most needed to be got rid of in 17th-century New England were the stones that rendered its newly rubbed-up field all but untillable, but few New Englanders thought to turn these nuisances into a blessing and make snug, fireproof, and verminproof houses of them; instead, they disposed of them in walls of a height and thickness that had little to do with their functions as fences. Wood was their old friend, and they would not let it go.

Eagerly, wisely, then as now, we have always contrived to look both backward and forward, but it wasn't until the 19th century that what we had to look back upon was wholly our own. The famous ''wedding-cake'' house in Kennebunk makes a festive, preposterous bridge between the centuries. It is an 18th-century Georgian box that, with an almost lunatic liberality of high spirits, has been tarted up in the 19th-century Gothic Revival mode. Little by little, we abandoned the architectural cosmetics of modes and began to put the genuine American Stamp—bold, brash, inexpungeable—on what Frost called the great land ''vaguely realizing westward . . . such as she was, such as she would become.'' We learned to build in a vernacular style that we have only recently come to prize as highly as it deserves—a style vigorous and exuberant, in which the touching ambition to be grand is often swallowed up in sheer bravado. With the shingle style in domestic buildings and the skyscraper in office buildings, we raised a shout that the Old World felt obliged to listen to. The frontiersmen had arrived.

''Those who forget the past,'' Santayana said, ''are condemned to repeat it,'' but the good news is that this is a threat we are taking care to avoid in our pell-mell rush toward the 21st century. It is not only the known, indisputable treasures—the Nathaniel Russell house in Charleston; the Moffatt-Ladd house in Portsmouth—that are in safe hands and will be spreading the benefaction of their rooms before our astonished eyes forever. And it is the young who, all unexpectedly, are taking charge of the hard and sometimes desperate task of preserving, in wood and brick and stone and iron and cloth and paper, evidences of those mingled traditions by which we made the land ours and became the land's.

IDEAS AND INSPIRATION FROM A DREAM HOUSE

Ménerbes, France, 1974

This is the dream house of Van Day Truex, teacher, president of the Parsons School of Design, and Design Consultant to Tiffany. The look of the house was controlled by the site: the top terrace almost 40 feet wide. He worked on the house with Henri-Alexandre Faure, a young and talented architect of the region, and together they planned just about the simplest solution possible—a house to be built in the centuries-old manner of stucco, stone and tile. It is a low rectangle

of two floors, of stucco inside and out, with cornices, window and door jambs of local off-white stone. The floors of both levels are of the same stone except in the kitchen and bath, which are tile. Everything is beige and white throughout. No wasted space, which means no dining room as such. "I preferred to have as generous a living room as possible, large enough to have a dining area. If a house has at least one generously large room, one minds less other rooms being medium or small . . ."

Above left: *The stone exterior. An Italian cypress shoots up like an exclamation mark.*
Above right: *The 13-foot-long refectory table seats 8 with ease—and rarely more. Mr. Truex doesn't like flower centerpieces, but endpieces, where the flowers and ferns go.*
Below left: *French doors open from the living room to the pebble-paved terrace outside.*
Above: *The living room is simple without being austere, ornamented with African masks and topiary bay trees—plucked occasionally to season a Provençal ragoût.*
Opposite page: *The entrance hall staircase—a fine example of Mr. Truex's preference for "beautifully proportioned cubes and circles."*

BEAUTY
AND HEALTH
IN A
SPA BATH

New York City, 1971

For the triple pursuit of beauty, rest, and relaxation, this is a superb example of the spa bath—far, far from the beaten path, and classic as a piece of sculpture. This spa bath was designed by architects Gwathmey/Siegel for Miss Faye Dunaway's remodeled New York apartment. A built-in chaise longue, a tiled, serpentine structure for reclining in a gentle curve under a sun lamp or resting after a sauna, ripples down at one end to join the tile-paved tub—massive, luxurious, wonderful for soaking away an hour in a cloud of scent. At the right of the tub is a cantilevered washbasin, and around the corner, a dressing room. Sauna, shower stall are on other side of the wall.

Left: *In the serene, healthful spa bath, only two surfacing materials are used: blue-black slate flagging, and white ceramic, 1-inch-square tile in a matte finish. A towel adds a touch of bright color.*

OPEN SPACE LIVING IN A CITY LOFT

New York City, 1971

Though originally tempted to break up the 75-by-100 foot, 1890s warehouse, *Artforum* publisher Charles Cowles realized he wanted the experience of living in one enormous room where big unobstructed spaces offer an almost Oriental serenity rarely available in city apartments, plus vast hanging space for a growing collection of work by young artists. Cowles went to Mark Hampton for advice on how to treat the space without using lots of furniture. Once having resolved where to put a free-standing, L-shaped wall that would mark out the functional parts of the space—bedroom, library, storage—he painted everything white, sanded the wood floor, then coated it in polyurethane, installed track lighting, and replaced window panes.

Right and opposite page: *A view of the enormous living space in the loft. Furniture, paintings, and plants are all movable.*
Opposite page, top: *A view of the library.*
Below: *Along a gallery of windows in the living room, a part of Mr. Cowles's collection of young artists: John Clem Clarke, Llyn Foulkes, Nigel Hall, Robert Hudson, Tom Holland, Gary Kuehn, Ronnie Landfield, Jeffrey Lew, Peter Reginato, Ed Ruscha, Keith Sonnier, John Tweddle, William T. Williams.*

NEW EXPERIMENTAL HOUSES

Breakaway houses that are heated by the sun; houses that are live-in sculpture; structures buried in the earth; computer wizardry adapted for living; face-lifts for beach houses; a three-bedroom modular house that arrives by truck—these are some of the exciting, revolutionary houses being built today by architects and designers who are ready to meet the challenge of new materials and new technology. But always, and finally, the merit of design in building must be measured against man; good design in a house must be a design for living.

This house, with no recognizable front façade, and jutting, angular walls, was designed by Peter Eisenman.

Left, from top: New solar house designed by architect Robert F. Shannon of the People/Space Company in Boston, with big insulated panels that drop down to hold heat in living room at night. Flat roof uses blanketing snow to hold heat in. 400 feet of collector, 320 square feet of reflector bounce sun into panels.

Shaped in a spectacular parabolic arch, this house, amid trees, looks like a huge bird, wings spread wide, hovering lightly over the land of Long Island, New York. The owners: Mr. and Mrs. Bert Geller; the architects: Marcel Breuer and Herbert Beckhard.

Bottom right: This house on the Pacific edge at Carmel, California, was designed by architect Mark Mills. Constructed of Gunite (a cement mix) sprayed over an elastomeric webbing stretched over insulation.

This molded fiberglass house is the sleek, colorful brainchild of a Finnish manufacturing company called Polykem, a lightweight, maintenance-free structure designed by architect Matti Suuronen. Shipped in three sections, the modular unit comes with or without glass window panels and bubble skylight, and with a choice of either a carpeted or vinyl floor. The shell, made in Finland, costs approximately $9000.

Opposite bottom left: Dr. and Mrs. Robert G. Milton worked themselves for two years to erect two domes (from kits) on a platform overlooking the Pacific in Southern California. Result: a practical and dramatic house.

Opposite bottom right: A playful architectural fantasy designed by architect Michael Graves for Dr. and Mrs. Paul Benacerraf in Princeton, New Jersey, contains a practical addition to the original (and more conventional) house.

This beach house in Atlantic Beach, Florida, has two identical living units. Architect: William Morgan.

Yellow and white dominate this New England house designed by Robert Stern and John Hagmann.

This brilliantly colored rear wall of a prairie house in Illinois was designed by Stanley Tigerman.

Stacked drums are used to heat this solar house in Albuquerque, New Mexico. Designer and owner: Steve Baer.

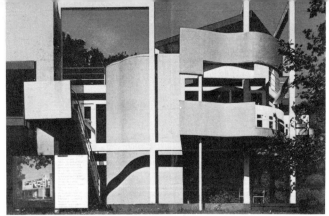

A complex glass-and-balconied illusion of a cluster of houses is to bring intimate scale. Architect: Michael Graves.

This house is a machine for living—its computor controls rotation of roof, garage doors. Architect: Stanley Tigerman.

A solar-heated house warmed by center bubbles, run by a computor. Designed and built by Mike and Ellen Jantzen.

A modular house that comes by truck and costs less than $15,000. Triad, by Hodgson Houses, architect: Edward Coplon.

Vertical concrete block house by Robert Whitton reaches up for views over Miami and also gives privacy.

A stimulating glass mini-car/environment designed in Paris by Quasar Khanh.

NEW SIMPLICITY IN A STRIPPED-DOWN SPACE

290

New York City, 1970

Controled colors and primary shapes create a walk-in still life in this stripped-to-the-essentials apartment. Designer John Saladino used furniture forms—cube, rectangle, circle, dome—as pieces of sculpture, along with textures and uncluttered space as the budget formula for Ruth Campbell's two-room apartment. Soft light streams in, and reflects off pale walls. A few textures—straw, a fur throw, living plants—add vitality.

Above: *In the bedroom, everything is in quiet, understated white. A wicker table, a bentwood chair, a wooden screen, are natural contrasts.*
Opposite page: *In the living room, the fireplace was painted white with the color extended up the wall and onto the ceiling in a giant, graphic circle. Vivid upholstery, the spool table, create a personal touch.*

BILLY BALDWIN'S TWO-ROOM APARTMENT FULL OF IDEAS FOR SMALL SPACE, BIG STYLE

Nantucket, Massachusetts, 1979

Luxury means something different to everyone. To Billy Baldwin, a man who's made a life of creating luxury in other people's houses and apartments, it has always meant living in a house that's perfectly suited to his taste and lifestyle: a house that's simple but comfortable, spare but full of warmth. "The most luxurious thing I can think of is having a window next to the bathtub," says Mr. Baldwin, and in this house he does. It's the two-room wing of a 19th-century shingled house, a country apartment "that, with two floors and two fireplaces, feels like a house, though rooms are small." Small space, however, is no match for the man who wrote the book on small-space decorating. He simply takes his own advice: "Uncomplicate." In the living room, just 15 by 16 feet, but in no way small-feeling because of its high ceilings and four big windows (each a wonderful garden picture)—linen-white paint lightened what was once dark maroon wainscoting and an old brick chimney. Tudor beams kept their natural ruggedness and, to give them strength and the room a proper dimension, the floor was stained dark and polyurethaned until it gleamed like glass. Mr. Baldwin brought a mix of furniture: some, like the sofa and the faux-bamboo coffee table, that had been in his New York apartment and some, the telephone table and the black lacquer Louis XV table by the stairs, from a summer cottage. The only acquisitions are the armchair, the Irish rug, and throw pillows, made from the lining of an Oriental coat. "If you're honest about your taste and buy only what's right for you, it will always be right, anywhere you put it."

Left: *1840s wing of an even older shingled house, Billy Baldwin's country apartment.*
Right: *The all-white living room with dark woodwork and floor that give dimension to the tiny space. The table beside the armchair was originally a stool until its upholstered seat was replaced by a marble slab. The deer-head on the chimney breasts is carved from wood—but the antlers on it are real.*

Left, from top: *Table arrangements, created by Billy Baldwin's logical eye:* On the marble-topped stool, *black and gold African tiger carrying a bird, lacquer ashtray, carved-head snuffbox, chestnut with an ivory base, and a tortoiseshell cigarette box.* On the living room's coffee table, *a turtle collection; one of Japanese wood, two of tortoiseshell.* On the Louis XV table, *a variety of greens; living in a Japanese cachepot, dried in a wicker-wrapped jar, painted on canvas.* On a Lucite table, *modern artwork, classical sculpture, beach stones embellished with gold beasts and ornaments, an oyster shell that opens to reveal a lizard.*

When something looks right to Billy Baldwin, it's because he's asked two questions: "How will it make the room look?" and "How will the room make *it* look?" In his bed-sitting room, for instance, he used the English coffee table and the Windsor chair, one of the few purchases made especially for this house, to enhance the two dark ceiling beams that point up the peaked roof and the fireplace. "Since it's my bedroom, I wanted as peaceful an atmosphere as possible. So, unlike the living room, almost all the woodwork is painted out." Even the blinds are painted white, making the five windows recede into space. "When you paint everything white, you bring in light, and a room filled with light is pure luxury." It is a simple luxury that is available to everyone.

Above: *The bed-sitting room. On the fireplace, a snipe decoy on driftwood. For andirons, silhouette horses in brass. An understated black and white pattern upholsters the daybed and armchair. "In small spaces, pattern should be used deliberately." Except for treasured presents from friends, all essentials are eliminated. "I may replace things, but I almost never add."*

New York City, 1976

The more Nature reveals to us, the more it has the look of an immense gathering with presents all around, and, despite the wild differences in form, a family affair as well. Giving things away is an ingrained habit among the living things of our planet; it is ordained, genetically determined. You could call it trading, I suppose, since everyone gets something in return, but there is such freedom and exuberance in the giving as to seem more like celebration than hard business.

Every kind of creature is dependent for his life on the life of other creatures nearby, and this meshwork of interdependency is spread over the surface of the whole planet. The most lavish of the presents, there for the asking, is the air itself. Oxygen is pumped into the atmosphere by green microorganisms, some free-floating in the sea, others living as permanent lodgers inside the cells of other organisms; the plants are green because of these creatures. Carbon dioxide, on which the plants depend for their use of solar energy, is pumped in by other microorganisms, the ones that use the oxygen; most of these also live as residents, called mitochondria, inside the cells of other animals. Were it not for these two great classes of microbe, dominating in benignity of the whole planet, none of the rest of us would be here.

Another mass of bacteria, the nitrogen-fixers, allow us to make the protein that we use for constructing ourselves, by taking nitrogen from the air and arranging it in molecular configurations within plants. They do this by "infecting" the roots of plants, but there is no disease, only the root nodules of beans. It is a model of interliving, a paradigm of the balanced complexity and intricacy needed for such arrangements. The bacteria invade the root-hairs of the plant and find a place where they can live and be nourished, and then they make the enzyme that the plant needs for incorporating nitrogen. The enzyme is fragile and needs protection from oxidation, and this is provided by a form of hemoglobin made in a collaboration between the bacteria and plant cells, two separate creatures assembling a single molecule. It is as intimate an exchange as one can find anywhere in nature: It has been suggested that the bacteria originally had all the DNA for this molecule, and donated some of the genes to the plant long ago. Bits of DNA are moved about in nature from creature to creature, with a lot more freedom than used to be thought possible.

Viruses can lift the genes from certain cells and carry them off, later attaching them to the genetic heritage of other cells. It is a way of passing information around quickly. Cells from totally different

THE ENORMOUS PARTY

BY DR. LEWIS THOMAS

species are capable of fusing to form single cells from single nuclei, hybrids, half man-half mosquito if you like.

Altruism used to be a puzzle reserved for philosophers, but it has recently become a specialized technical term for a central puzzle in biology. How can it be that creatures have evolved with sets of genes determining altruistic behavior? In the case of insects the current, acceptably Darwinian explanation is that this is a way of assuring the survival and replication of one's own genes, since it is the closest kin, with identical or nearly identical genes, who are enabled to survive by acts of altruism.

No such explanation will serve, of course, for altruism in our own species. We do not possess this degree of identity in our genomes, except for the identical twins among us. It may be that when it occurs among human beings, as it surely does, this has nothing whatever to do with genetics. Perhaps we are all as fundamentally self-obsessed and egoistic as Hobbes believed. Perhaps the only way of achieving altruism is to be instructed in the matter by society. This may be so, although it doesn't have to be so; anyway, who is to say that there are not biological determinants, genes and all, for constructing society? But it could be, you know, the other way around: We could be born with genes for altruistic behavior, and it is only in certain kinds of society (like, say, today's kind) that we can be systematically instructed to suppress the tendency.

I prefer the latter notion, for it helps explain something else about human behavior, which would otherwise be a bewilderment. It seems to me, based on no science at all but a lifetime of looking around in human company, that most people have an instinctive, biologically driven, ineluctable desire to be *useful*. I find it hard to explain this except by assuming that it is in the nature of human beings to be useful. I would not go so far as to say we have particular genes for encoding usefulness, but maybe, in the aggregate, our sort of DNA allows for a sensory receptor, perhaps a center somewhere in the right cerebral hemisphere, where the realization of being useful is received and recognized as pleasure.

Other creatures have evolved in what ecologists call niches. The various forms

of life inhabiting a coral reef, including the live coral itself, are preoccupied endlessly in adapting themselves to this kind of life. The environment is stable overall, but the whole thing moves with life. It is always engaged in growing, changing, and remaking parts of itself, always favoring the emergence of greater and more flexible varieties among the inhabitants. Fitness of an individual or of a whole species for environments like this, in the evolutionary sense, really means fitting in with all the other forms of life. Fitting in, by and large, means being useful.

I've been trying to think of the niche for human beings. Do we have anything like a niche, anything equivalent to a coral reef? You'd think not, to watch us in action. We can live anywhere, and do.

But there is one niche for us, rather like a coral reef, or more like the idea of a coral reef. We made it ourselves, for ourselves. It is language.

It is not known when the capacity for speech was built into our brain, but it must have been a very recent event, an eyeblink in evolutionary time. Whenever, it was probably then that we began to become a biologically social species, ultimately as compulsively communal as the famous social ants and termites. Early on, the evolutionary pressure on all humans to adapt quickly to the new environment of language must have been a powerful force. It is perhaps because of that sudden pressure that the astoundingly rapid evolution of the human brain occurred when it did.

Language became the environment in which humans live. It has a life, so to speak, of its own. And with it, we make gifts to each other. We give away, compulsively and without reluctance, the whole unique asset, for there is nothing else to do with it. Language is not designed for solitary selves; it is for others.

We are kept at this, and at one another, all our lives. We tell one another how the world seems, and the news and the images are passed around. We would empty out our minds for the people around us, if we knew how to do it. Poets appear to be talking for themselves alone. But it is an illusion; poets, good poets, are talking to, and for, the whole earth.

This is, I think, as much a form of altruistic behavior as anything else I've heard of in nature. We are biologically unique for having language, and because of this we have our minds, and are like the rest of nature in what we do with these treasures: We make them into presents, and give them away.

"The more nature reveals to us, the more it has the look of an immense gathering with presents all around." Photograph by Penn.

A GARDEN IS A SONG OF PRAISE

Italy, 1977

"**G**reen fingers are the extensions of a verdant heart,'' wrote Russell Page in his book, *The Education of a Gardener* (Collins, London). Gardening, he recognizes, is an evanescent art. But he believes a good garden can last. ''The skeleton has to be done in such a way that somebody 200 years later can see the traces. When I see the Villa Madama in Rome I recognize the magic and why it's there, although there's nothing much left of Raphael's plans except the great terrace.'' The technique of gardening has changed enormously in Mr. Page's lifetime. ''In the old days,'' he recalls, ''one thought of a garden as a complex of plants and patterns, with herbaceous borders, for instance. All that has become so difficult now from the point of view of maintenance. I see gardening today in a completely different light. Now I work with land modeling, with trees, with water. Land modeling used to be a huge undertaking with hundreds of men digging with wheelbarrows, like building the Great Wall of China. Now it's relatively simple. . . . If you plant a tree carefully and well, and look after it for the first year, after that there's no maintenance. So I'm very happy in my advanced station not to have to think about herbaceous borders or decide whether I like pink tulips rather than white tulips. Now I see trees and water and grass—these are main materials I am using.''

Top right: *Volcanic rocks were surrounded by water to make a focal point at the lowest level of Sir William and Lady Walton's garden on Ischia . . .*

Right: *A small formal pool is set off by a band of heavy-foliage Peltiphyllum in the garden Russell Page designed for Waltons. "Over the years the garden has become green and splendid with palms, chestnuts, cedars, bamboos, tree ferns—eccentric but visually successful neighbors supremely well-gardened.''*

Opposite page: *For an Empire villa in Northern Italy, Russell Page replaced a sloping vegetable plot with flights of steps leading down to three hedged enclosures, each on a different level and each with a different proportioned pool. "From the central stairway guarded by sphinxes you look down on panels of box and santolina clipped flat like a rug, with a box maze below.''*

INDUSTRIAL
MATERIALS
IN A HOUSE
OF GLASS

Toronto, Canada, 1976

The house can be described simplistically—two glass boxes supported by posts—or provocatively—an experiment in space. Built on the fringe of a park in Toronto, it is the home of Mr. and Mrs. Lawrence Wolf and their two children. Its designer, Barton Myers of Diamond & Myers, is an architect noted for his public and commercial buildings, which is why the Wolfs chose him. So here is their house, a strong yet airy structure built of industrial materials—in a way that opens up space for indoor-outdoor living.

Opposite page, bottom left: *The glass-fronted rear of the house.* Above, right, and opposite page, bottom right: *The wall storage between the kitchen and living room contains media equipment plus kitchen linens. Lined with mirror and marble, sliding doors can close off the whole unit from either side.*
Opposite page, top: *In the dining end of the living area, exposed beams, joists, steel ceilings, heating/cooling ducts look decorative with coats of paint. Mies van der Rohe chairs, marble-topped table designed by the Wolfs.*
Right: *In the sitting area, enormous Swiss-designed leather sofa faces view-sized windows.*

This house has no fixed, single-purpose rooms in the conventional sense. The living spaces are very open, yet by pulling accordion doors and movable panels installed in the right place, there is almost instant privacy. Twenty skylights and walls in motion provide light and air. Its openness to nature, its feeling of being an extension of the outdoors, make it almost like a grand family treehouse.

Opposite page, bottom from left: The parents' bath, with side by side tubs, faced in Carrara

marble. *Next to the tub unit is a storage area with two separate cabinets, his and hers, in white Formica. The Wolfs work in a study that is really a section of their bedroom, here closed off by accordion doors.*

Opposite page, above: In the skylighted bedroom, the headboard is built into a storage wall. The bed is covered with a 1910 quilt.

This page, from top: Each child's bedroom has a red double-decker bed with circular cutouts on each side, and a ladder. In the children's playroom, a sliding panel acts as blackboard on one side, pinboard on the other. The children's bath is a free-standing tiled compartment with a plastic bubble under two light-filled skylights.

A LIVE-IN KITCHEN WARMED BY WOOD

Pennsylvania, 1971

A love of cooking inspired this addition of a new wing on to a Pennsylvania house—a kitchen that opens onto a patio deck and into a second living room. Designer Melvin Dwork created the new live-in kitchen for Mrs. Herman Neissen, who is a great cooking enthusiast. Architecturally, the new wing became the heart of the house, adjoining the living room. In the kitchen, the island counter breaks up the large space, and high-up windows work like skylights. The barn siding on the walls adds a country feeling—like the country cooking the Neissens love.

Left: *Floor plan of the new wing.*
Above: *The living room, seen from the kitchen.*
Opposite page: *In the new kitchen, the long work counter has a high back to mask the work area. Counter-height windows afford light and country views. All of the appliances are stainless steel, the countertops covered in a slate-like vinyl laminate. Barn siding walls create warmth and a feeling of coziness.*

FLOWERING BEAUTY IN A GARDEN CIRCLE

U.S.A., 1978

In a sunny clearing in the woods, a circular garden is enclosed by flowers, a post and rail fence, and an inner ring of mixed flowers and vegetables. Edwin Eberman, an artist by profession and experimenter by inclination, designed this garden to grow vegetables and flowers for family and friends. Easy watering was a must, so garden size matches range of a revolving Rainbird sprinkler. Turned on once a week for 12-14 hours, it provides the equivalent of an inch of rain—just what most vegetables need.

To keep soil in good condition, a top-dressing of leaves from nearby woods is added each autumn.

Generous grass paths surround and separate two half-circle picking and cutting gardens (100 feet wide in all), one with a walk-in screenhouse to protect crops from birds. Wide gates at the front and back of the circle provide easy access for a rider-mower.

THE CLEAN LINES OF A RECYCLED AMERICAN BARN

Long Island, 1977

Elegance—there's no other word for a house with this kind of affectionate appreciation for natural materials combined with this kind of sophistication. The house is a new combination of assorted old buildings—a potato-picker's shack, an 18th-century barn, and various out-buildings—moved to the site from the surrounding countryside and linked together with a minimum of new construction. What remains from these venerable buildings are their expansive spaces and mellow woods. What is added are clean lines and light. Architect Donald R. Richey, who, with Carl Warns, designed this house for artist Arthur Williams, stripped the old buldings to their framework and filled in with wall and ceiling planes painted pure white. Flooring, too, is white—expanses of small hexagonal tile, with heating coils buried below. Skylights and new windows (with old frames) have been added everywhere, with no curtains to restrict light flow.

Opposite page, top: *The front of the house with old-fashioned flower garden—a touch of the past.*
Left: *In the living room, the fireplace seating is dominated by a Ward Bennett sofa in antelope suede and a pair of polished steel deck chairs once on the deck of the Mauretania. On the tile floor near the desk, a bronze armadillo.*
Right: *In the dining area, the rustic chairs are made by a Japanese woodcarver. At the far end, stands a giant bird from an old carousel, stripped down to its natural wood.*

The largest single element of the complex is the barn, which had been moved to the site from a nearby Long Island town. Rather than animals or farm equipment, the barn's main level now holds a wonderful surprise—a pool, heated for winter use. The barn's loft serves as owner Arthur Williams's studio. Walls have been opened to the woods through generous glass areas, and the barn is connected to the living-dining wing by a new passage which also leads to a sauna. White foam insulation fills all the non-glazed areas between wall studs and roof joists with a stucco-like texture, a seemly complement to the rough wood structure.

Right and opposite page: *In the barn, the original ladder to the loft has been replaced by a spiral steel staircase made in Mexico. The floor around the pool is bluestone (unlike some stone, it is not slippery when wet).*
Opposite page, bottom: *Outside the barn's new window wall, a cascade of wooden deck platforms projects out into the wooden site.*

INTO THE 80s

So many of the old barriers are down as we move into the last part of the century. Buildings for living range from space-age towers to earthbound energy houses. Rooms are no longer divided by traditional function. A growing obsession with health turns kitchens into nutrition centers, bathrooms into spas, and gardens into fruit and vegetable sources for the family. The emphasis on self-fulfillment makes "do-it-yourself" an ultimate expression. Everyone can be an expert. Every whim of personal taste can be satisfied in this increasingly personal age. The rage for collecting reflects this individualism, as many people reaffirm their faith in things in an unstable economy. Multi-purpose rooms and objects define the new style, while privacy becomes a precious commodity to be preserved. As time in the century runs out, so does space. Inner cities are being renewed in a humanizing spirit that recognizes man's continuing need for nature. In contrast, technological breakthroughs are bringing science into the home in a new form—the eighties will be the decade of domestic electronics and telecommunications. And dominating everything, the new wisdom—energy conservation, which will affect design in exciting new ways for decades to come.

Lake Michigan, 1976

Richard Meier's composition of all-white building, like a sculpture in the woods, rises authoritatively from its rugged site facing the lake. The house interior has drama of its own, with large glass areas facing the lake and with vertical penetrations of space from level to level. Curving rails celebrate the circulation.

ACKNOWLEDGEMENTS

We want to thank Lord Weidenfeld who first suggested we do this book. And there is a special group of people who helped to bring it to life. Denise Otis, Editor of House & Garden, helped with the editing of the material, particularly for chapters on the 1940s, 1950s, and 1960s. Professor Stanley Barrows, Chairman of the Interior Design Department at the Fashion Institute of Technology and an expert on decorating in this century, has been our consultant. Jay Holme did the original research—reading through 80 years of House & Garden issues. Diana Edkins coordinated the art work. Lorna Caine, Elizabeth Debry, and Susan Wilcox helped prepare the text and art for publication. All of this was overseen by William Rayner, Editorial Business Manager of Condé Nast Publications, and Paul Bonner, Director of Condé Nast Book Division. We want to thank Ralph Timm, Publishing Director of House & Garden, for his encouragement, and all the editors and publishers who have guided House & Garden through its 80 years. The book itself is made up of the work of hundreds of decorators, architects, landscape gardeners, photographers, and writers. We are most grateful to all of them.

Rohde, Gilbert 82, 118
Romantic Style 173
Rookwood Pottery Co. 34
Roosevelt, Dorothy 205
Roosevelt, Theodore 49, 54—55
Rosenberg & Futterman 253
Roenberg, Robert Hays 253
Rosenthal, Rena 121, 135
Rothko, Mark 230, 231
Rouault, Georges 228
Rubin, J. Robert 143
Rubin, William 228
Rudolph, Paul 240—241, 252, 253, 264—267
Ruhlmann, Jacques-Emile 78, 81
Runnels, Louise 247
Ruscha, Ed 286, 287
Russell, Harry B. 76—77
Russell, Nathaniel, House 281
Russell, John 228—229

S

Saarinen, Eero 188, 196—199
Sackville-West, V. 214—219
St. Regis, Hotel, New York 183
Saklatvala, P. D. 70—71
Saladino, John 290, 291
Saltzman, Ellin-Renny 242—245
Salzman, Stanley 252
Samarkand rug 182—183
Sandler, Ted 176, 205
Santayana, George 281
Sartorius 174
Scandinavia 118, 188
Schlee, Mrs. George 173
Schmidlapp, Mr. & Mrs. Carl J. 171
Schmidt, Julius 236
Schoen, Eugene 88, 89
Schumacher, F. 154
Schweinfurth, J. A. 18, 21
Scott, Irvin L. 130—131
Secession Spirit 86
Shannon, Robert F. 288
Sheff, Donald 262, 263
Sheraton furniture 97, 130
Shinoda, Morio 226
Sidney, F. F. 28—31
Silver
    French 88
    Modern 88—89
Sirugo, Sal 237
Sissinghurst Castle 214—219
Slee & Bryson 75
Sloane, John 97
Smith, David 226
Smith, Mr. & Mrs. Lloyd Hilton 208—209
Snelson 228
Solar houses 288
Sonnier, Keith 286, 287
Soriano, Raphael 126
Sorine, Savely 143
Spain 44—45
Stacey, George 170
Stnaford University 154
Starbird, Roy 202—203
Steel, Gardner 67
Steele, Mrs. Charles 101
Stern, Robert 289
Sterner, Harold 169, 176—177
Stevene, Louis 67
Stevenson, Harvey 126
Stickley, Gustave 16

Still, Clyfford 226
Stone, Edward Durell 136—137, 188
"Stonewall Farms" 288
Storrs, John 237
Strang, Elizabeth Leonard 115
Stubbins, Hugh 252
Stucco ornamentation 104
Sue et Mare 86—87
Suuronen, Matti 288
Sykes, James Greenleaf 66

Tamayo, Rufino 170
Tang 170
Taste, comings and goings 130—131
Tate, Diane 96, 97, 101, 171
Taylor, Mrs. Emma Flower 114
Taylor, Michael 211, 272—273
Teague, Walter Dorwin 118, 133
Technology 78
Tecton architects 126
Telephone, concealing 110—111
Tempchin, Dr. & Mrs. Stanley 248—249
Tempestini 167
Tennessee
    Knoxville 115
Texas
    Houston 188
Thomas, Lewis 296
Thonet
    Chairs 257
    Clothes tree 257
Tiffany 16, 282
    Lamp 34
Tigerman, Stanley 289
Tile 90
Tillett, Doris & Leslie 153
Toile de Jouy 105, 175
Topiary 32—33
Townhouse, replanned 150
Tropical patio garden 76—77
Truex, Van Day 282—283
Tudor style 75
Tuttle, Bloodgood 72—73
Tweddle, John 286, 287
"Twin Oaks" 16, 17

Uccello, Paolo 228
Ullman, Jane F. 212—213
Urban, Joseph 86, 120, 130—131
Utrillo, Maurice 176

Vanderbilt, Mrs. Emily 101
Van Gilder, G. S. 115
Van Nessen 160
Vass, John 218
Vernay 107
Victoria, Frederick P. 169
Victorian 16, 53, 90, 118, 171, 224, 238—239
    Camelback armcharis 208—209
    Flower montage 198
    Stained glass window 186
Vienna Workshop 154
    see also Wiener Werkstatte
Viennese Art 86—87

Vietor, Mrs. John 108
Villa Giulia 166
Villa Trianon 210
Villon, Jacques 257
Virginia
    Williamsburg 118
Vogue 233
Vollmer, Ruth 226

Wallpaper 84—85, 102—103, 105
Wall treatments 84—85, 102—103, 105
Walpole, Horace 56
Walton, Sir William & Lady 298
Wanamaker, Importer 88
Wanamaker, John 97
"Warbrook" 104
Warns, Carl 308—311
Washington, D.C. 16, 17
Washington
    Spokane 106—107
Waterford glass 171
    Chandelier 143
Weiller, Paul-Louis 183
Western Electric Co. 153
Westinghouse Electric Co. 112
Wharton, Edith 48
White, Mrs. Francis L. 169
White, Old, collecting 98—99
White, Stanford 181
Whitman, Walt 281
Whitney Museum of American Art 171
Whitridge, Mrs. Arnold 146—147
Whitton, Robert 289
Wickerwork 16, 46—47, 66—67
Widdicomb 152
Wiener Werkstatte 78
    see also Vienna Workshop
Williams, Arthur 308—311
Williams, Mr. & Mrs. Harrison 143, 180
Williams, Neil 236
Williams, William T. 286, 287
Wilson, Elsie Cobb 97, 101
Wilton, Dr. & Mrs. Robert G. 288
Winan, Hubert C. 122
Winckelmann, J. J. 130
Witkin, Isaac 226
Wolf, Mr. & Mrs. Lawrence 300—303
Wood, Ruby Ross 108—109, 144—145, 168—169
    see also Ruby Ross Goodnow
Woolf, Virginia 90—91
Work, Robert 96, 97
Wormley, Edward J. 155
Wright, Agnes Foster 67, 103
Wright Frank Lloyd 16, 126
Wright, Richardson 80—81, 130—131
Wright, Russel 134, 135
Wrought iron 66—67, 76—77, 169
Wyle, Mr. & Mrs. Frank S. 253

Yamamoto, Masahiko 253
Yeats, William Butler 281
Ysel, Inc. 144—145

Zaik, Saul 252
Ziegler, Gerhard 127

PHOTO CREDITS

Ameniya, 100; Martinus Andersen, 134, 135; Morley Baer, 288; Serge Balkin, 173; Ernst Beadle, 278, 279, 292, 293, 294, 295; Beals, 64; Hedrich Blessing, 127; Bodorff, 122,136,137; Bruehl-Bourges, 120, 121, 143; Michael Boys, 258, 259; Pierre Brissaud (paintings), 140, 141, 143; Campbell, 76, 77; Haanel Cassidy, 171, 173, 207, 212, 213; Clifford Coffin, 166, 167; Conigisky, 115; Marvin Culbreth, 204; Robert Damora, 119, 133, 151, 253; Emelie Danielson, 122; P.A. Dearborn, 176, 177; Anthony Denney, 184, 185, 186, 187, 214, 215, 216, 217, 218, 219; Drix Duryea, 96, 97, 100, 101, 108, 109, 116; Max Eckert, 262; Elliott Erwitt, 288, 289, 308, 309, 310, 311; Herbert Felton, 124, 125; Richard Fish, 252; John Fulker, 300, 301, 302, 303; Gillies, 52, 53, 56, 57, 74, 75, 94, 95; Gottscho, 145; Gottscho-Schleisner, 181; William Grigsby, 210, 225, 226, 227, 229, 230, 231, 236, 237, 290, 291, 304, 305; G.W. Harting, 83, 96, 97, 98, 99, 108, 117; Healey, 146, 147; Mattie Edwards Hewitt, 82, 100, 101, 103, 107, 109, 115, 145; E.O. Hoppé, 104; Horst P. Horst, 211, 232, 233, 234, 235, 272, 274, 275, 276, 277, 280, 282, 283; E.G. Hutchinson, 132, 133; Scott Hyde, 180, 181; Andre Kertesz, 158, 159, 160, 161, 168, 169, 170, 171, 173, 174, 175, 176, 177, 180, 182, 183, 190, 191, 192, 193, 194, 210, 211; Toshiharu Kirajma, 289; Klein, 109; John Krauss, 205; Clarence John Laughlin, 195; Robert Lautman, 289; Mark Lecroix, 254, 255; Leland Lee, 96, 101, 253; Leombruno-Bodi, 268, 269, 270, 271; Tom Leonard, 206, 208, 209, 210; Levick, 114; F.S. Lincoln, 131; Lofman, 178, 179; Fred Lyon, 172, 180, 202, 203; Russell Macmasters, 273; William Maris/Ezra Stoller Associates, 246, 247, 248, 249, 263; David Massey, 260, 261, 289; Herbert Matter, 152, 153, 154, 155; Norman Mcgrath, 288; Meisel, 189; Derry Moore, 298; Ugo Mulas, 256, 257; Emelie Danielson Nicholson, 172; P.A. Nyholm, 126, 127, 145, 183; Nyholm-Phillips, 121, 122, 123; David Payne (Drawings), 144; Irving Penn, 297; Alexander Piaget, 148, 149; Rada, 220, 221; John Rawlings, 170; Richardson (Illustrations), 110, 111; Ben Schall, 177; Marina Schinz, 306, 307; Maris-Semel, 289; Julius Shulman, 126, 162, 163, 181, 213; Shirk, 205; Soderholtz, 22; Ezra Stoller, 164, 165, 221, 222, 223, 252, 253, 254, 255, 262, 312; Sturtevant, 169; Tebbs, 50, 51, 58, 59; Tebbs and Knell, 117; Paul Thompson, 49, 54, 55; Trowbridge, 144; Watkins, 80, 81; Harvey White, 88, 89, 96, 101; Fred Whitsey, 299; Mary A. Williams, 102; Tom Yee, 238, 239, 265, 266, 267, 286, 287, 288, 289